Inter-Act

USING INTERPERSONAL
COMMUNICATION SKILLS

SECOND EDITION

Inter-Act

USING INTERPERSONAL COMMUNICATION SKILLS

SECOND EDITION

RUDOLPH F. VERDERBER / KATHLEEN S. VERDERBER

University of Cincinnati

Wadsworth Publishing Company
Belmont, California
A Division of Wadsworth, Inc.

Senior Editor: Rebecca Hayden
Production Editor: Kathie Head
Designer: Detta Penna
Copy Editor: Alan Hislop
Cartoons: Phil Frank

Printed in the United States of America
1 2 3 4 5 6 7 8 9 10—84 83 82 81 80

Photo credits: page 3, © Frederik D. Bodin/Stock, Boston; page 21, © Jean-Claude LeJeune/Stock, Boston; page 45, © Glenn Steiner, 1979; page 63, © Glenn Steiner, 1979; page 87, © Jean-Claude LeJeune/Stock, Boston; page 115, © D. A. Darrah/Stock, Boston; page 143, © George Bellerose/Stock, Boston; page 177, © Peter Southwick/Stock, Boston; page 199, © Tim Carlson/Stock, Boston; page 223, © Owen Franken/Stock, Boston; page 243, © Rose Skytta, 1978/Jeroboam, Inc.; page 265, © Carol Bernson, 1979; page 297, © Carol Bernson, 1979; page 319, © Glenn Steiner, 1979.

Library of Congress Cataloging in Publication Data

Verderber, Rudolph F
    Inter-act : using interpersonal communication skills.

    In the 1st ed. K. S. Verderber's name appeared first on t.p.
    Includes bibliographies and index.
    1. Interpersonal communication. I. Verderber, Kathleen S., 1949–   Inter-act. II. Title.
BF637.C45V47 1980   158'.2   79-21029
ISBN 0-534-00785-6

Preface

You are now starting a study of interpersonal communication. You may think interpersonal communication is a rather fancy label for something that you've thought of as just conversation, and perhaps it seems strange to be getting college credit for a course in something you've been working on for fifteen or twenty years. And indeed, in many ways, interpersonal communication *is* conversation. But as you work your way through this course and this book we believe you will begin to agree with us that, as with many subjects, there's more to interpersonal communication than there appears to be.

We believe that courses in interpersonal communication in general and this textbook in particular have a great deal to offer you, whatever your present level of communication skill. If you already see yourself as a good communicator, you can learn to identify what it is that you do so well and—by understanding your own success better—help others improve their communication. If you are like most people whose communication success is mixed, this study should introduce you to several new skills and to many others that you may know of but are not now using effectively. If you see yourself as a person who has trouble communicating, we believe that this book can teach you skills that will make major improvements in your communication.

In this second edition of *Inter-Act* we have tried hard to preserve and strengthen the material that made the first edition so useful. We have also tried hard to provide a better base for the skills development that is so fundamental to a basic interpersonal communication course. We continue to provide the material that will help you achieve interpersonal competence, with carefully considered changes directed toward making this goal easier.

Part 1 defines the bases of interpersonal communication. Chapter 1, "The Theoretical Base of Communication," discusses the transactional nature of interpersonal communication, how it works, and where it is used. Chapter 2, "The Perceptual Base of Communication," shows that all people "see" from a personal perspective; what you see is not an absolute reality, but a perception of reality. Chapters 3 and 4 consider the verbal and nonverbal bases of communication. They focus on the mistaken ideas that people have about the symbols they use.

Part 2, "Developing Interpersonal Skills," is the heart of the book. It presents basic interpersonal skills in a six-chapter unit. For each presentation, we define the skill, show its importance, consider procedures for using it, and guide you in practicing it. We believe we give one of the few comprehensive presentations of basic skills to be found in today's interpersonal textbooks. As we mentioned, you may at first think the skills are only common sense. What we believe you will discover is that even when you know or recognize a skill you may have trouble translating that understanding into behavior. You may also feel self-conscious about trying some of the skills that seem foreign to you or are hard to get right; but if you take time to practice seriously, you will soon see what a difference these skills can make in your communication.

Part 3, "Adapting Skills to Your Environment," gives practical insight into the variety of applications of the skills. Each of us lives in several worlds at the same time; each of us plays a variety of roles daily. Each of us finds a need to function in various contexts: male-female, family, cross-cultural, interviewing, groups, and, perhaps most important, in forming and maintaining relationships.

One of the features that you will appreciate in this book are the two appendixes. Appendix A is a glossary of the interpersonal skills. Appendix B is a glossary of the most common communication problems. In an easy-to-use, quick-review form, we have included the skill, its importance, the procedure for putting it into practice, an example of its use, and the pages in the text where the skill is discussed in detail. For the problems, we have included each problem, its potential harm, the kinds of skills that are most likely to solve or to help it, and the pages where each problem is discussed.

In the text we have tried to give both a means of practicing the skills and an opportunity for learning the skills by experience. These goals are accomplished in the communication sessions that follow major sections of each chapter. The sessions appear within, rather than at the end of, each chapter to encourage you to work with each concept or skill at the time you encounter it.

Each session has two or three kinds of activities: reflection, practice, and discussion. Reflections are mainly to stimulate thought. Although you may not want to write down your thoughts, our goal in asking you to write them is to get you to weigh and consider your own experience. The practices give you a chance to work with what you have learned. Practices sometimes call for pencil and paper work that you can do on your own; other times, they call for you to work orally alone or in groups. The discussions let you share your thoughts, ideas, and feelings with other members of the class; most are intended for small groups of from three to six persons.

Although you probably will not have time to complete every session, if you are intent upon learning the skills and concepts presented, you will find it essential to put in a reasonable amount of practice time. For your convenience, at the start of each chapter we have included a list of pay-offs—forecast statements of what you will learn and be able to do as a result of reading and working with the sessions in the chapter. We have also included a short list of suggested readings at the end of each chapter.

We hope that as a result of working with this textbook you find that we have met our goal in helping you learn the kinds of skills that will help you function more effectively in your day-to-day interactions.

We give our thanks to the many teachers and students who have offered suggestions while using the first edition. We also appreciate the challenging and thoughtful reviews of the manuscript by Roy M. Berko, Lorain County Community College; William H. Edwards, Columbus College; James E. Hasenauer, California State University, Northridge; Jo Ann Lawlor, West Valley College; Ronna Loewen, Evergreen State College; and William L. Robinson, Purdue University.

Contents

Part One

BASES
OF INTERPERSONAL
COMMUNICATION

Chapter 1
The Theoretical Base of Communication

PAYOFFS   *After you have read this chapter, you should be able to:*

1. *Define interpersonal communication.*
2. *Explain the transactional nature of interpersonal communication.*
3. *Define and show the interrelationships among context, rules, people, message, channels, and noise.*
4. *Explain why people need people.*
5. *Explain the relationship of exchange theory to undertaking interpersonal encounters.*
6. *Explain the decision-making function of interpersonal communication.*

"Marcia, I tried to call you last evening."

"Hm, I was in my house most of—oh, I remember, I was at the library from about 7:30 to 9:00. It must have been then."

"Yeah, I think it was about 8:30. Listen, I wanted to see whether you were up to a racquetball game Saturday at 10:00. I was able to reserve a court. Since I couldn't get hold of you, I thought I'd go ahead and get the court and then see if the time was okay."

"Hm, 10:00 isn't the best—oh, why not—I really need the exercise. I played only once this week. Shall we meet there about quarter till?"

"Great! You know I'm going to beat you this time!"

"We'll see about that! Thanks for getting the court—see you there."

This conversation between Marcia and Nancy, two college students who like to keep fit by playing racquetball, is an example of communication. More specifically, it is an example of *interpersonal* communication.

A person cannot get through even a small portion of a day without being part of some communication. Look at a painting and either it communicates something to you or it does not. Entering a friend's house, you are aware that the room communicates a feeling of warmth. You may try to console a friend who has a communication problem with her fiancé. From the television, the radio, or the newsstand, you see and hear stories about people trying to communicate with you and with others.

What ties all these examples of communication together is the effect of the communication—the meaning. If you get meaning from a person, an idea, an action, a painting, a building, or a room, communication has occurred. All communication requires an effect—the stimulation of some meaning.

Marcia and Nancy's conversation, however, is not merely an example of communication in general; it is interpersonal communication in particular. *Interpersonal communication* is the transactional process of people sharing meaning through the simultaneous sending and receiving of messages. It is the *transactional* nature of communication between and among people that sets it apart from all other forms of communication. A chat with your adviser about the problems of registration, a "heavy" talk with a friend about the direction your relationship has taken, a telephone call to your mother when you are lonely, as well as the conversation between Marcia and Nancy about setting up a racquetball date—all are interpersonal communication.

In this chapter we will look at the transactional nature of communication, and we will look at the social and problem-solving functions of interpersonal communication. Then we will discuss the interpersonal contract—a way for you to identify a major goal in improving your interpersonal communication.

Interpersonal Communication as Transaction

When you complete a transaction with someone, you have completed a deal that involves give-and-take and mutual agreement. A transaction implies an interdependency between those completing the transaction. Let's see how this applies to interpersonal communication. We have said that communication is a process; it is continuous and has no clear beginning or end. For example, from the moment that Clark and Alice enter the same environment, their clothes, gestures, movements, and other nonverbal factors are communicating. What they have said and what they have meant to each other before this encounter are also part of the communication process. As observers we can mark when they begin to speak and when a conversational episode ends, but the communication that takes place between them is affected by several factors that are not so easily detected.

Thus we said that this process is transactional, since the meaning that is shared during the conversation by the participants transcends what can be observed and includes context, rules, people, message, channels, and noise. The process is transactional because these elements occur simultaneously and because the people communicating are interdependent. Let's examine each element individually.

Context

Context is the physical and social setting in which communication takes place. The context affects expectations, meaning, and behavior. If you go out for an evening with friends of the same sex as yourself (the social context) and you end up at a disco (the physical context), your communication transactions will be different from what they would be if you went with your church group of men and women (social context) at the home of the minister (physical context). Why? Because the context provides a basis for the rules (the norms) operating within a transaction.

Rules

Rules are the guidelines that we establish or perceive as established for conducting our transactions. These rules exist at the beginning of an interpersonal encounter and grow, change, or solidify as people get to know one another better. Rules tell you what kinds of messages and behavior are proper in a given context and with a particular person. You may have a friend, Jack, who peppers his conversation with you with four-letter words. Yet when this same person talks with his parents or his teachers, he never uses such words. Jack's rules governing his talk with you are different from the rules governing his talk with parents and teachers. Do we always know the rules? Not always. We have to learn the rules through experience. For instance, Jack—who uses four-letter words in conversations with you—may do the same when he is talking with Annie, a person he has just met. From Annie's reactions—in speech or behavior—Jack may discover he must follow a different set of conversation rules if he wants to be friends with her.

The rules of interpersonal communication may be formal (such as parliamentary procedures); they may be proven social guidelines (such as the cliché, "never discuss religion, politics, or sex at a party"); or they may simply develop within the context of a particular relationship.

People

The *people* in an interpersonal transaction play the roles of sender and receiver—sometimes simultaneously. As senders, we form messages and attempt to communicate them to others. As receivers, we process the messages that are sent to us and react to the messages both verbally and nonverbally.

Each person is a product of his or her individual experiences, feelings, ideas, moods, sex, occupation, religion, and so forth. As a result, the meaning sent and the meaning received may not be exactly the same. For instance, when Art speaks of a good job, he means one that is highly paid; to Glen, his listener, a good job is one that is stimulating, regardless of pay. A successful communicator must take advantage of every skill available to present and interpret meanings as clearly as possible.

Message

The *message* is the content of the transaction. Messages have at least three parts: meaning, symbols used, and form or organization.

Meanings are ideas and feelings. You have ideas about how to study for your next exam, where to go for lunch, and whether marijuana should be legalized. You have feelings such as hunger for an ice cream cone, anger with your roommate for borrowing your favorite sweater, and love for a friend. Pure meaning, however, cannot simply be moved from one person's mind to another. We need some method to communicate our meaning and create similar meaning in the mind of someone else.

To communicate meaning, you must express your ideas and feelings in symbols. *Symbols* are words or actions that represent meaning. Symbols can be communicated with both voice and body. As you speak, your mind chooses words to convey the messages. However, at the same time, facial expressions, gestures, and tone of voice—all nonverbal cues—accompany your words and affect the meaning of the message. As we listen, we take both the verbal and nonverbal cues and assign meanings to them. The process of transforming ideas and feelings into symbols is called *encoding;* the process of transforming symbols into ideas and feelings is called *decoding*. You have been communicating for so long that you probably don't consciously think about either the encoding or the decoding processes. When your eyes grow bleary and you say, "I'm tired," you aren't thinking, "I wonder what symbols will best express the feeling I am now having." When you hear the words, "I'm tired," you are not likely to think: "*I* stands for the person doing the talking, *am* means that the *I* is linked to some idea, and *tired* means growing weary or feeling a need for sleep; therefore, the person is feeling a need for sleep." At the same time, you are not likely to worry about whether you have the same mental picture of "tired" as the person using the word. You are probably aware of the encoding process only when you must grope for words, especially when you feel the right word is just on the tip of your tongue.[1]

The messages in our communication may be either intentional or unintentional. The person sending an intentional message makes a conscious effort to select the correct symbols—the message he or she sends has a purpose. Yet, at the same time, that person may be unintentionally sending a conflicting message through nonverbal cues. For instance, if someone says, "That was a great movie," the meaning you actually receive depends upon whether the expression "great" was accompanied by a smile that was real, faked, or forced, and upon whether the tone of voice was pleasant or sarcastic. Regardless of what the speaker intended to communicate, you may interpret the message differently. Both the intentional and the unintentional messages are important to the sharing of meaning.

---

[1]R. W. Brown and D. McNeill, "The 'Tip of the Tongue' Phenomenon," *Journal of Verbal Learning and Verbal Behavior* 5 (1966): 325–337.

When an idea or feeling has many parts, the sender may need to communicate it in sections or in a certain order so that the receiver will not become confused. Thus another part of the process of communicating meaning is choosing a form or organization for the message. For instance, when Julia tells Connie about the apartment she looked at yesterday, her message takes a certain form. If her description moves logically from room to room, the message is likely to be clearer than if she attempts to describe bits and pieces drawn from all over the apartment in a random order. The context in which the message occurs, the rules of that context, and the messages you are receiving in return—all influence how you will shape, form, and organize your ideas.

Channels

The *channel* is both the route traveled by the message and its means of transportation. Words are carried from one person to another by air waves; facial expressions, gestures, and movement by light waves. Usually, the more channels that can be used to carry a message, the more likely the communication is to succeed. Although human communication has basically two channels (light and sound), people can and do communicate by any of the five sensory channels—a fragrant scent and a firm handshake are both forms of communication.

Noise

A person's ability to interpret, understand, or respond to symbols is often hurt by noise. *Noise* is any stimulus that gets in the way of sharing meaning. Much of your success as a communicator depends on how you cope with external, semantic, and internal noises.

External noises are the sights, sounds, and other stimuli that draw people's attention away from the message. For instance, during a lecture in American history, your attention is drawn to the sound of a power lawnmower outside the window. The sound of the lawnmower becomes external noise. Trying to concentrate on the lecture might be fruitless unless the noise is eliminated. Physical noise such as this does not have to be heard, however. Perhaps during the same lecture a particularly attractive man or woman looks toward you, and for a moment your attention turns to that person. Such visual distraction to your attention is also physical noise.

Semantic noises are those message symbols that inhibit or prevent shared meaning. Because your perceptions and experiences differ from those of a person speaking to you, you may hold different meanings for even relatively simple words. Suppose your instructor excitedly tells you that she will be reading a paper at a forthcoming convention. If you think "reading a paper" just means what people do to find out the day's news (rather than giving an oral report on research), you may not understand her enthusiasm. Since meaning depends on your own experience, you may at times decode a word or phrase differently from the way the sender intended. When this happens, you get semantic noise.

Semantic noise can also occur when you attach to particular words some emotional significance that others are unaware of or are insensitive to. For instance, a friend who recently moved from the Midwest to the Southwest was appalled to hear the Mexican-Americans in the area called *Chicanos*. Having had almost no experience with Mexican-Americans, she mistakenly thought that *Chicano* was an ethnic slur, like *Dago* for Italian. She reacted by tuning out people who used *Chicano* in their conversations—the word *Chicano* created noise for her. When she finally confronted someone with his use of what she thought was racist language, she was politely informed that Mexican-Americans preferred *Chicano* and used the word in talking about themselves. This explanation at once cleared away the semantic noise.

Semantic noise is the basis of our deliberate use of double meanings. John says he bought his new car primarily because of the body style, and Mary looks at John and says, "I'm pretty wild about the style of your body myself." Mary is using semantic noise on purpose.

Internal noises are the thoughts and feelings that interfere with the sharing of meaning. Have you ever found yourself daydreaming in class? Perhaps you let your mind wander to thoughts of the good time you had at a disco last night or to the argument you had with someone this morning. If you have tuned out the lecture and tuned in a daydream or a past conversation, then you have created internal noise.

Let's review the elements of an interpersonal transaction by looking at a specific example. At breakfast, Joe says to his wife, Gloria, "What do you say we go out to dinner tonight?" Gloria frowns and says, "I don't know that I want a hamburger . . ." "Not for hamburgers," Joe interrupts with a lilt in his voice. "I meant let's go to the Chalet!" A startled Gloria replies quickly, "The Chalet—wow—you have a deal!"

In this example we have the social context of a marriage and the physical context of a home. Joe encodes his thought into the words "What do you say we go out to dinner tonight?" Gloria decodes his words, gets a meaning she perceives as accurate, and responds with a frown and a verbal "I don't know that I want a hamburger." Joe sees that his message was not decoded accurately, so he tries to correct the faulty interpretation. Nonverbally he gets a lilt in his voice, and verbally he says, "I meant let's go to the Chalet!" Now Gloria responds with a nonverbal gasp and says verbally, "The Chalet—wow—you have a deal!" Meaning shared—communication complete. On the first statement of the message Gloria's incorrect decoding was a function of some semantic noise associated with knowing the kinds of restaurants Joe frequents.

Communication Session

Reflection

Consider a short communication transaction you had some time today. Focus on the dialogue of the conversation. Can you identify the six communication elements within that conversation?

Practice

1. See whether you can write out an analysis (like the one in the review of the process above) of the following encounter: Rita and her mother are shopping. As they walk through an elegant dress shop, Rita sees a dress she wants. With a look of great anticipation Rita says, "That's a beautiful dress—can I have it?" Her mother frowns, shrugs her shoulders, and says hesitantly, "Well . . . yes . . . I guess so. . . ." Rita continues, "And it's only forty dollars!" Her mother brightens and says, "Yes, it is a beautiful dress—go ahead and buy it."

2. Your instructor will ask for a volunteer to describe a diagram to the class.

   a. The volunteer will stand with his or her back to the class. You may not ask the describer any questions, but you must try to draw exactly what he or she is describing.

   b. The same volunteer will now describe a second diagram to the class. This time he or she will face you and you may stop the describer at any time to get clarification or additional information on how to draw the second diagram.

When both are finished, check to see how much of the first diagram you got correct versus how much of the second.

Discussion

In groups of three to six, discuss the differences between the first and the second situations. List as many differences as you can. Discuss why the two situations differ. Record your list on paper. At the end of discussion time, pass paper to the front of the room to allow the whole class to view it. Be prepared to defend your list.

Functions of Interpersonal Communication

It is unlikely that any other behavior is as important to you as your interpersonal communication. Each day you communicate for social and decision-making purposes that affect every aspect of your life.

Social Function

Human beings are social animals. People need other people. Of course we have all heard of hermits who choose to live and function alone, but they are an exception. Most of us need to talk to people and have them talk to us; we need to show affection and have it returned; and we like to affect others and have them affect us.

Let's look at some of the research that establishes these facts. Rene Spitz studied two groups of children who were institutionalized. The first group received little personal attention because the nurse was responsible for the care of eight to twelve children. In the second group, each child, although institutionalized, was cared for by its mother. The group that received little human contact showed an intellectual decline, were more prone to sickness, and had a higher death rate than did the group that were cared for by their mothers.[2] In another study, Harriet Rheingold found that babies who were held, played with, and interacted with regu-

Each day you communicate for social and decision-making purposes.

[2]R. A. Spitz, "The Role of Ecological Factors in Emotional Development in Infancy," *Child Development* 20 (1949), 145–156.

larly were more advanced intellectually and socially and more developed in motor skills than were babies who received less care.[3]

But people need people even after childhood. William Schutz, a psychologist, theorized that people have three needs that can be satisfied only by interacting with other people: affection, inclusion, and control.[4] Schutz believed that people vary both in the degree to which they are willing to fulfill these needs for others and in the degree to which they need others to fulfill their needs.

AFFECTION

Affection The need for affection is the need to express and to receive love. The "personal" individual is one who can express and receive affection effortlessly. He or she gets joy out of relationships with others, and his or her communication reflects that joy. People you know probably run the affection gamut. At one end are the "underpersonal" individuals. You have met them: they avoid close ties; they seldom show strong feelings toward others; and they shy away from those who show or who want to show affection. At the other end are the "overpersonal" individuals. You have probably encountered them, too: they thrive on establishing "close" relationships with everyone; they think of all others as their close friends, and they are free with use of terms of personal endearment; they confide in persons they have met for the first time; and they want all others to think of them as friends and to be interpersonally "open" with them.

INCLUSION

Inclusion The need for inclusion is the need to be in the company of others. Everyone has some need to be social. Yet again, because people are individuals, their inclusion behavior varies widely. At one extreme is the "undersocial" person who wants to be left alone. Although this person may occasionally seek company or may enjoy being included with some others if he or she is specifically invited, being around people is not the normal behavior. Whether this person finds the company of others threatening, whether he or she treasures solitude, or whether he or she has some other reason, much time is spent alone. At the other extreme is the "oversocial" person who needs constant companionship and dislikes or even fears being alone. If there is a party, this person is there; if there is no party, then he or she starts one. The door is always open—everyone is welcome, and the oversocial person expects to be welcome as well. The ideal, of course, is to be comfortable alone or with others. The social person does not need constant company to feel fulfilled. His behavior is a cross between the loner and the social butterfly.

---

[3]Harriet Rheingold, "The Modification of Social Responsiveness in Institutional Babies," *Monograph of the Society for Research in Child Development* 21 (1956).

[4]William C. Schutz, *The Interpersonal Underworld* (Palo Alto, California: Science and Behavior Books, 1966), pp. 18–20.

CONTROL

Control   The need for control involves the need to feel that one is a responsible person successfully coming to grips with his environment. Again, how you respond to this need may vary somewhere between extremes. At one end is the person who shuns responsibility—he does not want to be in charge of anything. The "abdicrat," as he is called by Schutz, is extremely submissive and is afraid to make decisions or accept responsibility. At the other end is the person who likes to be—indeed who needs to be—in charge. The "autocrat" must dominate others at all times. He usurps responsibility and makes every decision. The ideal could be called the "democrat." He is comfortable either leading or following. He can take charge when need be, but he can follow equally well. He stands behind his ideas, but he is not reluctant to submit when someone has a better idea.

On all three of these needs most of us fall somewhere along a continuum rather than at either of the extremes. Through our communication we display where we stand relative to each of these needs. As we interact with others, we see whether their affection, inclusion, and control needs seem compatible with ours. As you see your relationships with others forming and breaking apart, you may well see your communication display of these needs determining or at least playing a part in the defining of the relationship.

How or whether you are going to have your needs met is partly determined by how you behave when you are with someone who might be willing to meet these needs.

On one social level, people communicate for the sheer pleasure of interaction. At such times, the subject of the conversation is unimportant. Two people may sit for hours interacting about apparently inconsequential matters. When they part, they may have exchanged little real information, but they may carry away from the interaction a truly good feeling caused solely by the experience of talking with another human being.

On a second social level, people communicate to demonstrate their ties with other people. Why do you say, "How're you doing?" to a man you sat next to in class last quarter but haven't seen since? You may get pleasure out of the interaction—you may also see it as meeting a social need. When you see people you know, you overtly recognize them so that they will continue to recognize you. By saying, "Hi, Skip, how's it going?" you conform with our societal norms—you acknowledge a person you recognize with one of the many statements you have learned to use under these circumstances. Failure to communicate is seen as a slight—the person may think you are stuck up. Recognition serves to demonstrate your ties with people.

On a third social level, people communicate to *build* and to *maintain* relationships. When you do not know a person at all, you may communicate with that person to try out the relationship. If you find that you have things in common, the relationship may grow. Depending upon the results of the interaction, you may be content with an acquaintance relationship or a school-friend relationship, or you may seek a deeper, more intimate relationship. Some conversation is conducted for purposes of moving the relationship to higher levels of intimacy; some, for reinforcing the satisfactory nature of the relationship that has been achieved. Few relationships stay the same—especially during college years. You may find yourself moving in and out of a variety of relationships even within a single term. This is part of living—and it is an important purpose of interpersonal communication.

William Schutz's theory helps to explain the basic reasons why people communicate. But it does not explain why a person chooses to talk to another person or what determines how long that communication will last. For an explanation of these conditions we turn to exchange theory.

John Thibaut and Harold Kelley explain social interaction in terms of rewards received and costs incurred by each member of an interaction.[5] Rewards are the benefits received. Some common rewards are good feelings, prestige, economic gain, and fulfillment of emotional needs. Costs are considered in terms of the time, energy, and money spent to accrue the rewards. Whereas a person may be willing to spend a minute of time if he expects to have some good feelings as a result, he may not be willing to spend an hour of time to receive the same amount of good feelings.

According to Thibaut and Kelley, each of us seeks interaction situations in which our preferred behaviors will yield us a high reward and low cost outcome to help us satisfy our needs. For example, if Jill runs into Sarah on campus, there are several communication options available to Jill: she can ignore Sarah; she can smile; she can say, "Hi!" in passing; or she can attempt to start a conversation. What Jill does will depend in part upon her appraisal of the reward-cost outcome of the interaction. For instance, if Jill has been thinking about giving Sarah a call to arrange a game of tennis, she will probably take the time now to attempt to seek that outcome—she will be willing to pay the cost of taking time and using energy in hopes of receiving a suitable reward, a tennis date. If Jill and Sarah do talk, the duration of the interchange will continue until one or both realize that the interaction is falling below the satisfactory level. For Jill this might mean until a tennis game is set. For Sarah this might mean something else. Thibaut and Kelley suggest that the most desirable ratio between cost and reward varies from person to person and within one person from time to time.

If a person's net reward (reward minus cost) is below a comparison level, he will experience an unsatisfactory or unpleasant interaction; but,

[5]John W. Thibaut and Harold H. Kelley, *The Social Psychology of Groups* (New York: John Wiley, 1959), pp. 100–125.

if his net reward is higher than the comparison level he sets as satisfactory, he will experience a pleasant and satisfying interaction. Moreover, if a person has a number of interactions that give him a good reward-cost ratio, the comparison level he sets will be high, and he is not likely to be satisfied with low-outcome interactions. If Joan gets along well with four or five other men, she is not likely to put up with Charley, who irritates her. On the other hand, the person who does not have many positive interactions will be satisfied with interactions that the person with a wider choice would find unattractive. If Joan felt that Charley was the only man who could provide the benefits she sought, she would be inclined to put up with his irritating habits.

While the ratio of outcomes to the comparison level determines how attractive or unattractive an interaction might be to a person, it does not determine how long a given interaction will last. Although it seems logical to leave an interaction in which costs exceed rewards, circumstances are sometimes such that a person will stay in a relationship that is plainly unsatisfactory.

The variable that may intervene is what Thibaut and Kelley call the *comparison-level alternative*. They explain that whether a person stays with a particular relationship may depend on what alternatives or other choices he perceives himself to have. Thus durability of a relationship is also dependent upon possible alternatives. If his outcome level drops below the level he can attain elsewhere, the person will leave the relationship or interaction in order to engage in his next-best alternative. If, however, a person is not satisfied with the outcome level, he may continue in the interaction because no feasible alternative exists. The experience, as unsatisfactory as it may seem, is the best he believes he can get *at this time*.

Decision-Making Function

In addition to being social animals, humans are also decision makers. Starting with whether or not you wanted to get up this morning, through what you had for breakfast, to whether or not you decided to go to class, you have made countless decisions already today. Some of these decisions you made alone; others you made in consultation with one or more persons. Even more important, every one of the decisions involved some kind of language use. Communication during the decision-making process has two major purposes.

One important purpose of communication is information exchange. It is impossible to function in our society without data. Some of these data you get through observation, some through reading, some through television, and a great deal through interpersonal communication. Jeff runs out to get the morning paper. As he comes through the door hurriedly, Tom asks, "What's it like out there this morning?" Jeff replies, "Wow, it's cold—it couldn't be more than twenty degrees." Tom says, "I was going to wear my jacket, but I guess I'd better break out the old winter coat." Such a conversation is typical of countless exchanges that send and receive information. Since decisions generally are better when they are based on information, anything that you can do to improve the accuracy of your information exchange is to your benefit in decision making.

A second important purpose of communication is to change attitudes and behaviors. After making a decision, you must be able to carry it out, which often requires that you effectively influence others. You try to get your friends to go to a particular movie; you try to win the commitment of an acquaintance to vote for you; you try to persuade your father to let you use the car this weekend; or you try to get an instructor to change your course grade. These are but a few examples of attempts to influence people in order to make and carry out decisions. Some theorists argue that the purpose of all communication is to influence behavior of others.

Just as there is a direct relationship between communication and human relations, so is there a direct relationship between communication and decision making. The better understanding you have of the means of processing information, sharing information, and persuasion, the better your decisions will be. Likewise, the more understanding you have of the problem-solving method, the more likely you are to cope with your problems systematically and to arrive at the best decisions possible.

Some of these decisions you make alone.

For any decision, it is important that you go through the various steps of problem awareness, problem analysis, possible solutions, and selection of the best solution. Unless the decision is a spontaneous emotional reaction, it requires processing information, sharing information, and in many instances persuasion.

The Communication Contract

In this chapter we have looked at the main goal you can hope to achieve in this course: to improve your interpersonal communication so that you are better able to meet both your social and decision-making responsibilities. An important question to ask yourself at this time is: What one specific communication goal would I like to achieve? You are an individual, and your needs are likely to differ in many respects from those of your classmates. This is your chance to express your individuality. Whether you do it now or after you have done more work with the material in this book, we would like you to identify your personal communication goal and write it in the form of a contract.

Why a written contract? A familiar saying is "The road to hell is paved with good intentions." However serious you may be about completing a long-term project, you are often likely to turn your attention to immediate needs. Before long, you have forgotten both your original resolve and the project. If, however, you write out a description of the project and a plan for completing it and then sign it and date it and have another person witness it, you are more likely to honor the commitment you have made.

Identify your personal communication goal and write it in the form of a contract.

Writing the Contract

Your contract includes four parts: (1) a statement of your goal, (2) a description of the communication problem, (3) a step-by-step action plan to reach the goal, and (4) a method of determining when the goal has been reached. Let's look at each of these four parts in detail so that you can see how to proceed:

1. *Statement of the goal:* Perhaps now, before reading another word of this book, you may have your major communication goal in mind. On the other hand, you may need to do some reading and some thinking before you are able to verbalize your principal need. As a help in self-analysis, turn to Appendix A. Read through the communication skills listed there. Is there one that seems particularly important to you that you are not now practicing? Then read the communication problems listed in Appendix B. Perhaps you will discover that some communication behavior of yours is creating a problem. When you have determined a specific change you need to make, write your goal specifically. *Example:* "Goal: To increase my listening efficiency with my parents—especially with my mother."

2. *Description of the problem:* Here you describe to the best of your ability the specific nature of that communication problem. *Example:* "Problem: Currently when my mother tries to say something to me, I find myself daydreaming or rehearsing my replies. Consequently, I sometimes miss important points or misinterpret what she is telling me."

3. *Step-by-step action plan:* By reading the procedures in the appendixes for implementing a skill or coping with a problem or by referring to the pages in the text where the skill or problem is discussed, you can gain insight into the various elements you may wish to include in your plan. When you have a plan in mind, write it out in sufficient detail. *Example:* "Step-by-Step Action Plan: (1) I will consciously attempt to clear my mind when my mother is speaking. (2) I will learn to employ the skill of paraphrasing in order to check the accuracy of what I've heard."

4. *Method of determining when the goal has been reached:* Here you will write the minimum requirements for having achieved your goal. *Example:* "Test of Achieving Goal: This goal will be considered achieved (1) when I have completed two weeks of listening during which my mother never has to repeat something for me to get it; (2) when I have internalized paraphrasing to the extent that I remember to do it and do it well."

After completing the contract you should sign it. We also suggest that you have another person in class witness the contract. (Perhaps you can witness his or her contract in return.) At the end of the term, you can meet with the witness to determine whether your contracts have been fulfilled.

Communication Contract

1. Statement of the goal:

_____

2. Description of the problem:

_____

3. Step-by-step action plan:

_____

4. Method of determining when the goal has been reached:

_____

Signed: _____

Date: _____

Witnessed by: _____

_____

Figure 1-1

Communication Session

Practice

Write a communication improvement contract. Use the form in Figure 1-1.

Summary

We have defined interpersonal communication as people sharing meaning. Because interpersonal communication is a transactional process, we looked at the nature of the transaction and at the functions of interpersonal communication.

Interpersonal communication is transactional because it is a dynamic process that relies on the interdependency between those completing the transaction. Transactions consist of context, rules, people, message, channels, and noise, all happening at once.

Interpersonal communication has important social and decision-making functions. People interact with others because they must. Each person has interpersonal needs that must be met. Interactions are determined in part by need fulfillment and in part by cost-reward satisfaction. On one social level, people communicate for the sheer pleasure of interaction; on a second level, people communicate to demonstrate their ties with other people; and on a third social level, people communicate to build and to maintain relationships.

People also communicate to meet important decision-making functions. People communicate to exchange information, and they communicate to change attitudes and behaviors. Information is used as a basis for making decisions, and attempts to change attitudes and behaviors are made to influence others to carry out the decisions that have been made.

Suggested Readings

Dean C. Barnlund (Ed.). *Interpersonal Communication: Survey and Studies*. Boston: Houghton Mifflin Co., 1968.

David K. Berlo. *The Process of Communication: An Introduction to Theory and Practice.* New York: Holt, Rinehart and Winston, 1960.

Gerald R. Miller and **Mark Steinberg.** *Between People: A New Analysis of Interpersonal Communication.* Chicago: Science Research Associates, 1975. See pp. 3–86 for a comprehensive discussion of communication as transaction.

Paul Watzlawick, Janet H. Beavin, and **Don D. Jackson.** *Pragmatics of Human Communication.* New York: W. W. Norton & Co., 1967. This book and Barnlund's and Berlo's books are becoming classics of communication theory.

Chapter 2
The Perceptual Base of Communication

PAYOFFS   *After you have read this chapter, you should be able to:*

1. *Define perception.*
2. *Explain the processes of selection, organization, and interpretation.*
3. *List and explain the factors that affect perception.*
4. *Recognize the difference between facts and inferences.*
5. *Define self-concept and discuss the ways it is formed.*
6. *List and explain four functions of self-concept.*
7. *List and explain attitudes and feelings that affect the accuracy of a person's perception of others.*

> *As was traditional at Robley College, the freshman class was celebrating the end of orientation week at a Friday afternoon party in the gym. On Monday, classes would begin. Pat was meeting many people for the first time. His attention was drawn to a person on the opposite side of the room. There, talking with some other students, was the woman he knew he'd been looking for. There was something special about the expression on her face; the sparkle in her eyes told Pat she was the one he had to meet. Excusing himself from the group he was talking with, Pat walked slowly toward her.*

You have probably read many stories and seen many movies and television programs that began much like Pat's story. Pat's thoughts, his actions, and his anticipated conversation with the woman he hopes to meet all grow from his *perceptions* of her. Will his encounter with her meet his expectations? Will he be disappointed? Whatever happens, his perceptions will play an important part.

We'll begin this chapter by taking a brief look at the process of perception; then we'll focus on how perception of self and of others affects our communication.

Perception

Perception is the process of assigning meaning to sensory information. Your eyes, ears, nose, skin, and taste buds gather information; perception is what your brain does with that information. Because people believe in the accuracy of their senses, they often say such things as, "Of course you can believe what I tell you about the bank robbery—I was there, *I saw it.*" However, we know that, when two people see the same event, their reports of the event can differ significantly. Why? Because the reality each person reports is a product of his individual perceptions. When someone sees something happening, his brain responds in three stages: it selects, it organizes, and it interprets. The result is perception.

Stages of Perception

Although the three stages of perception happen almost all at once, let's consider each separately.

Selection   Every second you are bombarded by millions of sensory stimuli. If you were consciously aware of each sensory stimulus, you could go mad. You have learned to cope with this bombardment by focusing attention on relatively few of these stimuli. Right now you are reading this book, so your attention should be focused on making sense out of the visual data you are seeing on this page. Stop for a minute and look around—try to become aware of all the sights and sounds you could be focusing on right now. If you have ever had difficulty reading in a noisy room, you can appreciate the need to be selective in the sensory data you choose to attend to. Once you focus on a particular set of stimuli, the rest

*We know that when two people see the same event,
their reports of the event can differ significantly.*

of the sights and sounds blend into an indefinite background. In the language of visual experience, what you focus on is called the *figure* and the rest of what you see is the *ground*.

The interesting point is that you can focus on only one part of the total at any given instant. The scope of the focus may vary (you can use a wide lens or a narrow lens—a close-up or a distance shot), but the focus is still limited. For instance, in a televised football game, an instant replay reveals detail that you missed the first time around. The isolated replay permits focus on actions that you may have missed entirely as the play originally unfolded. The experienced eye can enlarge the focus—the football commentator may see more than you did in the play the first time around, but even this expert generally misses more than he or she sees.

Since the focal point of any given scene may be at any of an infinite number of places, depending upon what each selects as the focal point, ten persons viewing the same scene may have ten different perceptions. Let's show the importance of focal points with a drawing that is often used to illustrate the figure-ground concept. Look steadily at Figure 2-1. What do you see?

Figure 2-1

At first you will probably see either the goblet or the faces. You will never see them both at exactly the same time. As you look at the picture, notice that each comes in and out of focus—although you may have the impression that sometimes you see them both at once, actually you are focusing briefly on one, then the other. When two actions occur simultaneously, you can see only one of them; when two persons are talking to you at the same time, you can listen to only one of them. Sometimes you can switch focus rapidly to give yourself the impression you are seeing or listening to both—but you can *focus* on only one at a time.

Organization   Data are received from the senses by the brain. The brain selects certain stimuli, and then it must try to sort the data into some intelligible order. This process of *organization* is a second major element of perception. The brain organizes sensory input by grouping similar stimuli in three ways: by patterns, by proximity, and by good form.

Let's consider organizing by *patterns*. When people group by patterns, they focus on characteristics that are similar. Look at the three sets of shapes in Figure 2-2. In Figure 2-2a, the dots and circles may seem to separate into two groups because of the similarities of the dots and circles. In Figure 2-2b, you may see four columns of figures rather than sixteen individual figures. In Figure 2-2c, you may perceive an X surrounded by small circles. Similarly, when you consider a group of people, depending upon your organizational frame of reference, you may perceive the group in terms of subgroups. Instead of perceiving a number of individual human beings, you may think of them as males and females, or marrieds and singles, or young, middle-aged, and elderly.

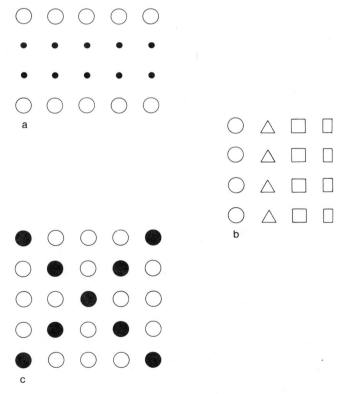

Figure 2-2

A second way of grouping is by *proximity*. We tend to group those things that are physically close together. Look at Figure 2-3. What do you see? Figure 2-3a probably appears as three pairs of parallel lines rather than as six individual parallel lines. Figure 2-3b probably appears as four sets of circles rather than as sixteen individual circles or as horizontal rows or vertical columns of circles. In a classroom, if you see a group of five students sitting apart from the rest of the class, you may decide that they have something in common.

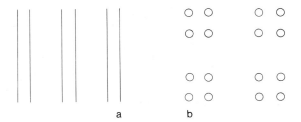

Figure 2-3

A third element of grouping has been called the *law of Pragnanz*. This law states that people tend to perceive a stimulus as a "good" form. The law has two ramifications for visual perception: (1) If a figure approximates a geometric form, you will probably see it as that form; and (2) if the figure has a gap in it, you are likely to see it as a closed figure. Look at Figure 2-4. Because of this tendency to modify what you see, you probably perceived Figure 2-4a as a triangle, 2-4b as an oval, 2-4c as a circle, and 2-4d as a square. This same tendency explains why you may read a neon sign correctly when a portion is burned out and why you may finish a sentence correctly when a speaker leaves out a word.

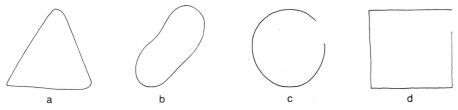

Figure 2-4

Interpretation   As the mind selects and organizes, it completes its perception by interpreting the information it receives. The interpretation gives the perception meaning.

If, as a result of the selection, organization, and interpretation process, your mind has a distorted perception, then the communication that follows the perception is likely to be distorted as well.

Let's consider the link between perception and communication. Examine Figure 2-5. Describe aloud the woman you see. Talk about her age, her features, how attractive she is, what she is wearing, and what you believe she is thinking.

Figure 2-5

If you saw a picture of a young woman, your description was much different from what it would be if you saw a picture of an old woman. Which did you see? Look again. Keep looking at the picture until you have seen both women. "Ah," you say, "but this is just a trick. No real-life situation could possibly fool me like this one." Don't believe it. People are fooled every day. You have probably at one time been momentarily fearful of a threatening person or animal only to discover that what you saw was actually a shadow or reflection that only suggested the feared creature. Are flying saucers real? Many people have seen objects they

Many people have seen objects they thought were flying saucers only to find out they had seen flocks of flying geese, weather balloons, or cloud formations.

thought were flying saucers only to find out they had seen flocks of flying geese, weather balloons, or cloud formations. Was the communication based on such misperceptions accurate? Probably not.

Factors That Affect Perception

Why do you perceive as you do? Let's consider several of the factors that affect your perceptions. Among the most important are the following:

1. *Limitations of the senses.*   If your eyes are weak, you are going to have trouble accurately recording what you see. So it is with all the senses: any problem in sight, hearing, touch, taste, or smell will affect perception. Even when the senses are working properly, they have limitations. For example, human eyes perceive only certain rays—you do not see the infrared or ultraviolet ends of the color spectrum. Likewise, human ears cannot pick up many of the sounds that come to them—they are limited to a range between 20 and 20,000 cycles per second. This is why you cannot hear certain kinds of dog whistles.

2. *Expectation.*   Basically, we perceive what we expect to perceive. For instance, spectators expect the players on a college basketball team to wear uniforms of the same color and design; they expect each player to have his own number—but not a distinctive uniform. Why? Because of past experience. A starting player in one game we saw had a blue bobcat sewn on the pants of his uniform, but all the other players had a white bobcat sewn on theirs. When we pointed this out to the couple sitting next to us, they had trouble seeing the difference; it defied their expectation.

Expectation is largely determined by what your experience has shown you to be true: uniforms are supposed to be *uniform*. When experience does not conform with expectation, expectation sometimes wins out. On a day that bus drivers are on strike, you may still believe you saw buses running; if a friend does not usually wear earrings, you may not notice them when she does.

Observing accurately is a learned activity. It takes mental effort to record data that override your expectations.

3. *Desire.*   Sometimes people see only what they want to see. A small child sees a man with a red suit, a white beard, and a pillow under his belt and perceives him as Santa Claus. Some children recognize *any* man with a white beard as Santa during the Christmas season. When fooling yourself is a harmless, pleasurable activity, perhaps it's not so bad. But if you want to see only the bad or evil in a person, a place, or an event, then the limited perception can be harmful to you and your communication.

4. *Interest.*   A factor related to desire is interest. People are likely to look for and to see those things that are of interest to them. Among those crossing a college campus at noon, an architecture student may be primarily aware of the beauty (or ugliness) of the buildings; a person in a wheelchair is keenly aware of steps and curbings she has to negotiate to get from building to building; a naturalist focuses on the trees that grace the campus. You may have had the experience of buying a new car, then suddenly noticing that make and model of car wherever you looked. Ownership creates interest, and with interest comes awareness.

5. *Context.*   The perception you have can be affected greatly by the context of the perception. If you see a flashy sports car in front of a suburban mansion and then see the same car in front of a dilapidated inner-city building, you are likely to *see* a different car! Why? Because the context has affected your expectation, and, as we have already seen, expectation affects perception.

   The more complex the context, the more likely there will be distortion in your perception. Remember, you are able to focus on only one aspect of a setting at a time. The more complicated the picture, the more focuses you will need in order to perceive the total. To walk across a street when the traffic light is green, you must focus on the color of the light, the "walk" signal, the possible presence of cars either running the red light or turning the corner, and the people coming toward you from the other side. Your total perception will depend upon what you focused on and in what order.

6. *Ambiguity of input.*   Even when a person is perceiving an object or group of objects under the best of circumstances, that person may perceive inaccurately. When what the person is looking at is for some reason ambiguous, or capable of being seen in more than one way, the chances of misperception greatly increase. Most people have been startled by something they saw from the corner of their eye, only to discover that what they thought they saw was far different from what was actually there. Similarly, most people have mistakenly recognized a stranger as someone they knew because they saw what seemed to them a familiar coat or hair style or gesture. Sometimes perceptions are formed before the mind has had the time to select, organize, and interpret. The more ambiguous the input, the more time it takes to go through the stages of perception, and the more likely the chance for error.

7. *Emotions and attitudes.*   Your perception is likely to be affected by how you feel at the moment of perception. We'll explore these two factors later in the chapter when we focus on perception of people. For now, let's consider one example that has probably happened to you. When you are hungry—really hungry—you will often see everything in terms of food. You perceive a red Corvette not as a luxury sports car, but merely as a means of transportation to a grocery store or restaurant. Likewise, you

can walk down a street and be oblivious to nearly everything but places to eat.

Improving Perception

You know that perception is a product of selection, organization, and interpretation and that many factors affect perception. What can you do to improve the accuracy of your perceptions? One, by recognizing the causes of misperceptions you can avoid or lessen them. Two, you can concentrate harder on what you see, hear, feel, taste, or smell. And three—and this is especially important—you can learn to separate fact from inference. Failure to distinguish fact from inference will lead to difficulty in thinking logically, shaping messages, and communicating. Research studies show that many people are unable to make this distinction in their communication.[1]

A fact is a verifiable statement—usually a statement about something that can be or has been directly observed. An inference is a conclusion about what has been observed. Separating fact from inference means being able to tell the difference between a verifiable observation and an opinion or conclusion based on or related to that observation. Let's clarify this contrast with an example: Ellen tells a friend that she saw her neighbor Hector run from his house, start his car quickly, and without pausing race his car down the street. She tells only what she saw—she relates an accurate perception. If, however, in addition, she had chuckled and said, "Hector is late again," she would be making an inference because she would be concluding—without actually *knowing*—that Hector was late again. Her interpretation of what she saw may be true, but it may not be. Suppose, for example, that Hector had just been notified of a sudden illness in his family and was rushing to the hospital. Not only would Ellen's inference be wrong, it could result in inappropriate action on her part.

There is nothing wrong with drawing inferences—people must make them in order to make sense out of the world. However, (1) you should know when you are inferring and when you are reporting observation; (2) you should recognize that, although your inferences may be true, they may not be, and they should not be stated as if they were; and (3) you should not act as though your inferences are facts.

Failure to separate fact from inference can cause embarrassment, discomfort, and occasionally disaster. If Jane and Marsha cross the street to avoid the forbidding-looking man standing in the doorway, they may be embarrassed to find that the menacing "man" is only a shadow. In this case the embarrassment is a small price to pay for caution.

---

[1]For a discussion of one such study, see "How Hints Are Transformed into Facts," *Psychology Today*, Vol. 9 (April 1976), p. 114.

Confusing inference with fact can be disastrous, however. Consider this situation: Tom and Larry are driving north in a hurry because Tom is late for an appointment. Larry, the driver, stops at the stop sign at the intersection of Main and Corry. Cars coming east-west on Corry have no stop sign at the intersection. As Larry pulls to a stop, a car appears from Larry's left traveling west to east—the car's right turn signal is blinking. Tom nudges Larry and says, "Go on, Larry, he's turning here." The result of Tom's confusion of inference and fact could be hundreds of dollars in repair bills and possible injury. The blinking turn signal does not guarantee that the car will indeed turn right onto Main. The signal could have been turned on by accident; it could have been turned on because the car was going to turn into a driveway just beyond the intersection; or the signal could have been turned on early to designate a turn at the next intersection.

What communication effect does the skill of separating fact from inference have? (1) It helps you eliminate embarrassment; (2) it helps you keep from creating the impression that what you are saying is fact; and (3) it helps you avoid making statements that may be costly for both you and others.

Accuracy of perception depends on your ability to separate fact from inference. The following exercises give you a chance to practice making this distinction.

Communication Session

Reflection

What are your most frequent confusions between fact and inference? What kinds of problems result?

Discussion

In groups of four to six, share past experiences where fact-inference confusion caused problems.

Practice

Read the following statements. Assume that all information presented in them is true. Then follow the instructions given below no. 1.

1. The only vehicle parked in front of 725 Main Street is a red truck. The words "Bob Jones TV Repair" are spelled in large white letters across the side panels of the truck.

Read the following statements made in reference to the data above. Indicate each statement as F–Fact, or I–Inference.

____ 1. "Tom, there's a red truck parked in front of 725 Main."

____ 2. "Yes, I see it. It belongs to Bob Jones, the TV repair man."

____ 3. "Looks like the people living at 725 need their TV fixed."

____ 4. "Well if it can be fixed, Bob Jones will fix it."

2. Two people came hurrying out of a bank with several large bundles, hopped into a long black car, and sped away. Seconds later, a man rushed out of the bank waving his arms and looking quite upset.

____ 1. "The bank's been robbed!"

____ 2. "Yes indeed—we saw the robbers hurry out of the bank, hop into a car, and speed away."

____ 3. "It was a long black car."

____ 4. "The men were carrying several large bundles."

____ 5. "Seconds after they left a man came out of the bank after them—but he was too late, they'd already escaped."

3. Tom and Susan walked side by side across campus. A man with long hair came running down the walk panting, bumped into both Tom and Susan as he squeezed between them, stumbled slightly, and then disappeared into the crowd.

____ 1. "That man sure seems in a hurry."

____ 2. "Well, he's lost whoever was chasing him."

____ 3. "He sure was panting."

____ 4. "He'd been running for a long time."

____ 5. "He stumbled as he squeezed between them."

____ 6. "That's when he hurt his leg."

____ 7. "He really gave them a good shove as he went between them."

Answers to 1: 2. Fact. (Beware of inferences in fact clothing! Just because it says "I don't see it," don't be fooled. Bob Jones may have just sold this truck and the new owner may not have had time to change the lettering.) 3. Inference. (Someone may need his TV repaired, but from the statements we don't know that as a fact.) 4. Inference. (If there is something wrong, the repairman may fix it—the repairman may or may not be Bob Jones.)

Answers to 2: 1. I; 2. I; 3. F; 4. I (men?); 5. I.

Answers to 3: 1. I; 2. I; 3. F; 4. I; 5. F; 6. I; 7. I.

Perception of Self: The Self-Concept

Now that we have defined and discussed perception, we want to see how your perceptions combine to form your self-concept and how your self-concept affects your behavior in general and your communication in particular.

Formation of the Self-Concept

Your self-concept is a collection of perceptions of every aspect of your being: your appearance, physical and mental capabilities, vocational potential, sexual capabilities, size, strength, and so forth. Your self-concept is formed by (1) your view of yourself and your experiences, (2) other people's comments to you about you and your behavior, and (3) your selection of roles.

View of self and experience   You form impressions about yourself partly because of what you see. You look at yourself in the mirror and make judgments about your weight and size, the clothes you wear, and your smile. These judgments affect how you feel about yourself. If you like what you see, you may feel good about yourself; if you don't like what you see, you may try to change—perhaps go on a diet, buy some new clothes, or begin jogging. If you don't like what you see and you cannot or are unwilling to change, you may begin to develop negative feelings about yourself.

Other impressions of yourself are a result of your reactions to your experiences. Through experience you learn what you are good at and what you like. If you find that you can throw a ball or a stone from distances of as much as twenty or thirty feet and hit the target you aimed for, you are likely to see yourself as having a good arm. If you can read a recipe, modify it, and produce a dish that tastes good, you are likely to think that you are a good cook. Now, a single satisfying experience may not give you a positive perception of your throwing or your cooking, but if additional experiences produce similar results, then the initial perception is strengthened. The greater the number of positive experiences you have—whether as a cook, lover, decision maker, student, or parent—the more positive your self-concept becomes.

Others' comments to you about you and your behavior   Your self-concept is also a result of how others react and respond to you. Suppose a person looks at you and says, "You really have beautiful hair." Or suppose that, after you've given your opinion on the energy crisis to your study group, someone says to you, "You're a very convincing speaker." Even one comment like either of these might be enough to cause you to think that you have beautiful hair or that you are a persuasive and influential speaker. If you respect the person making the comment, the comment will have an even greater effect. You may have heard someone repeat with pride a comment about his personality, ability, or behavior that was made years ago and has never been forgotten.

You are likely to use other people's comments to validate, reinforce, or alter your perceptions of who and what you are. The more positive comments you get about yourself, the more positive your total self-concept becomes.

Roles you play   A third way you define yourself is by the roles you choose or are forced to play. Roles are products of the value systems of society, of groups, and of the self. Society's value systems are easy to illustrate. Consider, for example, some of the roles that society expects you to play. In this era of the women's rights movement, we hope that sex-role expectations are changing. Nevertheless, in many cultures, little girls are still expected to play with dolls and other homemaking toys to prepare them for the nurturing roles of wife and mother; little boys learn that it is unmanly to cry, and they are encouraged to play aggressively in rough and tough sports and to play with mechanical toys—all in preparation for their roles in society of he-man husband, father, and bread-winner. If a child in such a family is caught playing with "inappropriate toys," a boy is called "sissy," a girl is called "tomboy"—both are derogatory terms and can be injurious to self-concepts.

In addition to social values, the value system of a specific group may also determine your role. Your family, your social organizations, your service organizations—every group you belong to approves or disapproves of things you do or say and of what you are. They "let" you be a certain kind of person in their presence, and you soon come to see yourself as that kind of person. For instance, if you are the oldest child in a large family, your parents may cast you in the role of model child, disciplinarian, or brothers' and sisters' keeper depending upon how they see family relationships. Your peers may look upon you as a "joker"; and you may accommodate them by playing your role: laughing and joking when you are really hurt and want to cry.

Other roles are products of your own value system. "Easygoing," "fashion model," "sincere student" are just a few examples of the roles you may adopt either to fit your perception of experience and feedback or to reflect a role you have chosen to play.

Each of us has a number of on-stage and off-stage roles—roles we play in public may differ from the roles we play in private. Although you may not be Superman hiding your real identity in Clark Kent, you often show yourself as different from what you perceive yourself to be. In each new encounter, you may test a role you have been playing or you may decide to play a new role. If you perceive the role as meeting some need, you may alter your self-concept on the basis of that particular role.

So *perception* of experience, others' comments about you and your behavior, and roles that you play work together to create a self-concept that may be anywhere on the continuum from very negative to very positive. How real or accurate are your self-estimates? The answer depends upon the accuracy of your perceptions! All of us experience both successes and failures at things we do. If in determining your self-concept you think about mostly successful experiences, your perception of self will be positive and your self-concept will probably be high. If, on the other hand, you think about mostly negative experiences, your perception of self will be negative and your self-concept will probably be low. Whether you are really "successful" or "a good person" is not as important as your *perceptions*.

Of course, very few persons have a completely high or a completely low self-concept. Most of us see ourselves as quite good at some things, average at many things, and fair to poor at others. For instance, your experience and feedback may give you the perception of being good as a cook and in relating to others, average in appearance, and fair to poor as a problem solver. If, however, you see yourself negatively in many ways, this emphasis on the negative is likely to result in a generally low self-concept.

Functions of Self-Concept

You have a self-concept—everyone does. What part does this self-concept play in your communication? It serves at least four basic functions: (1) it predicts behavior, (2) it moderates competing internal messages, (3) it filters messages from others, and (4) it influences your word selection and tone of voice.

Predictor of behavior   An important function of your self-concept is to predict what will happen to you: the higher your self-concept, the more likely you are to predict positive experiences; the lower your self-concept, the more likely you are to predict negative experiences. Soon your self-concept begins to shape reality—you begin to profit or lose by what are called "self-fulfilling prophecies." A self-fulfilling prophecy is an accurate prediction of behavior based on self-concept. For example, Clifford sees himself as a good test taker; he says, "I'm going to do well on the economics test." Then, as a result of his positive self-concept, he remains relaxed, studies, takes the test confidently, and does very well. Gordon, on the other hand, who believes himself to be a poor test taker, says, "I just know I'll blow the economics test!" Then, because he fears tests, his study is interrupted by negative thoughts; he goes into the test tired, irritable, and very worried; and, just as he has predicted, he does poorly. Positive thoughts and positive language produce positive results; negative thoughts and negative language produce negative results.

Moderator of competing internal messages   When you are thinking, you are talking to yourself. When you are solving a problem, you may be especially conscious of the different voices in your head. In the morning when the alarm goes off, Carl might say something like this to himself: "There goes that blasted alarm. I'm so tired—maybe if I lie here just a few more minutes. Hold on—if I don't get up now, I'll go back to sleep. Oh, who cares—it feels so good. Let's see, what if I slept just another fifteen minutes. No, it's already later than I like to get up. Come on, Carl—move it!" Several of the messages in this short internal conversation are competing. Which will Carl listen to? Which will determine his behavior? Self-concept is likely to be a moderator in the choice. If he feels good about himself and the day he has in store, Carl will probably get up right away. If, on the other hand, things aren't going well, if he doubts himself, Carl might seek to escape reality in sleep.

Let's examine another situation in which the nature of self-concept can be seen to influence a decision. Suppose Louise's boss at work says to her, "I'd like you to be in charge of the new program on . . ." As she hears her boss speak, she may hear herself thinking any one or more of the following:

"You've got to do it—it's your duty."

"What would being in charge of the program do for me personally?"

"Won't people ever leave me alone?"

"Another request for work—I think I'm going to scream!"

"Great, Louise—you know the botch you made of the last job."

"How much time will this really take?"

"I'm never going to get out from under what I have to do now."

Will Louise panic and try to get out of the job? Will she listen to the voice of duty that demands she accept at any cost? Or will she think the decision through rationally and make a choice based upon the best evidence she can gather? It is likely that Louise's decision will be at least partly a product of her self-concept. If she feels weak, insignificant, a pawn to be manipulated by anyone in authority, she will accept the position without further thought. "You have no choice," she says to herself. If she feels so bad about herself that she sees everything she does as ending in disaster, she might panic and refuse even to try, regardless of the possible benefits to her personally and to the organization. If, on the other hand, she sees herself as able to make decisions calmly and without being pushed, she will weigh the advantages and disadvantages and make a choice that she can justify rationally. The decision may turn out to be good or bad, but if she has listened to the voices of reason, she can be assured that she was in control of her right to make her own decision.

Eric Berne, a psychologist, developed a system of analyzing these internal messages. He called his system transactional analysis (TA).[2] Thomas Harris's book *I'm Ok—You're OK*,[3] a best seller a few years ago, is a readable popular treatment of Berne's theories. In brief, TA says that the kinds of thoughts that Louise had come from three ego states: the *Parent*, the *Child*, and the *Adult*. Statements from the *Parent* ego state are critical, evaluative statements; they are the voice of conscience. Statements from the *Child* ego state are emotional reactions. Statements from the *Adult* ego state encourage rational decision making. Using TA to analyze the thoughts quoted in response to the statement, "I'd like you to be in charge of the new program on . . .," we arrive at the following classification:

1. Parent *(critical-evaluative):*
   "You've got to do it—it's your duty."
   "You know the botch you made of the last job."

2. Child *(emotional or "gut" reactions—either positive or negative):*
   "Won't people ever leave me alone?"
   "Another request for work—I think I'm going to scream."
   "I'm never going to get out from under what I have to do now."

3. Adult *(rational statements that attempt to weigh and consider):*
   "What would being in charge of the program do for me personally?"
   "How much time will this really take?"

Although we do not believe that transactional analysis is the only way to understand the kinds of statements people make, students have found some of its concepts helpful in understanding or identifying certain communication events.

Filter of statements of others   Self-concept also filters what others say to you. Even though you receive all messages equally, you do not listen equally to each, and what you choose to hear reinforces your self-concept. For instance, if you have decided that you are not a good cook, you will look for and listen to statements that reinforce this perception. If someone says something that contradicts your perception, you are likely to ignore it—you are likely to act as if it were never said. Then you prepare lunch for your study group, and one of the people says that you're a pretty good cook. Because this remark contradicts your self-concept, you may ignore it, not really hear it, or perhaps reply, "No, this was more like a lucky accident" or, "Thanks for being kind to me, but it really wasn't that good." On the other hand, if you have decided that you

---

[2]See Eric Berne, *Games People Play: The Psychology of Human Relationships* (New York: Grove Press, 1964).

[3]Thomas A. Harris, *I'm OK—You're OK: A Practical Guide to Transactional Analysis* (New York: Harper & Row, 1967).

are in fact a good cook, you will seek out those messages that reinforce this positive view and screen out those that don't.

Perhaps you have spotted what appears to be a contradiction in our analysis of self-concept. Earlier we said that your self-concept is formed partly by listening to other people's statements. Now we are saying that it is the self-concept that determines whether you listen to those statements or screen them out. The fact is that your self-concept is *both* a result of others' comments and a filter of others' comments. It seems that certain comments help to form a self-concept. Then the self-concept begins to work as a filter, screening out certain messages. At times, however, new comments will get past the filter and change the self-concept, and then the newly changed self-concept begins to filter other comments.

Influencer of word selection and tone of voice   Self-concept also affects a person's word selection and tone of voice.[4] A person's self-concept is revealed by the statements he makes about himself. Emphasis on self-criticism, weakness, and self-doubt is often a sign of low self-concept. Such comments as, "I never was any good at . . .," "If only I could," are examples of statements suggesting a low self-concept. On the other hand, positive evaluations and confidence are signs of a high self-concept. "I like a challenge" and "I'll be going all out to do a good job" are examples of positive approaches. Signs of self-concept are especially prevalent in statements about competition. People with a low self-concept are often pessimistic about competition and are likely to say such things as, "Why should I try? I won't win." People with a high self-concept are likely to look forward to competition and make statements showing their confidence. You may also notice that people with low self-concepts are likely to be quick at blaming others when something goes wrong and quick to discount the value of an accomplishment. Remarks such as, "We've got to find who is responsible for this," and "Well, he gets A's only because he butters up the instructor," are common examples. Moreover, people with low self-concepts often speak in a whining voice when they are being critical or explaining behavior.

Perception of Others

When people meet, they form quick impressions of one another. As they interact, their impressions may be changed, reinforced, or intensified. These impressions determine such things as how much they like one another and how much they will try to talk with one another.

Many of these impressions are based on limited information. A per-

---

[4]In his material on "Developing a Healthy Self-Image," Don Hamacheck offers a lengthy analysis of the symptoms of inferiority and self-acceptance. See Don Hamacheck, *Encounters with the Self* (New York: Holt, Rinehart and Winston, Inc., 1971), pp. 232–237.

son may meet and talk with another person for only a few minutes. For instance, after a party in which Jack talks to Charlie while he is standing at the buffet table making a sandwich, Jack may later say, "Charlie really has a good head on his shoulders—he's a good analyst." Or, after a brief exchange in the hall with a co-worker that consists of no more than, "Morgan, how are you?" and "Fine," Morgan replies as he moves quickly down the hall, Jeff says to his friend Al, "Morgan seems so aloof—I just don't think I'd like him very well." In some instances a person does not even need an in-person encounter to form an impression—a mere photograph may do. Show your friend a picture of your uncle or grandmother and your friend is likely to form some perception of the person's personality on the basis of that photo alone.

Since so much of your interpersonal communication depends on impressions—perceptions—you need to assess how accurate your impressions are likely to be. The research results are inconclusive: some people consistently make reasonably accurate judgments; others make judgments that are neither consistent nor accurate. We believe that people have better interpersonal communications if they do not rely solely on their impressions to determine how another person feels or what that person is really like.

We can improve the accuracy of our impressions (or at least find out why we are unlikely to be accurate) if we understand the variables that affect perception. In the first section of this chapter we said that accuracy of perception is influenced by (1) limitations of the senses, (2) expectation, (3) desire, (4) interest, (5) context, (6) ambiguity of input, and (7) emotions and attitudes. As we examine the factors that affect the accuracy of our perception of others, we want to take a closer look at factor seven: emotions and attitudes.

We often let our emotions influence the way we see others. For example, if a person is afraid for some reason, he is more likely to perceive others as menacing than if he is joyful and happy. If it is a dark night and you are walking frightened and alone down an almost empty street, you are more apt to see the faces of those walking toward you as menacing than if you saw the same people with the same expressions walking toward you on a busy street in the middle of the day.

Our perceptions can be influenced by our emotions and attitudes in a number of ways. The following paragraphs discuss six of the major types of influence.

Assumed Similarity People usually perceive other personalities as similar to their own when they detect similarities in age, race, national origin, and income. If you are a very social person, if you like parties and plenty of action, you will probably perceive another person as social if that person is your own age and sex and from a similar background. This kind of perception is similar to what psychologists call *projection:* your perception of another person may not be influenced as much by what that person is like as it is by what *you* are like.

Expectation of further interaction   You are likely to think highly of a person that you would like to be with. If Donna sees Nick as a man with whom she would like to develop a strong relationship, Donna will give weight to her positive perceptions of Nick. Donna will look only at the positive side of Nick's personality and overlook or ignore the negative side that is apparent to others. When we are in love, we are oblivious to a person's faults. Once two people have married, however, they may begin to see the negative traits of their partners, traits that may have been apparent to others all along.

Confusing wishing with reality   When we began our discussion of perception, we noted that people often see what they want to see. For example, when a person wishes that another person shared his feelings, the results of this wish can be fascinating. Consider the following situation: Don loves Jane. As a result, Don wants to perceive Jane as loving him; that is, he wishes she would. His belief that Jane probably really loves him is wrong, but Don looks for ways to confirm it, however bizarre his efforts may seem to others. Jane can tell Don she does not love him; she can insult him to his face, yet Don may see every one of her insults as a reinforcement of his wish. Matthew says, "Don, she doesn't love you—she's refused to go out with you five times in a row, she won't talk with you on the phone, and she crosses to the other side of the street when she sees you!" Don replies, "She loves me all right—she's just trying to play hard to get. Give her time—she loves me; you'll see." Seeing the world through rose-colored glasses has not improved the accuracy of Don's perceptions of Jane's feelings.

The next three influences on our perceptions are similar in that they all derive from some misuse of reasoning by generalization. *Generalization* is a form of reasoning that assumes that what is true in some instances is true in all (or almost all) other instances. If the last five suits you bought at a department store were good buys, you might reason by generalization that all suits bought there or the next suit you buy there would also be good buys.

Relying on central traits   You are likely to perceive companion traits in a person when you have verified the presence of a central trait. Let's take the quality of *warmth* as an example. *Warmth* is a central trait because people often begin to perceive companion traits after they have identified the presence of warmth. For instance, if Nancy sees Marsha as a "warm" person (that is, Marsha always smiles and seems considerate of the feelings of others), then Nancy may also decide that Marsha is friendly, empathetic, easygoing, and likable, whether or not Marsha actually has these qualities. Although no one knows which traits are always seen by others as central, the tendency to link traits still exists.

Awarding value traits   People tend to award value traits to others on the basis of whether the other people are perceived as good or bad. This tendency is known as the halo effect. Consider the following situation: Joan perceives Susan as a "good" person. As a result, she may award Susan those traits that accompany goodness, such as honesty. At the same time, Joan perceives Gloria as a "bad" person. As a result, she may award Gloria those traits that accompany badness, such as dishonesty. One day Joan, Susan, and Gloria are eating lunch together. Each person leaves her books, notebooks, and other belongings on the end of the table. Susan and Gloria finish eating first and leave the table. When Joan is finished, she gathers up her belongings and notices that her purse is missing. Only two people could have taken it. Whom is Joan likely to accuse? Certainly not Susan, who is "good."

Stereotyping   Stereotyping is assuming that a single member of a group has the same characteristics as all other members of the group. Stereotyping is a judgment about an entire group with little or no regard for individual differences within the group. You are likely to develop generalized opinions about any group you come in contact with. Your opinions may be true in a very broad sense, partially true, or totally false, depending on the accuracy and breadth of your perceptions. When you learn that a person is a member of a given group (recognition may come as a result of perception of skin color, a religious medal, grey hair, or many other signs), you may automatically project your general opinions to the individual person. If Allen stereotypes Jews as pushy, greedy, and insensitive, as soon as he learns that Dave is Jewish, he automatically perceives Dave as pushy, greedy, and insensititve.

Stereotyping is a problem for two reasons. First, it is extremely likely that the stereotype is wrong. That one person or five persons who happen to be Jewish are greedy does not mean that *all* Jews are greedy. Second, even if 90 percent of all Jews were greedy, that does not mean that Dave, a Jew, is greedy. Stereotyping is hard to combat because a person can always find in a group one or more members with the characteristics that gave rise to the stereotype.

Let's examine the contrasts among these last three influences on our perceptions. First, Pam sees Midge as a considerate person—she has seen her pick up a coat that had fallen on the floor and hang it up, even though she didn't know to whom the coat belonged. As a result, Pam also perceives Midge as kind, gentle, and gracious. This example illustrates a reliance on a central trait. Second, Pam also sees Midge as a "good" person. Perhaps the evaluation of good came as a result of her seeing Midge pick up the coat. Because she is a good person, Midge could not do anything bad. When Pam is told that Midge cheated on her college entrance exam, Pam won't believe it. On the other hand, Pam *will* believe a story she's heard about Midge lending her roommate money for tuition. This example illustrates the awarding of value traits. Third, Pam finds out that Midge is a member of Alpha Alpha sorority. Pam knows no other Alphas, nor does she know anything about the group. When Pam meets another Alpha Alpha, she immediately perceives her as having many of the same traits that Midge has. This last example is stereotyping. It so happens that this example of stereotyping has a positive outcome, but whether the outcome is positive or negative, the stereotype is still inaccurate.

You are probably aware by now that you are not always accurate at perceiving what a person is like or how a person feels. What can you do to make your perceptions more accurate? You do not have to be a mind reader. You do not have to draw conclusions based solely on a facial expression, a shrug of the shoulders, or tone of voice. In Part 2, Communication Skills, we will consider several specific skills designed to help you test the accuracy of your perceptions before you act. Pay special attention to the discussions of behavior description, paraphrasing, and perception checking. These three skills will help you clarify perceptual information so you can then behave appropriately.

Communication Session

Practice

Your instructor will ask for three volunteers, who will leave the classroom. One at a time they will reenter the room and describe to the class a full-page magazine ad that the instructor has given them. On the basis of their descriptions, you are to try to visualize the picture as clearly as you can. Then, again using the three descriptions, you are to determine your perception of the person or persons in the picture.

When the three have finished, your instructor will show you the ad.

Discussion

What were the differences among the three descriptions? How did your image differ from the actual picture? How can you account for the differences? Did your perception of the person or persons in the picture change after you actually saw the picture? Why?

Summary

Perception is the process of assigning meaning to sensory information. Our perceptions are a result of our selection, organization, and interpretation of sensory information. Inaccurate perceptions cause us to see the world not as it is but as we would like to see it or as we want it to be. The accuracy of our perceptions is based on such factors as limitations of senses, expectation, desire, interest, context, ambiguity of input, and emotions and attitudes.

A person's self-concept is a collection of perceptions that relate to every aspect of that person's being. The self-concept is formed by views of self and experiences, other people's comments about self and behavior, and roles played. The self-concept serves at least four basic functions: it predicts behavior, it moderates competing internal messages, it filters messages from others, and it influences word selection and tone of voice.

Perception also plays an important role in forming impressions of others. Because research shows that people vary considerably in the accuracy of their perceptions and judgments, we take the position that people would have more successful interpersonal communications if they did not rely entirely on their impressions to determine how another person feels or what that person is really like. Additional factors that affect the accuracy of a person's perception of other people are feelings of the perceiver, assumed similarity, expectation of further interaction, confusing wishing with reality, relying on central traits, awarding of value traits, and stereotyping.

Suggested Readings

Gerald M. Goldhaber and **Marylynn B. Goldhaber.** *Transactional Analysis: Principles and Applications.* Boston: Allyn and Bacon, 1976. A good contribution to the theory of transactional analysis that combines the Goldhabers' explanations with a representative selection of readings.

Don E. Hamachek. *Encounters with the Self.* 2d ed. New York: Holt, Rinehart and Winston, 1978. A good analysis of self-awareness and self-concept.

R. D. Laing, H. Phillipson, and **A. R. Lee.** *Interpersonal Perceptions: A Theory and a Method of Research.* New York: Harper & Row, 1966. An analysis of the interaction of perception between two people.

Lawrence S. Wrightsman. *Social Psychology.* 2d brief ed. Monterey, California: Brooks/Cole Publishing Co., 1977. One of the many excellent social psychology books available.

Ruth C. Wylie. *The Self-Concept.* (2 volumes.) Lincoln: University of Nebraska Press, 1974. This work provides a comprehensive analysis of research related to formation and evaluation of self-concept.

Chapter 3
The Verbal Base of Communication

1. *Explain the statement, "Meanings are in people, not in words."*
2. *Explain the Sapir-Whorf Hypothesis.*
3. *Explain the difference between denotation and connotation.*
4. *List and explain the factors that affect denotative meaning.*
5. *Explain the semantic triangle.*
6. *Explain the purpose of a semantic differential.*
7. *List and explain the major goals of language usage.*
8. *List and explain three pitfalls of usage.*

You have spent a portion of each year of elementary and high school education studying the English language. As a result, the basics of English are a part of your general knowledge. Even so, many of the communication problems you encounter can be traced directly to language problems. In this chapter we'll look at the relationship between language and meaning, and we'll discuss the important difference between word denotation and word connotation. We'll also consider language use as it applies to the learning of communication skills.

Language and Meaning

The English language is a system of symbols used for communicating. Our language system consists of the words we know (vocabulary) arranged in certain learned ways (grammar and syntax). If we have a vocabulary that is large enough and an understanding of basic English grammar and syntax, we can communicate with other speakers of English. Given the right words and the right order for the words, communication is pretty well guaranteed. But the relationship between language and meaning is not as simple as it appears. Let's look at four facts about words that are important to an understanding of interpersonal communication: (1) the meaning of words is arbitrary, (2) the meaning of words is conventional, (3) the meaning of words is learned, and (4) the meanings of words and perception are interrelated.

The Meaning of Words Is Arbitrary

When we say that meaning of words is *arbitrary*, we mean that the words in our language that are used to represent objects, ideas, feelings, and actions are a result of the *preference* of the person or persons who used the word the first time. For example, why is the word *chair* used to stand for an object to sit on? The English word *chair* derives from the Latin *cathedra,* which means *seat* or *bench*. There is reason, therefore, for an English word that sounds something like cathedra, but why *chair*? Why not *chaum* or *cathdra,* or simply *cath*? The choice of *chair* over any other similar word was a purely arbitrary decision—it represents the preference of someone at some time and place.

The arbitrary nature of language helps explain a saying well known to students of interpersonal communication: meanings are in people, not in words. At first glance, the saying may sound nonsensical. Why do you spend all that time in school studying vocabulary if words don't mean anything! But if you examine the saying for a moment, it becomes clear.

Words only represent meanings—the words themselves are not the meanings. Moreover, words may represent meanings accurately or poorly, depending on many circumstances. If, for instance, a person says to you, "I took a bus to work this morning," you know that the person did not ride a three-letter word with the oral sounds *b, u,* and *s.* What the person meant was that she rode in a four-wheeled vehicle, the size and shape of which is symbolized or represented by the word *bus.* In addition, you know that whatever the person called the four-wheeled vehicle she rode in, the reality of the ride would not be changed. Thus the word *bus* expresses the person's meaning; the word *bus* is not itself the meaning.

The meaning of words is arbitrary: the choice of a certain word to stand for a certain object is a matter of preference. The question then becomes, whose preference?

The Meaning of Words Is Conventional

When we say that the meaning of words is *conventional,* we mean that the selection of a particular word to express a particular meaning is agreed upon by a large number of individuals. By using words that other Americans use and by using them to represent the same or similar meanings that other Americans use them to represent, we are, in effect, agreeing to that usage. When Marge says, "Tom, will you please bring in another chair?" Marge assumes that Tom will bring something to sit on because *chair* is one of the words that we have "agreed" to use when we name an object that can be sat on.

How does agreement come about when a word is first used? The procedure goes something like this: a person uses a new word, and, from the context, sound of voice, bodily action of the user, and other clues, those listening understand the meaning that the user is trying to communicate with the new word. If the listeners like that word, they may begin to use it to represent the same or similar meaning. At some point, enough people have used the word the same way so that those within the culture accept that word as representing that particular meaning. For example, at some point in the history of the English language, someone began calling four-legged creatures with certain other common characteristics *dogs*. The choice of the word *dog* was an arbitrary one. For some reason, whether it was the prestige of the person using the word, or the appealing sound of that word, or the repeated use of the word, more people began to use *dog* than any of the other expressions. Eventually the word *dog* caught on with enough people to gain acceptance.

If you begin using a new word as a matter of preference, you should not expect it to become a part of the language until other people have used the word often enough to make it conventional.

The Meaning of Words Is Learned

Each new generation must learn the language anew. Children's brains enable them to think, and they have a vocal mechanism that allows them to form any number of sounds. But how to determine which sounds go together to form which words must be taught from generation to generation.

During their first year or so of life, children begin to use object words (words that name people, places, and things) they have heard frequently. Usually one of the first words a child learns is *mommy*. At about the same time, children learn a few action words like *drink, walk,* or *kiss*. As the child gains a mastery of a small functional vocabulary of a few dozen words, he begins to struggle with word order. Toddlers speak abbreviated sentences such as, "Go potty," "Me fall down," "No go bed,"

During their first year or so, children begin to use object words they have heard frequently.

and "Me kiss doggy." Remarkably early, children learn that "Me kiss doggy" says something far different from "Doggy kiss me."

By the time children are between three and five years old, they have learned enough vocabulary to communicate almost all their basic ideas and feelings and have mastered enough grammar to be understood. From then on, they enlarge their vocabulary and sharpen their understanding of grammar.

The implication of the point that meanings are learned is that all people do not learn exactly the same meanings for words, nor do they learn exactly the same words. A person must never assume, therefore, that another person will know what he is talking about just because he has used the "right" words.

The Meanings of Words and Perception Are Interrelated

That the meanings of words are arbitrary, conventional, and learned are well-accepted facts. That the meanings of words and perception are interrelated is a theory of language that is still being tested. We discuss this theory here because of the implications it has for interpersonal communication. When we say that two or more concepts are interrelated, we mean that they affect each other. One part of the theory that perception affects language is easily supported. If we encounter a situation that no word in our vocabulary can describe, we are likely either to form a new word or to use an old word in a new way to describe the situation. Likewise, if we see an object different from any other known object, we choose a new word to label it. The other part of the theory—that the words in our language shape our perceptions—is the part that is being tested. Let's consider this part in more detail.

The concept of the interrelationship between language and perception was developed by Benjamin Lee Whorf with suggestions from Edward Sapir. In the early 1950s Whorf presented what is now called the Sapir-Whorf Hypothesis. The gist of the hypothesis is that your perception of reality is determined by the language system that controls your thought system. For instance, Eskimos have different words for different kinds of snow, such as *gana* (falling snow) and *akilukak* (fluffy fallen snow). Each of these words is different from the other. In English we say simply *snow*. We can add words (fallen snow, fluffy snow, hard-packed snow), but in each case the word *snow* is included. The Sapir-Whorf Hypothesis suggests that, when confronted with many different samples of frozen moisture, the American will perceive all the different sizes, shapes, and densities as *snow*. Eskimos, on the other hand, perceive snow in many different ways because they have the language flexibility to do so.

What does this hypothesis mean for the student of interpersonal communication? The Sapir-Whorf Hypothesis allows us to see how different people from different places will *think* differently and *communicate* differently because of differences in both language and perception. Although you are not likely to be communicating much with Eskimos unless you live in Alaska, a lot of your communicating does cross cultural and socioeconomic boundaries. As a result, you must not assume either that the words you use will mean the same to others that they mean to you or that you will see the same realities that others see. We will explore the implications of this hypothesis later when we discuss cross-cultural communication.

The Difference between Denotation and Connotation

The words we use have both denotations and connotations. Because these concepts are so important to our own word use and to the understanding of others' use of words, we'll look at each in some detail.

Denotative Meaning

Denotation means the direct, explicit meaning or reference of a word; denotation is the simplest meaning given in a dictionary. If a person

The gist of the hypothesis is that your perception of reality is determined by the language system that controls your thought system.

wants to find out the denotation of *dog*, he looks in a dictionary, where he finds, "any of a large and varied group of domesticated animals related to the fox, wolf, and jackal."[1] Although knowing dictionary definitions is useful in communicating accurately, even with a firm grasp of word denotation we can still encounter many problems. Let's examine a few:

Multiple meanings   The 500 most common American words have over 14,000 definitions listed in the dictionary. The more common the word, the more dictionary meanings it is likely to have. Let's illustrate this by examining a common, frequently used word, *low*. You know what is meant by the word *low*, or do you? *Webster's New World Dictionary* offers the following twenty-six meanings for *low*:[2]

1. *Of little height or elevation*

2. *Depressed below the surrounding surface of normal elevation*

3. *Of little depth; shallow*

4. *Of little quantity, degree, intensity, value*

5. *Of less than normal height*

6. *Below others in order, position, rating*

7. *Near the horizon—the sun was low*

8. *Near the equator*

9. *Cut so as to expose the neck or part of the shoulders, chest, or back*

10. *Prostrate or dead—in hiding or obscurity*

11. *Deep; profound*

12. *Lacking energy; enfeebled; weak*

13. *Depressed in spirits; melancholy*

14. *Not of high rank; humble; plebeian*

15. *Vulgar; coarse; debased; undignified*

16. *Mean; despicable; contemptible*

17. *Poor; slight; unfavorable*

18. *Containing less than a normal amount of some usual element*

---

[1]With permission. From *Webster's New World Dictionary*, Second College Edition. Copyright © 1978 by William Collins + World Publishing Co., Inc., p. 414.

[2]With permission. From *Webster's New World Dictionary*, Second College Edition. Copyright © 1978 by William Collins + World Publishing Co., Inc., p. 839.

19. *Not advanced in evolution, development, complexity; inferior*

20. *Relatively recent*

21. *Designating or of that gear ratio of a motor vehicle transmission which produces the lowest speed and the greatest power*

22. *Not well supplied with; short of—not having any or much money; short of ready cash*

23. *Of little intensity; not loud*

24. *Designating or producing tones made by relatively slow vibrations; deep in pitch*

25. *Very informal and permissive in matters of ceremony, doctrine, etc.*

26. *Phonet. Produced with the tongue held relatively low in the mouth.*

When a person says, "I'm low," there's at least the chance you do not know what the person means. Our forgetting this simple fact may lead to misunderstandings—little ones and big ones—resulting in minor embarrassment, loss of friendship, and career problems.

Changes in meanings   As time goes on, words acquire and lose meanings. According to W. Nelson Francis, in the 700 years it has been in the English language, the word *nice* "has been used at one time or another to mean the following: foolish, wanton, strange, lazy, coy, modest, fastidious, refined, precise, subtle, slender, critical, attentive, minutely, accurate, dainty, appetizing, agreeable."[3]

We're all familiar with words that have changed their meaning over a period of time. Usage problems come when these changes are quick or dramatic. A common word that has changed meaning considerably in just ten years is *gay*. In the fifties and sixties, people often spoke of having a "gay old time," of Jack being a "gay blade," and the state of "being gay" as desirable for a person who wanted to have friends. In each case *gay* meant joyous, merry, happy, or bright. Today having a "gay old time," being a "gay blade," and the state of "being gay" refer to a person's sexual preference. Although the first meaning is still sometimes heard, it is becoming obsolete. If you describe yourself as a "gay person" and you mean happy or joyous, it is likely that your meaning will be misinterpreted.

Influence of context   The position of a word in a sentence and the other words around it may change the denotation. When a young girl says, "Dad, you owe me a dime," the meaning is somewhat different

---

[3]W. Nelson Francis, *The English Language* (New York: W. W. Norton & Company, Inc., 1965), p. 122.

from when she says, "Dad, I need a dime for the machine." In the first case, she is looking for two nickels, ten pennies, five pennies and a nickel, or a single ten-cent piece. In the second case, she is looking specifically for that small copper coin wrapped in that oh so little bit of silver that we call a *dime*.

Level of abstraction   Denotation is also dependent on the word's level of abstraction. The more specific a word is, the less chance of error in understanding; the more abstract, the greater the chance of error. An example of a series of words moving from specific to abstract is: Dutch elms, elms, deciduous trees, trees, plants, vegetation, organic matter.

People are likely to achieve the greatest accuracy by using specific object language. For example, if a person says she bought a new carpet for the living room, we get a picture of a floor covering made of some fabric. By adding other specific words, the person can sharpen the image. For instance, the phrase "blue, thick carpet" conveys a sharper image than the word carpet alone. "New, steel blue, plush nylon carpet with a one-inch pile" is sharper still. All object language gives some picture. The more specific and concrete that language and the more specific and concrete the qualifiers, the sharper the image. Misunderstandings can still happen: a rug may be a hair piece as well as a floor covering. The problems with object language, however, are relatively easy to cope with.

The most difficult problems with language denotation come with the use of non-object language. Simple verbs like *run, walk,* and *talk* have many variations in meanings; nouns like *integrity, motivation,* and *happiness* have meanings that are often hard to pin down. For instance, what do you understand a person to mean when he says, "Clemons is basically an *honest* man," or, "Don't worry, Judge Simmons is a strong advocate of *justice*"?

We should also remember that a word that is specific in one context may be general or abstract in another. If someone says to Jane, "What is your favorite kind of food?" and Jane replies, "Italian," she would be giving a specific reply. In a restaurant, however, Jane would not get very far ordering *Italian* food. She must choose among ravioli, spaghetti, lasagna, and other selections.

Communication Session

Practice

1. Make a list of current "slang" or "in" words. How do the meanings you assign to these words differ from the meanings your parents or grandparents assign?

2. Write your own definition of each of the following words, then go to a dictionary and check to see how closely your definition matches the dictionary's.

   1. rabbit   4. ring
   2. cloud   5. love
   3. freedom   6. justice

Discussion

Discuss the implication of the Sapir-Whorf Hypothesis with regard to the commonly accepted practice of using the masculine pronouns (he, him, his, himself) when the sex of an individual is unspecified. For example, "Each person should do his own work."

Connotative Meaning

Whereas denotation refers to the most basic, explicit definition of a word, connotation refers to the feelings that a particular word arouses.

Whereas denotation refers to the most basic, explicit definition of a word, connotation refers to the feelings that a particular word arouses.

Let's look at three simple sentences: "She wants a *dog*," "She will treat you like your own *mother*," and "We're going *home* for the holidays." Each of the three words in italics, *dog*, *mother*, and *home*, has a clear dictionary definition. Yet the meaning of those three sentences will differ for different people because of word connotations. Let's look at some possible connotations for each word.

1. *Dog.*   If, when you were a child, you had a dog that was a constant companion, that slept with you at night, licked you when you came home from school, lay at your feet as you watched television, and wagged its tail at the sight of you, you will have emotions and values aroused by the word *dog* that would be entirely different if you never had a dog as a pet and your next-door neighbor's dog bit you five different times and always barked at you no matter what you said to it or how you acted.

2. *Mother.*   If your mother was a warm, loving person who treated you fairly, praised you, and provided for your emotional and physical needs, the meaning you attach to the word will differ from that of a person whose mother was indifferent, busy, unconcerned, and provided only for physical needs and ignored emotional needs.

3. *Home.*   If home to you is a place filled with fun, love, understanding, warmth, and good feelings, it means something far different from what it does to a person to whom home means fighting, bickering, punishment, confinement, and harsh rules.

Each of these three words is a highly emotive and value-expressive word. That is, the meanings of these words are colored by the emotions and values of the person using them. As a result, people who use these words carelessly may have great difficulty understanding one another.

To illustrate connotation we can use I. A. Richards's Semantic Triangle.[4] You can see from Figure 3-1 that, when a word is stated, the

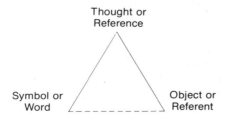

Figure 3-1

[4]C. K. Ogden and I. A. Richards, *The Meaning of Meaning* (New York: Harcourt Brace Jovanovich, 1923), p. 11.

meaning does not go directly to the object or referent but instead goes by way of thought or reference. Both the sender's and the receiver's meaning can be shown using the triangle. For instance, Pat tells Mark he is going home for Christmas. The meaning of *home* for each of them is shown in Figure 3-2.

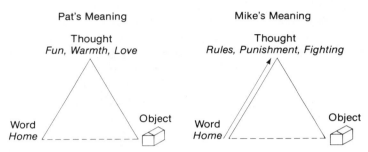

Pat's Meaning

Thought
Fun, Warmth, Love

Word
Home   Object

Mike's Meaning

Thought
Rules, Punishment, Fighting

Word
Home   Object

Figure 3-2

Pat says *home* and Mark hears the word *home*; both may think they have communicated. But because the feelings each has about the place they call *home* differ and because these feelings are not revealed by their statement, they may not be communicating at all. Real communication, sharing meaning, will occur only if one or both of them state how they feel about home.

The Semantic Triangles shown in Figures 3-1 and 3-2 illustrate connotation, but they do not describe the nature of the feelings an individual may have about a word. Charles Osgood and his associates developed an approach to word connotation that focuses on dimensions of meaning.[5] Each of these dimensions is a part of the total feeling a person has about a word. Their method involves describing feelings about words through bipolar adjectives (adjectives that are the opposite of each other).

Why did they focus their study on adjectives? If you list the responses that come to your mind when someone says the words *home, dog,* or *mother,* you will see that many, if not all of them, are adjectives. You may think of *home* in terms of happy or sad, big or small; *mother* in terms of attractive or unattractive, strong or weak, good or bad.

As they studied the various responses, Osgood and his associates grouped them in identifiable categories called *dimensions.* There are many of these dimensions, but the three most prevalent are adjectives of evaluation, adjectives of potency or intensity, and adjectives of activity or

[5]Charles E. Osgood, George J. Suci, and Percy H. Tannenbaum, *The Measurement of Meaning* (Urbana, Illinois: University of Illinois Press, 1957).

movement. They found that *good–bad, awful–nice, ugly–beautiful,* and *valuable–worthless* are most revealing of the evaluation dimension; *strong–weak, light–heavy,* and *large–small,* are most revealing of the potency dimension; and *hot–cold, active–passive,* and *fast–slow,* are most revealing of the activity dimension. The end result of their work was a Semantic Differential test that can be administered to groups and individuals alike.[6] Of the three dimensions, the evaluative seems to be by far the most important, because people choose evaluative adjectives more often than any other in revealing their feelings.

The value of categorizing these dimensions is that it gives us the ability to compare results. First, it enables us to compare one person's feeling with another's. Is one person's feeling more or less positive? Stronger or weaker? More or less active? Second, it enables us to compare a person's reaction to several different words. Does the person see *home* differently from *resort, farm,* or *camp*? Third, it enables us to compare a person's feeling about a word at different times. Does a person feel differently about *camp* after she has spent six weeks at one?

What is the value of this kind of knowledge to you in your interpersonal communication? If you know how others feel about the words they use, you understand and communicate better with them. Consider a schoolteacher who wants to develop a teaching unit on the theme "A community is a group of people who help each other." It would be useful for that teacher to discover how the class feels about such words as *community, home, police,* and *businessman* before beginning the unit. Or consider the value of the semantic differential to the congresswoman who would like to know how the people in her district feel about words like *bussing, schools,* and *taxes*.

Since giving a Semantic Differential test to everyone you talk with would be impracticable, what can you do to ensure your awareness of others' meanings? First, just being conscious of the potential for differences in feelings may prevent you from always assuming that, because a person uses an easily defined word, you will know what that person means. Second, take conscious note of the nonverbal cues that accompany the word. How the person sounds and looks may well tell you as much—or more—about his feelings as what he says. In the next chapter we will explore aspects of voice, gesture, and movement that affect meaning. Third, use the skills that are designed to help you double check the accuracy of your perceptions. In Chapter 7 we will discuss guidelines for paraphrasing, describing behavior, and perception checking. These three skills are indispensable to your understanding of meaning.

---

[6]Ibid., pp. 36–38.

Communication Session

Reflection

Are you aware of your feelings about the words you use? How do you know?

Practice

Working in groups of three, select several common words like *home* and *dog.* Each person will list at least five adjectives that he or she associates with the word. When you have finished, compare the results. In what ways are your meanings different?

Language Use

We have looked at the relationship between words and meaning; now we want to consider the goals of using language and point out a few common pitfalls you need to look out for as you begin to practice your interpersonal communication skills.

Goals of Language

The main goal of language use is the development of the behavioral flexibility that is achieved when language is clear and appropriate.

Clarity is the basis of using language successfully. Messages must be sent using verbal symbols that accurately reflect the sender's meaning, that are specific enough to clarify the differences between similar ideas, and that are free from contradictory or annoying nonverbal cues. In later chapters we'll look at several elements that contribute to clarity and at several of the skills that can help you clarify meaning.

In addition to being clear, language must be appropriate. One way to achieve appropriateness is to make your language fit the knowledge, interests, and attitudes of your receiver. Another way is to adapt your language to the context in which you are interacting. Use language that a receiver can understand. A five-year-old child has a smaller vocabulary than his mother; a ditch digger may not understand abstract language as well as a lawyer. Use language that a receiver will feel comfortable with. Many college students both know and use profanity in conversation with their fellow students. These same students use a different vocabulary when talking with their parents, their instructors, or their bosses. Many problems in communication arise when a person unthinkingly uses a vocabulary that meets the norms of one group when he is speaking to a different group. Any student of communication should understand that groups differ in their norms for member behavior, and that if a person is to be effective in communication with different groups, he will have to adapt his vocabulary to the norms expected by a particular group.

For some people certain words have a hidden power. Words themselves are neither good nor bad—it's the connotative meanings the users of words assign to them that may be good or bad. Yet, some people react emotionally to certain words as if the words themselves had power. With any group there are words that will cause strong reactions whether the speaker intended to arouse that reaction or not. Such expressions as, "I tried to *jew* down the price," or "Old Marshall is a *red-neck*," or "You're apt to see a lot of *libbers* applying for jobs today," are going to create problems whether the speaker intended them to or not. Everyone makes mistakes on occasion. And even though any inappropriate vocabulary will hurt your communication, changing your vocabulary when you sense a strong reaction may help repair the damage. The continued use of objectionable language in the face of adverse reaction, however, will lead only to more problems.

Pitfalls of Language Use

We should always try to use language clearly and appropriately. Where are we likely to go wrong? How do we get ourselves into trouble? Let's consider a few of the most common problems of language use:

1. *Limited vocabulary.*   A limited vocabulary can affect both your message formation and your ability to listen. In general, the smaller your vocabulary, the greater the potential difficulty in communicating effectively. Meanings may be in people, not in words, but if we know which words are most likely to communicate accurate pictures of what we are thinking or feeling, we greatly simplify communication.

A person whose use of words is vital to her occupation (a writer or a journalist, for instance) will have a vocabulary of at least forty thousand words. A college student may have a vocabulary of as many as thirty thousand words or as few as ten thousand words. A standard college dictionary includes about one-hundred thousand words. These figures make it clear that most of us are likely to run across words that we cannot define.

Some scholars argue that the standard American vocabulary is getting smaller because people spend more time watching television than they do reading magazines, newspapers, and books. The argument is that, since television and mass circulation printed matter use a vocabulary that twelve- to fourteen-year-olds will be able to understand, the average adult American is seeing fewer words. As vocabularies get smaller, the mass media use even fewer difficult words. If this trend continues, there may be a time when the English language is reduced to only a few thousand commonly used and commonly understood words.

The vocabulary of people whose occupations require them to use *jargon* (words that have meaning only in a particular context) may cause problems for their listeners. For example, an instructor of public speaking may say that Martin Luther King's strength was his *ethos.* "His what?" a student asks. "You know, his ethos—his credibility, his charisma." "Now I see," the student replies. *Ethos* is a standard word in the teacher's vocabulary because he is a scholar in public speaking; he forgets that the student in a beginning speaking course has no reason to have heard of the word *ethos.*

We cannot guarantee that our listeners will know all the words we use, but we can try to use words that they are likely to understand.

2. *Pressure.*   Under pressure a person is likely to make mistakes in word choice. If a person is relaxed and confident, communication is likely to flow smoothly—the person is likely to select words that communicate. If this same person is put under pressure, the accuracy of word selection begins to deteriorate. If you come from a large family, you may have seen your mother or father go through the names of all the children before getting the right name. If, for instance, it's dinner time and you are setting the table incorrectly, your mother might say in a moment of frustration, "Pam, er Chrissie, er Jack, I mean Kathie, what are you doing!" Your mother knows your name, but under pressure accuracy of word choice often fails.

Your brain is like a computer: it is a marvelous instrument, but it does fail to work sometimes. More often than not, the failures happen when you are under pressure or when you speak before you think. Sometimes you think one thing and say something entirely different. Consider a familiar scene: The math professor says, "We all remember that the numerator is on the bottom and the denominator is on the top of the fraction, so when we divide fractions . . ." "Mrs. Jones," a voice from the third row interrupts, "you said the numerator is on the bottom and . . ." "Is that what I said?" Mrs. Jones asks, "Well, you know what I meant!" Did everyone in the class know? Probably not.

3. *Double meanings.*   The person listening to you may detect a contradiction in your message. As you speak, you are at the same time sending your message on the nonverbal channel. When you say "ouch," you are likely to have a pained expression on your face and a pained sound in your voice. But the verbal and nonverbal messages are not always complementary. For example, a person may answer the question, "Do you still love me?" with the words, "Of course I do," but nonverbal signals may contradict the words. In this situation the listener is more likely to pay attention to the nonverbal cue than to the meaning of the spoken words. Why? Because words can be controlled much more easily than facial expression or tone of voice. We'll explore this subject in greater detail in the chapter on the nonverbal base of communication.

Summary

Language is a system of symbols used for communicating. Language communicates when words are arranged in certain learned ways. Even though you have worked years to develop a good vocabulary and to understand the grammar of the English language, you are still likely to have problems.

You will be a more effective communicator if you recognize that the meaning of words is purely arbitrary (meanings are in people, not words), the meaning of words is conventional, the meaning of words is learned, and words and perceptions are interrelated.

A word's denotation is its dictionary meaning. Despite the ease with which we can check a dictionary meaning, word denotation can still give us problems. Why? Because most words have more than one dictionary meaning, changes in meanings occur faster than dictionaries are published, words take on different meanings as they are used in different contexts, and meanings can become obscured as words become more abstract.

A word's connotation is the emotive and value significance the word arouses. Regardless of what a dictionary says a word means, we carry with us meanings that are a result of our experience with the object, thought, or action the word represents. Connotations can be understood by tracing the course of a word on a Semantic Triangle. Word connotations can be quantified and tested by comparing scores achieved on a Semantic Differential test.

You can make your communication more effective if you take into account the goals of language use. You can achieve a reasonable level of success in your language use if you strive to make word choice as clear and appropriate as possible. You should also be aware of common pitfalls of language use: limited vocabulary, pressure, and double meanings.

Suggested Readings

Stuart Chase. *The Power of Words.* New York: Harcourt Brace and Jovanovich, 1953. A pioneer work in general semantics. A good place to begin the study of problems with meaning.

Joseph DeVito. *The Psychology of Speech and Language.* New York: Random House, 1970. A short work that you will find quite informative.

W. Nelson Francis. *The English Language: An Introduction.* New York: W. W. Norton & Co., Inc., 1965. An excellent introduction to linguistics.

Edwin Newman. *Strictly Speaking: Will America Be the Death of English?* Indianapolis: Bobbs-Merrill Co., Inc., 1974. A popular book that is well worth reading.

Charles E. Osgood, George J. Suci, and **Percy H. Tannenbaum.** *The Measurement of Meaning.* Urbana: University of Illinois Press, 1957. Good for a complete discussion of the Semantic Differential.

Chapter 4
The Nonverbal Base of Communication

PAYOFFS *After you have read this chapter, you should be able to:*

1. *Discuss the differences between verbal and nonverbal communication.*
2. *Explain the three most important functions of nonverbal communication.*
3. *Discuss how fixed-featured and semi-fixed-featured space affect communication.*
4. *Arrange semi-fixed-featured space that will invite effective communication.*
5. *Explain how territoriality affects communication with others.*
6. *Explain your use of the four categories of personal space.*
7. *Discuss how color, temperature, and lighting may affect interpersonal communication.*
8. *Explain how you use time and how you react to others who use it differently.*
9. *Define kinesics.*
10. *Discuss the use of emblems, illustrators, affect displays, regulators, and adaptors in interpersonal communication.*
11. *Define paralanguage.*
12. *Discuss vocal qualifiers, vocal differentiators, and vocal interferences.*

Helen moves forward smoothly on the tennis court to take the high, easy bounce and put the ball away. Instead of the super shot she anticipates, she hits the ball into the net. She groans and throws her racket on the ground in disgust.

As he picks up his fifth card in the hand of draw poker, George breaks into a wide smile—quickly he looks around the table to see whether anyone caught the smile, and then he resumes his "poker" face.

"No doubt about it, Maggie, you were terrific," Suzi says with a sarcastic sneer in her voice.

Allison rushes through her bath, hurries her make-up job, dresses frantically, and finishes at the stroke of eight. "Made it!" she says to herself as she moves down the stairs and into the living room to await Jeff. As 8:30 comes and goes, Allison is doing a slow burn as she paces the floor in front of the door.

In each of the preceding paragraphs, the people use nonverbal channels as the primary means of communication. Discussing nonverbal communication separately from verbal communication may seem somewhat artificial because in the real world both occur simultaneously. Nevertheless, in order to stress the importance of nonverbal communication, we will analyze it separately.

Everyone has heard the saying, "Actions speak louder than words." Actions are so important to our communication that researchers have estimated that in face-to-face communication as much as 90 percent of the meaning may be carried by the nonverbal message.[1] Because people are so much less aware of the nonverbal structure than the verbal, we'll begin with a basic analysis of the differences between verbal and nonverbal messages. We'll then look at the various elements that make up nonverbal communication.

Verbal and Nonverbal Communication

Verbal and nonverbal communication differ in at least three major ways. First, whereas verbal communication is discrete, nonverbal communication is continuous. Speech communication begins when sound comes from the mouth and ends when the sound stops. Nonverbal communication, however, continues for as long as a person is in your presence.

Second, whereas verbal communication is single-channeled, nonverbal communication is multichanneled. Have you ever tried to participate in a conversation when you were wearing ear plugs? If the plugs worked properly, you could not hear, and there was little if any communication. Verbal symbols—words—come to us one at a time, in sequence; we hear the spoken words, see the printed or written words. We send and receive various kinds of nonverbal messages simultaneously—in, for example, tone of voice to be heard or a raised eyebrow or a hand gesture to be seen. By nonverbal messages we communicate more than most of us realize.

Third, whereas verbal communication is almost always under your voluntary control, you may not be aware of, let alone control, your nonverbal communication. You are likely to think about or to plan what you are going to say—verbal communication is usually well under control. On occasion words will "slip out," but in most instances you determine what you want to say. In your nonverbal communication you may consciously control some of your "body language," but more often than not you are unaware of all the nonverbal signals you are sending.

These contrasts are not meant to give the impression that you have two communication systems, verbal and nonverbal, operating totally apart from each other. Actually, verbal and nonverbal communication are usually both operating as you send and receive messages.

---

[1]Albert Mehrabian, *Silent Messages* (Belmont, California: Wadsworth Publishing Company, 1971), p. 44.

In the ideal relationship, nonverbal communication *supplements* verbal communication. Gesturing to show the size of a ball or the direction a car went reinforces the words. The dejected look accompanying the words, "I lost" or the smile that goes with the exclamation, "Congratulations!" are complementary. When the coach grips your arm and says, "I want you to try harder," the grip emphasizes the meaning of the word.

Under some circumstances, nonverbal communication is sufficient by itself—no verbal communication is needed. When the team comes into the dressing room after a game, the looks, posture, and tones of voice tell the story of who won the game—no one needs to ask. And when the umpire jerks his thumb into the air, you know the runner is out.

The most important point about nonverbal communication, however, is that nonverbal communication can contradict verbal communication. When you slam the door behind you but say you don't care; when you perspire profusely but claim you are not nervous; when you shout and say you are not angry, your verbal and nonverbal messages are contradictory. Which is to be believed? According to most communication scholars, nonverbal communication defines the meaning in most situations. This means that observers are more inclined to believe what is expressed nonverbally because it is less subject to conscious control. You are not likely to fool anyone if you should say, "Oh, I'm so sorry!" and your eyes are dancing and a smile is twitching at the corners of your mouth. You are not fooled by someone who says, "Let me help," then disappears when there is work to be done. The contradiction of verbal statements is carried to an art when the tone of voice is sarcastic. Such statements as, "Great play, George!" said in a sarcastic tone are always perceived as negative, regardless of the positive nature of the words themselves.

In this next section we'll examine several elements of nonverbal behavior. Larry Barker and Nancy Collins[2] have identified some eighteen separate elements; we will group the most important ones under the four headings of environment, personal style, body motions, and paralanguage.

The Environment

Not until we analyze some of the elements of nonverbal communication do we become aware of how much meaning we place in them. Meanings gained through the environment are a case in point. How fixed-featured, semi-fixed-featured, and informal space, as defined by Edward T. Hall,[3] are

---

[2]Larry L. Barker and Nancy B. Collins, "Nonverbal and Kinesic Research," in Philip Emmert and William D. Brooks (Eds.), *Methods of Research in Communication* (Boston: Houghton Mifflin, 1970), pp. 343–372.
[3]Edward T. Hall, *The Hidden Dimension* (Garden City, N.Y.: Doubleday, 1966).

structured makes a great deal of difference in how we react to them. Moreover, color, temperature, and lighting further affect those meanings.

Fixed-Featured Space

Fixed-featured space includes the elements in your environment that are relatively permanent. The buildings that you live and work in and the parts of those buildings that cannot be moved are all fixed-featured space. Architects communicate something about themselves and their environment through the design of buildings. People who buy or rent homes or who rent space for offices seek a compatible environment. Many elements of fixed-featured space affect your interpersonal communication. The amount of time neighbors spend talking with each other is likely to differ between people whose homes are less than twenty feet apart and those whose homes are a quarter of a mile apart. Moreover, people who live in apartment buildings tend to become acquainted with neighbors who live across the hall and next door but are less likely to know those who live on other floors. Also, your chances of knowing people who live in your building are greatly enhanced if you live near an elevator, a staircase, or a door.

Not only does fixed-featured space often determine with whom you will communicate, it also can help or inhibit the kind of communication that will occur. Have you ever gone to an informal dinner for six or eight people in a formal dining room? The environment is too formal for the guests to develop the intimate atmosphere that such a party needs. Or have you ever attended a formal dance in a converted barn? The guests feel foolish because the setting does not match the occasion.

Semi-Fixed-Featured Space

Semi-fixed-featured space consists of objects that remain in a fixed position unless they are moved. Your desk, your chairs, and your table are objects in your room that are positioned to create an environment. How you arrange these objects reveals a great deal about your interpersonal relationships. The atmosphere of a classroom in which several rows of chairs face the lectern differs from that of a room in which chairs are grouped into one large circle or four or five smaller circles. In the first environment, most students anticipate a lecture format. In the second, they might expect a give-and-take discussion, with the instructor and members of the class participating. In the third setting, they might expect the class to be working on group projects.

The arrangement of furniture in your living room creates an effect. The presence of a television set in that room often determines that all chairs and sofas face toward the set, with none turned toward other seats.

This room arrangement invites television viewing but discourages conversation.

Consider a situation that may be well known to you—the talk with your professor during his office hours. You can tell a lot about him and about the kind of climate he is trying to establish just by the arrangement of his office and where he asks you to sit. If he shows you to a chair across the desk from him, he may be implying, "Let's talk business—I'm the professor and you're the student." If you would like to be more personal, the barrier of space (and the table) could hinder communication. If he shows you to a chair at the side of his desk, he may be indicating, "Don't be nervous—let's just chat." Although we must be somewhat tentative about the conclusions we draw, the use of space is nevertheless a pretty good index of how a person is going to treat you and how he is going to expect you to treat him. We expect space utilization to conform with our perception of the nature of the setting. When we do something that appears to violate norms or is different from expectation, the result may be harmful to communication.

Informal Space

Informal space refers to all the space around us: how we use it and how we feel about it. Students of *proxemics*, the study of space, are concerned with such questions as why people tend to sit in the same chair in class each day even when seating is not assigned. Or what determines the behavior of people in a crowded elevator or trying to get on a crowded bus. As communicators we need to be aware of how people regard space and how we can use knowledge of space to improve our communication.

We are well aware that our communication is influenced by the distance between us and those with whom we communicate. Edward T. Hall, a leading researcher in nonverbal communication, has discussed the four different distances that can be used to determine four different communication situations.[4] By far the most important is the intimate distances, up to about eighteen inches, which we regard as appropriate for intimate conversation with close friends, parents, and younger children. What happens when we are forced into spatial relationships that violate this intimate distance? Consider your last ride in a crowded elevator, for example. Most people get rather rigid, look at the floor or the indicator above the door, and pretend that they are not touching. Being forced into an intimate situation is acceptable, provided all involved follow the "rules." When closeness is not required, having someone encroach on your personal space is cause for a form of alarm reaction. For instance, in

---

[4]Edward T. Hall, *The Silent Language* (Garden City, N.Y.: Doubleday, 1959), pp. 163–164.

a movie theater that is less than one-quarter full, couples tend to leave a seat or more between them and another couple. If you are sitting in a nearly empty movie theater and a stranger sits right next to you, you are likely to be upset. If a person you do not know violates this intimate distance in conversation, you may instinctively back away.

The other three distances are personal—one foot to two and one-half feet—appropriate for casual conversation; social—four to twelve feet—for impersonal business (a job interview, for instance); and public distance—more than twelve feet. These norms have grown out of typical behavior. What do these distances mean to you? Test them against your own use of space.

One way of looking at informal space is as territory. Territory is a space over which a person claims ownership. A violation of this space will cause the person to react defensively. Although we no longer look at territory controlled as the principal means of determining personal value (at times in the past—and still occasionally in the present—the amount of land owned determined status), we certainly still subscribe to the so-called territorial imperative in much of our daily routine. Whether we are functioning in an office, a classroom, a dormitory, or our home, one of our first actions is to try to define a territory that is ours. How do you deal with your territory? Have you and your roommate divided your sleeping room in half? How about closet space? desk space? When you go into a

Misunderstandings between people of different cultures often occur as a result of their different ways of perceiving territory.

classroom, do you establish a territory that is yours? When you go to the library, do you spread out your books and papers so the limits of your territory are defined? Have you ever used a "marker" (a notebook, an umbrella, your coat) to identify your space in a dining hall, a classroom, a movie? Or have you ever asked someone to hold "your" seat or "your" place in line while you were gone? Or when you have occupied the same space over a long period, do you expect people to recognize it as yours? For most people, the answer to *all* of these questions is "yes."

What does this have to do with your communication? Mostly, we expect others to respect our territory, and we are expected to respect the territory of others. When our territory is invaded, we usually act defensively toward the invader. For instance, a person sitting too close to us in the dining hall or the person dropping books on our space is apt to be met with a cold stare or a harsh comment. Of course, persons who are not considered threatening do not provoke the same defensive action— still, if your guy or girl pushes his or her books onto your side of the table, you might feel at least a little twinge.

Our needs for territory are culturally determined, and therefore what an American would consider the boundaries of territory may be different from what an Arab or an Oriental would consider to be territorial boundaries. Misunderstandings between people of different cultures often occur as a result of their different ways of perceiving territory.

Color, Temperature, and Lighting

When it comes down to it, almost every facet of the environment has a communication potential. Three facets that people seem sensitive to and over which people have considerable control are color, temperature, and lighting. *Color* is particularly important to how we behave. For instance, people are likely to react predictably to various colors: red is accepted as exciting, stimulating; blue as secure, comfortable, tender, soothing, calm, peaceful; yellow as cheerful, jovial; black as strong, masterful. Interior designers who are trying to create a peaceful, serene atmosphere will decorate in blues rather than in reds and yellows. If, on the other hand, they want to create a stimulating atmosphere, as for a playroom, they will use reds and yellows.

Of course, much of our reaction to color comes from expectation: mashed potatoes are supposed to be white; butter, yellow; and broccoli, green. When a color does not meet expectation, reactions are unpredictable. Mashed potatoes tinted green in honor of Saint Patrick's Day may nauseate diners who are not color-blind, before they even attempt to eat.

Temperature acts as a stimulant or deterrent to communication. The ideal temperature for communication is one that is perceived as neither too high nor too low. Americans seem most comfortable when temperatures are between 70 and 75 degrees. If you doubt the importance of temperature, recall your grade school days when the June or September heat made listening to the teacher especially difficult. During the brutally cold winter of 1977, Americans began to learn by hard experience some of the discomforts of the energy crisis. Most citizens complied—some willy-nilly—with requests that thermostats be lowered to 65 degrees. For many who were conditioned to more "reasonable" temperatures, the cold acted like noise in the environment, making the sending and receiving of messages difficult.

Lighting can also act as a stimulant or deterrent to communication. In lecture halls and reading rooms, bright light is expected—it is conducive to good listening and comfortable reading. In a chic restaurant, a music listening room, or a television lounge you expect the lighting to be soft and rather dim. Such soft, dim lighting is conducive to a cozy atmosphere and to intimate conversation. You can create a communication climate by adjusting the variables of color, temperature, and lighting.

Communication Session

Reflection

1. Think of where you live (dorm, apartment, house). Which of your neighbors do you know best? Can you account for interactions with neighbors by the proximity of your fixed-featured space?

2. Make a list of territories that you defend. What do you do when those territories are invaded? What are your expectations about space when you are talking with an instructor? When you are talking with a good friend? When you are talking with a person for the first time?

Practice

1. Work in pairs. Start on the opposite sides of the room (at least 20 feet apart). Begin to walk toward each other. (a) Stop at 12 feet apart and hold a conversation. (b) Stop at 7 feet apart and hold a conversation. (c) Stop at 1 or 2 feet apart and hold a conversation. (d) Continue until you feel *too* close. Step back until the distance seems comfortable. Notice how far apart you are.

2. Before your instructor arrives at class, change the semi-fixed-featured space in the classroom. For example, remove the lectern, change the arrangement of the chairs, and the like. Note the instructor's reactions to these changes.

3. Next time you are standing and talking with a friend, slyly take one step toward him. He will probably step back in order to reestablish conversationally comfortable distance. Try the same thing with two or three different people.

Discussion

1. In groups of four, discuss what happened as people walked toward each other. What changes in behavior occurred as distances became smaller? Was there any difference in behavior of male to female? male to male? female to female?

2. Discuss how individuals in the group react to different colors and variations in heating and lighting. Under what conditions do you work best? rest best? listen best?

Personal Style

Your personal style is a presentation of yourself through such elements as the clothes you wear, the way you wear your hair, your body shape and how you react to it, and how you treat and react to others' treatments of time. Most people know by now that not all long hairs are anti-Establishment, that short skirts are not indicative of promiscuity, and that size is not related to brutality—at least people say they know. Still, long hair, length of skirts, and size as well as numerous other physical qualities can and do communicate to your benefit or to your detriment. When a woman has her hair done, buys a new outfit to wear, and takes a maximum amount of time to make sure she looks just right, she is saying something about her attitude toward a job interview; likewise, the man who does not bother to shower and shave and puts on his rumpled sport coat over a dirty shirt is saying something about his attitude toward a job interview.

We sometimes laugh at Emily Post's and Amy Vanderbilt's statements on etiquette, but what they do is verbalize cultural norms. How a person acts in relation to those norms does communicate.

Clothing

You have the power to help yourself or hinder yourself by the way you dress for a particular occasion. Times change and values change, so what was proper dress ten years ago is not necessarily proper today. It is up to you to determine what is appropriate or expected; then you can deviate from expectation at your own risk. The man who goes into an interview with a major oil company in a rumpled sweatshirt, levis, and tennis shoes had better have quite a lot going for him if he expects even to be heard, let alone hired.

People have the right to their individual differences, and we believe modern society is moving in the right direction in allowing a person to express himself individually. Nevertheless, your clothes are still perceived by others as clues to your attitudes and behaviors—clothes do communicate, however accurate or inaccurate you may believe that communication to be.

Body Shape

More basic than the clothes we wear is the body type the clothes adorn. There are three basic body types: endomorph, mesomorph, and ectomorph. The endomorph is soft, round, and fat; the mesomorph is muscular, hard, and athletic; the ectomorph is thin, fragile, and brittle.

In a study by Wells and Siegel,[5] 120 adult subjects were shown silhouette drawings of the three body types and asked to rate them on such paired adjectives as lazy–energetic; intelligent–unintelligent; dependent–self-reliant. The results showed that endomorphs are seen as older, lazier, weaker, but more warmhearted, good-natured, agreeable, and trusting; mesomorphs are seen as stronger, more masculine, better looking, younger, taller, and more mature; ectomorphs are seen as younger, more ambitious, more suspicious, more tense and nervous, more stubborn, and quieter. Thus how you are physically proportioned affects others' perceptions of you.

You have the power to help yourself or hinder yourself by the way you dress for a particular occasion.

---

[5]William D. Wells and Bertram Siegel, "Stereotyped Somatypes," *Psychological Reports,* Vol. 8 (1961), pp. 77–78.

In addition to body type itself, height, skin color, and body hair also communicate. Americans seem to prefer tall men to short. Within races, skin tone from lighter to darker is also a variable. We are affected by the amount of hair on face, arms, and body, as well as the length of hair on the head.

Clothes, body type, hair, skin color, and height are all part of the personal style that you communicate to others. Whether your approach to these elements is conscious or unconscious, the interrelation of these elements still affects your relations with people around you.

Time

Because time belongs to no one in particular, it may seem a peculiar topic to include in a discussion on personal style. It is not time itself, however, but your attitude toward time and the use you make of time that we are concerned with. The way you *handle* time is truly a matter of personal style.

For each of us, there are durations of time that we regard as appropriate for certain events. For instance, Sunday sermons are twenty to thirty minutes long, classes take fifty minutes (Tuesday and Thursday classes of seventy-five minutes never seem right to many students), a movie runs roughly two hours. Television programs last thirty minutes and sixty minutes *unless* they are movies or sporting events. When the duration of an event does not meet expectations, that time itself becomes an obstacle to communication. You may get angry with the instructor who holds you beyond normal class time; likewise, you may become hostile if someone asks you to cut short your lunch hour or coffee break.

In addition to an appropriate length of time, there is also an appropriate time of day for certain things to happen. People work during the day, sleep at night, eat at noon, have a cocktail at five o'clock, and so on. You may make judgments about people who accept times for events that differ from yours. Joe is strange if he gets up at 4:30 A.M. The Martins eat dinner at 4:30 P.M.; the Smiths do not dine till 8 P.M.—you may consider both families peculiar. Adam works on his books from midnight till 4 A.M. and then sleeps till noon—you are aware that he is "different." So, *when* people do things communicates something to you.

Finally, and perhaps most basic to your perception of people, is how they treat time designations. For instance, suppose you are having a party. When you invited people, you told them to come at about 8 P.M. What do you think of Rob if (1) he arrives at 7:30? (2) he arrives at 8 P.M. exactly? (3) he arrives at 8:30? (4) he arrives at 10 P.M.? Now, for the sake of argument, let's change the setting. Suppose you have a test scheduled for tomorrow. After today's class, suppose that a group of five of you decides to study together. Because your place is as good as any, you say, "Stop by about 8 P.M." Now what do you think of Rob if he arrives at (1) 7:30? (2) 8 P.M. exactly? (3) 8:30? and (4) 10 P.M.? Depending upon how *you* see time, you will make a value judgment on the basis of when he comes; moreover, you may see his arrival time differently depending upon the occasion or your past experience with him.

Time does communicate. You must be sensitive to your own perceptions of time as well as to those of others so that the variable of time facilitates or at least does not inhibit your communication.

Communication Session

Reflection

1. Do you dress to achieve any special goal? If so, what? If not, does how you dress still affect your relations with others?
2. What is your body type? Do you believe the generalizations about body types on pages 73–74 accurately reflect your personality? If so, how? If not, why not?

Practice

1. Next time you go to class, dress completely differently from your normal dress. Notice what effect, if any, this has on your communication with those around you.
2. Working in groups of four to six, have two people role-play various situations related to time, and the rest of the group will share their reactions. Examples: A student is late for an appointment with a professor; your date is fifteen minutes late for your first date; your steady is fifteen minutes late for a date.
3. Each person in class should bring in a colored picture of a person taken from a magazine article or advertisement. Divide into groups of six. Each person in the group should write three to five adjectives about each of the pictures. Then the persons in the group should compare their assessments and discuss them on the basis of perception of clothes, body type, height, hair, and skin color.

Discussion

In your groups, consider how each person handles someone who violates his or her time boundaries.

Body Motions

Of all nonverbal behavior you are probably most familiar with *kinesics*, the technical name for body motions. These include facial expression, eye behavior, gestures, movements of the limbs and body, and posture. To the unobservant, all body motion may appear to be random

movement growing from peculiarities of culture, personality, or national-
ity (Italians talk with their hands; the British use few gestures). By careful
study, however, you can begin to interpret with some accuracy these
nonverbal clues. To analyze the various body motions, we will adopt the
Ekman and Friesen categories of emblems, illustrators, affect displays,
regulators, and adaptors.[6]

Emblems

These body motions or gestures take the place of a word or two or a
phrase. Emblems are the exception to the rule of the nonsymbolic nature
of nonverbal communication. Their meanings are every bit as clearly defined and generally accepted as are verbal dictionary definitions. Thumbs
up for "everything is Go"; extension of first and second finger in V shape for
"peace"; the waved hand for "hi" or "how are you doing"; shaking the head
for "no" and nodding for "yes"; shrugging the shoulders for "maybe" or "I
don't care"; or rolling the eyes for exasperation are but a few of the nonverbal emblems that people consistently use to replace speech.

Just as your verbal vocabulary consists of words that you know and
use regularly in your daily speech, words that you can recognize if others
use them but that are not in your working vocabulary, and words that
you have to look up, so your nonverbal vocabulary has these same three
classifications. For instance, nearly everyone in our culture nods his head
for "yes"; this is an example of a nonverbal emblem that each of us
knows and uses regularly in daily communication. Examples of emblems
that you recognize but do not use are those that do not fit your personality, or do not have enough meaning for you. Many obscene emblems may
be in your understanding vocabulary even if you rarely or never use
them. Likewise, there are many emblems that are just not familiar to you.
New emblems come into vogue just as new words are constantly being
coined (the generation gap is reinforced by both verbal and nonverbal
language usage). Moreover, some ethnic groups have sign languages
whose meaning is known only to members of the group.

When do you rely on emblems to carry your messages? Emblems are
probably used most when you are too far away for speech to be heard
and when there is so much noise that you cannot hear, or when you just
do not feel like verbalizing. Emblems also are used nearly exclusively when
auditory receptors do not work properly (the deaf have developed an extremely elaborate sign language) or when people are trying to exclude
someone who is not a member of the "in" group.

---

[6]Paul Ekman and W. V. Friesen, "The Repertoire of Nonverbal Behavior: Categories, Ori-
gins, Usage, and Coding," *Semiotica*, Vol. 1 (1969), pp. 49–98.

Illustrators

Illustrators are sets of nonverbal body movements or gestures used to accent or emphasize what is being said verbally. Often when a person says, "He talks with his hands" or "She couldn't talk if we tied her hands," he means that the person's speech and body movements are totally complementary.

Researchers have classified illustrators as serving six different functions. *Batons* are movements that accent or emphasize a particular word. If you said, "I don't want to go to the movie," you might make a sharp downward gesture with one or both of your hands when you said, "want." Nearly everyone has different gestures he uses as his batons. It is not the nature of the gesture that is important so much as where or how it is used. *Ideographs* sketch a path or direction of thought. If you said, "The progress of this class goes from good [and you pointed to an imaginary extreme] to poor [and you pointed in the opposite direction]," your pointing would be a form of ideograph. Again, the gesture itself is not so important as where or how it is used. *Deictics* are movements that point to present objects. If when you said "Take this chair, for instance," you pointed to it by extending your forefinger, the act of pointing was a deictic gesture. *Spatial movements* depict a spatial relationship. You might hold your hands about a foot apart when you said, "The fish I caught was only about this long," or you might hold your hand parallel to the ground as you said, "She already stands about this high." *Kinetographs* are movements that depict a body action. For instance, you might chuckle and say, "Did you see the way he was nodding?" and while you were talking you would show the kind of nod you had been observing. The last classification is *pictographs,* which are actual drawings of their referents to illustrate such statements as "Here's the shape of the window."

Like emblems, illustrators are used intentionally, and receivers process their use in determining meaning. Also, illustrators are socially learned and can be taught. Body action used in public speaking or lecturing consists largely of illustrators. In the old days, training of public speakers involved detailed study of illustrators. You have probably heard older people talk about "elocution," which was in part a study of how to gesture "properly." Today, when we teach public speaking, we talk of letting the body action follow naturally from the thought. We are not, therefore, advocating that you learn and put into practice a set of illustrators. Our goal is to raise your awareness of their use, and, if you use them inappropriately, or if your use calls attention to them rather than facilitating meaning, you should try to correct the use.

Affect Displays

When you feel a strong emotion, you are likely to affect-display the nature of that feeling through a facial configuration or some concurrent body response. For instance, you get out of bed in the morning and, as you walk sleepy-eyed to the bathroom, you stub your toe. You are likely to show the pain with some verbal comment (do you have a pet word for these occasions?) and with an accompanying grimace. More often than not, these reactions—spur-of-the-moment emotional displays—are not intended as conscious communication. One of the apparent reasons for labeling the body motion a "display" is that your reaction takes place automatically whether you are alone or with others, and it will probably be quite noticeable.

Of all the body motions we have considered thus far, affect display is the kind by which you reveal most about yourself. Although the response you make is automatic, it is conditioned by a set of cultural, familial, and personal norms that alter the nature of the display. You can learn a lot about a person by how he displays his emotions. The behavior you witness will probably be of four different kinds. Consider these carefully— they are very important to increasing your awareness of nonverbal communication.

1. *A person may deintensify the appearance of clues.*   For instance, when Jane is extremely afraid, happy, or hurt, she may feel she must attempt to look only slightly afraid, happy, or hurt. Perhaps Jim bangs his head very hard on the door frame getting into the car, but acts as if it hurt only a little.

2. *A person may overintensify or amplify.*   When a person is only slightly afraid or happy, she may show extreme fear or happiness. A child (and sometimes an adult) who suffers a little pain may scream as though grievously injured.

3. *A person may take a neutral position.*   If a person is happy, afraid, sad, or angry, he shows no difference. We call this the poker face.

4. *A person may mask the clues.*   This means that the person purposely looks different from what we would expect. If a person is happy, he may sneer or look angry. If he is angry, he may smile.

These display rules are usually learned—perhaps at home, perhaps in a social group, or perhaps in keeping with a self-image a person is trying to project. Especially in relation to the family or social group, a person tries to conform to the established norms. For instance, if in your family it is considered bad form to show fear, then you learned from early childhood to deemphasize your display when you were afraid, or to adopt a neutral posture or perhaps to mask the display. Of course, the stronger the stimulus, the harder it is to follow your personal rule. When you step sleepily out of bed and stub your toe, the display is likely to be directly proportional to the degree of pain. Ordinarily, however, your rules are your guide. Of course, you may portray yourself differently under different circumstances depending on how well you know the people present, what you think of them, and what you want them to think of you.

In this area of affect display, you as a student of communication need to be very careful about the conclusions you draw. For if you do take the nonverbal behavior as the true meaning of the communication, you can be fooled. In Chapter 6 we will discuss the skill of perception-checking, which can help you to understand nonverbal behavior.

Regulators

A less dramatic but equally important category of body motion is called the *regulators*. These are nonverbal actions that regulate the flow of conversation by telling the speaker to continue, to repeat, to elaborate, to hurry up, and the like. Think for a minute. How do you know when someone has finished speaking? or when someone will continue speaking for a while longer? How do you know when you should talk more slowly? or faster? We pick up such communication clues from movements such as nodding of the head, shifting eye contact, slight head movements, shifts in posture, and raised eyebrows.

Regulating occurs on the periphery of your awareness. You usually do not know when you are doing these things, and you are not necessarily conscious of others' doing them. But, if you were restrained from doing them, you would probably become quite frustrated—we expect and need these regulators.

Regulators penetrate your awareness when their usage reaches a state that is described as rudeness. If, while Maria is talking, Carl gives signs of impatience, she may think, "How rude of him to do these things when I'm talking!" Or, if in the midst of what you think is a good conversation the other person gathers his things, puts his coat on, and starts to leave while you are in the middle of a statement, you probably would be upset. Yet, on a subtler level you do regulate communication constantly.

Adaptors

The fifth classification, which is the most difficult to define, is the *adaptors*. Researchers have called them adaptors because they are thought to be a response that satisfies needs, performs actions, manages emotions, develops social contacts, or performs many other functions. Of all the nonverbal movements we have discussed, these are the least capable of being coded—yet, in some ways they are the most fascinating. You may be familiar with one or more of the books that trade on the mystery of adaptors. Fast's *Body Language*[7] was the first in a long line of books designed to encourage people to try to "psyche out" the hidden messages

---

[7] Julius Fast, *Body Language* (New York: M. Evans & Company, 1970).

that people were unaware of or were trying to repress. Such books heighten general awareness of the fact of adaptors, and many readers ponder such problems as, for example, if Maggie crosses her knees, it may have something to do with her attitude toward the man she is with (or it may not) or the crossing of her arms may have something to do with her rejection of her boss's proposed budget (or it may not). Usually, we are just not aware of adaptive behavior.

Yet, if people believe they sense something in your nonverbal behavior, their belief may greatly affect communication. When you talk with a person, you may get an instinctive feeling of what he is like, what he is thinking or feeling. For instance, supervisors who take off their coats, roll up their sleeves, and pitch in to help in an emergency tell something about themselves that is somewhat different from the messages sent by supervisors who dress rather formally, stand apart from workers, and shrink from getting their hands dirty. You have probably been attracted to persons who are vibrant with sex appeal or move with an easy grace or just seem relaxed and comfortable to be with. Sometimes you may have been repelled by persons who seem stern, strict, formal, and uptight. Many of these impressions are responses to adaptive behaviors on the part of the persons in question.

In the following exercise, the goal is not to try to codify adaptors but to determine your own reactions to nonverbal behavior. Of course, in normal conversation you should check out the accuracy of your perceptions.

Communication Session

Reflection

Do you use many gestures when you speak? What emblems are most common to your usage? What kinds of illustrators do you use most frequently? What are your normal nonverbal means of displaying such emotions as anger, pain, surprise, boredom, and others? What do you do to show others that you have finished talking?

Practice

1. Working alone, compile a dictionary of emblems. Classify them as (1) emblems used consistently and (2) emblems understood but seldom used.

2. Working in groups of three to six, share your lists. Is there any similarity? What are the bases of the differences? As a result of the comparison, develop a third classification: (3) emblems not known. Have you put any in this classification?

3. Working in groups of four to six, have each individual describe a game he or she has played, a place he or she has just been, where he or she had lunch, or the like. Give the person a maximum of two minutes to talk. Note the nature of the illustrators: Was body action used as a baton, ideograph, deictic, spatial movement, kinetograph, or pictograph? Was the usage above average, average, or below average? You will begin to establish a norm for average as others continue with the assignment. Compare the use of body movement as illustrators. Who uses more than others? Under what circumstances?

4. Working in groups of four to six, have each person role-play various emotional incidents—for instance, stubbing your toe, getting angry with a person for slighting you. In these role-playing situations, what displays are shown?

5. Locate a book on hand language for the deaf. Try to carry on a conversation with this elaborate system of emblems. What problems do you encounter?

Discussion

Working in groups of four to six, discuss the following:

1. What kinds of adaptive behavior seem to be conscious, or in the control of the person? What kinds seem unconscious?

2. What kinds of facial expression, posture, gesture, or movement are suggestive of being "sexy," "fun loving," "boring," "pushy," and the like?

3. What seems to account for some people being more likely to use various kinds of body motions? Under what circumstances, if any, should people attempt to change the body motions they use?

Paralanguage

Kinesic behavior relates to the bodily movements we see; *paralanguage* relates to the sounds we hear. In simple terms, the study of paralanguage deals with *how* something is said and not with *what* is said. We have all developed some sensitivity to the clues people give with their voices. Let's consider three major categories of paralanguage.

Vocal Characteristics

The four major characteristics of voice are *pitch* (highness or lowness of tone), *volume* (loudness), *rate* (speed), and *quality* (the sound of the voice). Each of these by itself or in concert with one or more others either complements, supplements, or contradicts the words used. People talk loudly when they wish to be heard at a distance, but some people also talk loudly when they are angry and softly when they are being loving. People tend to raise and lower their pitch to accompany changes in volume. They may also raise pitch when they are nervous or lower pitch when they are trying to be forceful. People may talk more rapidly when they are happy, frightened, or nervous; they will talk more slowly when they are unsure or trying to emphasize a point.

In addition to combined changes in volume, pitch, and rate, each of us uses a slightly different quality of voice to communicate a particular state of mind. We may associate complaints with a whiny, nasal quality; seductive invitation with a soft, breathy quality; and anger with a strident, harsh quality. To each of these different qualities, we assign some kind of value judgment about how persons are feeling or what they are thinking.

None of these particular differences in voice quality necessarily has the meaning we assign. Some people have high-pitched or breathy or nasal or strident voices all the time. Perhaps some people use these different qualities for reasons other than those we assign. Nevertheless, *how* the person says what he says does convey meaning, whether intended or not. Although paralanguage is learned, it is quite difficult to change. If you have some vocal characteristic that works to contradict the meanings you intend to send, you may need professional help in changing those patterns. Our purpose here is to make you more aware of the meanings received through paralanguage rather than to suggest the need for change of your own paralanguage. If you have concerns, talk them over with your professor. If he or she believes you do in fact have some problem, he or she can refer you to a speech therapist for help.

Vocal Differentiators

Differentiators are special vocalizations. Such things as crying, laughing, belching, yawning, swallowing, and clearing the throat may have a definite meaning in and of themselves. Yawning may show boredom. Of course, some of these are related to phenomena that have nothing to do with communication; we also yawn when we need more fresh air in our lungs.

One set of vocal differentiators that we must become attuned to is the set we call the breakers. For instance, the nervous giggle and the quivering voice of emotion are both forms of breaking. Breaking refers to loss of control or insecurity. When you perceive these becoming a part of a person's speech, you should realize he is coming under extreme stress for one reason or another.

Vocal Interferences

Interferences are vocalized pauses (such as "uh-uh," "um," and "ah") that may have meaning but may be nothing more than space fillers. By and large, they have a negative role in communication and should be avoided as much as possible. A person who uses vocalizations of this kind excessively becomes quite annoying. If you find yourself falling into habits of "uh," "ah," or "um" throughout your speaking, you should consciously try to hear them. When you can actually hear yourself using these, you can consciously prune them from your speech.

In Chapter 6, Message Formation Skills, we will consider in some detail a program for limiting or ridding yourself entirely of these annoying interferences.

Communication Session

Reflection

1. What happens to your voice in stress situations? When does your pitch go up? down? When do you talk loudly? softly? When are you likely to talk fast? slowly?

2. Are there any vocal interferences that you use frequently? Are you always aware of their use? Are you making some effort to reduce or eliminate their use?

3. What are the emotions you read in other voices? For instance, how do you know when a person is being sarcastic? angry? condescending? humble? happy? sad? spiteful? Are there consistencies? Can you be sure?

Practice

1. Go around the room having each class member say the word "yes." Each member should have in mind a specific question he or she is answering "yes" to. After each person has said "yes," try to figure out what his or her reaction to the question was. Was he or she excited? tentative? angry? What other emotions?

2. Divide into groups of three to six. Have two persons role-play various situations: for instance, a student has received a low grade on her theme that she worked on for hours and she wishes to confront her instructor, a person who does not have much patience when talking with students. The rest of the group should listen for paralanguage.

Summary

Although verbal and nonverbal communication work together best when they are complementary, nonverbal communication may take the place of or even contradict verbal communication.

The environment is one aspect of nonverbal communication that is often overlooked. Yet the way a person arranges and reacts to space and the way he controls or reacts to color, temperature, and lighting contribute to the nature of the communication that will occur. Likewise, a person's own style as manifested by such things as clothing, hair style, and use of time further affects communication.

Perhaps the most obvious of the nonverbal means is what and how a person communicates through body motions and paralanguage. Movements of hands, arms, and other parts of the body act as emblems, illustrators, affect displays, regulators, and adaptors. Likewise, a person's vocal characteristics and vocal interferences affect the meaning communicated.

Nonverbal communication is not easily controlled, but it can be understood and taken into conscious consideration by those who understand its various aspects.

Suggested Readings

Judee K. Burgoon and **Thomas Saine.** *Unspoken Dialogue.* Boston: Houghton Mifflin, 1978. This relatively new book provides a comprehensive analysis of nonverbal communication.

Edward T. Hall. *The Silent Language.* Garden City, New York: Doubleday, 1959 (paperback). This classic work by Hall is fundamental to any comprehensive study of time and space.

Mark L. Knapp. *Nonverbal Communication in Human Interaction,* 2nd ed. New York: Holt, Rinehart and Winston, 1978 (paperback). Excellent analysis of research studies.

Dale G. Leathers. *Nonverbal Communication Systems.* Boston: Allyn & Bacon, 1976 (paperback). Another detailed account with an excellent bibliography.

Albert Mehrabian. *Silent Messages.* Belmont, California: Wadsworth, 1971 (paperback). A short, highly readable book focusing on the role of nonverbal communication in social interaction.

Part Two

DEVELOPING INTERPERSONAL SKILLS

Chapter 5
Positive Climate Development Skills

PAYOFFS   *After you have read this chapter, you should be able to:*

1. *Define empathy.*
2. *List and explain the forces that promote and limit empathy.*
3. *Define trust.*
4. *Discuss elements that affect trust.*
5. *Define self-disclosure.*
6. *Discuss the importance of self-disclosure in developing and maintaining relationships.*
7. *State guidelines for determining appropriateness of self-disclosure.*
8. *Explain methods of demonstrating openness to feedback.*
9. *Define describing and explain why it is so difficult to put into practice.*
10. *Contrast provisionalism with dogmatism.*
11. *Contrast equality with superiority.*
12. *Contrast spontaneity with hidden agenda.*
13. *List and discuss three nonverbal elements for creating a positive climate.*

Do you recall those times when in the midst of an interpersonal encounter you thought to yourself, "Something's wrong—I can feel the tension in the air." If you later analyzed the situation, you may have decided the tension was the result of something that was said or something that was done, or perhaps the *way* something was said or done. Perhaps you were bewildered by why things went wrong this time when things went so smoothly at other times. Perhaps you felt a victim of circumstances beyond your control. In reality, you—and the others involved—have the potential for control over the kind of climate that will prevail in any communication setting.

Communication encounters take place within an interpersonal climate—an atmosphere comprised of the tones, the moods, and the attitudes of those communicating. Your effectiveness as a communicator may depend on the type of interpersonal climate you help create. The more positive the climate, the more likely that the participants will have satisfactory outcomes.

Jack Gibb is a leading authority on communication climate. He has stressed that a positive communication climate occurs when behaviors are *empathic* rather than *neutral*, *descriptive* rather than *evaluative*, *provisional* rather than *dogmatic*, *spontaneous* rather than *strategic*, *problem solving* rather than *controlled*, and *equal* rather than *superior*.[1] Although our discussion is based on Gibb, we will add another behavior we believe is equally important in developing a positive climate, *openness*.

When a person tries to develop a positive climate, he must be concerned with both positive attitudes and appropriate behavior. If, for example, Bruce feels that social conversation is a waste of time, he will probably never develop the skills necessary for casual conversation. Those he meets socially may see him as a "cold fish" or unfriendly, and the communication climate around him will probably be strained.

Even if a person has positive communication attitudes, however, her behavior may create a negative climate. For instance, although Paula may believe that openness between friends is important, she may be shy and have trouble behaving in a way that is consistent with her belief.

In this chapter we'll look at six behaviors: empathy, openness, describing, provisionalism, equality, and spontaneity.

Empathy

In their discussion of fundamental interpersonal skills, Bochner and Kelly say that empathy is the basis of successful communication.[2] We agree. Empathy is a quality or attitude that is the starting point of a positive interpersonal climate. Empathy requires a series of skills that will be discussed in part in this chapter and also in Chapter 7.

Empathizing is being able to detect and identify the immediate affective state of another and to respond in an appropriate manner. The first part of this definition, the ability "to detect and identify the immediate affective state of another,"[3] describes the quality or attitude that is basic to building a positive climate. A person who has this quality understands another person's feelings as a result of his own experience in a similar situation or his fantasized reaction to that situation. Empathy is a "you" orientation that makes the likelihood of successful interaction probable, rather than an "I" orientation that may prevent a positive climate from developing.

Let's look at an example. George approaches Jerry. Empathy, a "you" orientation, allows Jerry to see the look on George's face, and see the cues that his gestures, movements, and posture may be giving. He

[1]Jack R. Gibb, "Defensive Communication," *Journal of Communication*, Vol. 11 (September 1961), pp. 141–148.

[2]Arthur P. Bochner and Clifford W. Kelly, "Interpersonal Competence: Rationale, Philosophy, and Implementation of a Conceptual Framework," *Speech Teacher*, Vol. 23 (November 1974), p. 289.

[3]Robert J. Campbell, Norman Kagan, and David R. Krathwohl, "The Development and Validation of a Scale to Measure Affective Sensitivity (Empathy)," *Journal of Counseling Psychology*, Vol. 18 (1971), p. 407.

also hears the words George speaks, hears the changes in vocal quality and pitch, and detects the presence or absence of interferences in his speech. From all of these cues he not only perceives what George is saying, but feels and understands George's total meaning. If George says, "And out of the blue he slugged me right on the jaw," and from words and nonverbal cues Jerry is able to feel what it is like to be hit on the jaw, Jerry is empathizing. Even if Jerry had himself never been hit on the jaw but could imagine both the pain and the bewilderment of being unexpectedly struck, Jerry would be empathizing. On the other hand, if Jerry had an "I" orientation—that is, if he was so wrapped up in his own thoughts, feelings, and experiences that the sense of George's words and nonverbal cues didn't reach him—then he would be unable to empathize.

Empathy also requires the ability to "respond in an appropriate manner" to the feelings of others. Appropriate responses take many forms, several of which we'll be discussing in detail when we talk about listening and responding skills in Chapter 7. When George says, "And out of the blue he slugged me right on the jaw," Jerry's sensitivity to the words and nonverbal cues enables him to have an appropriate empathic feeling. Jerry supplements this feeling with a verbal response such as, "That must have really jolted you," spoken in a way that suggests understanding of the pain and surprise that George must have felt. This kind of response (called a supportive statement) shows George (1) that Jerry understands what happened, (2) that Jerry shares in the emotions George is feeling—what it is like to be suffering pain or surprise—and (3) that Jerry is willing to talk with George and offer what help he can.

People sometimes confuse *empathy* with *sympathy*. Empathy is an understanding of another person's feelings that derives from the ability to detect and share those feelings. Sympathy is either a similarity of feeling or a feeling of pity or compassion for another person's trouble. When George says, "And out of the blue he slugged me right on the jaw," Jerry may have had some experience that enables him to share George's feeling; this sharing is empathy. Or Jerry may actually develop a strongly similar feeling, a "sympathy"—just as when an object begins to vibrate, an object near it develops a "sympathy" vibration. In addition, Jerry may simply feel sorry for George—nobody likes to see a friend be a victim. Empathy and sympathy often go hand in hand, but they are not the same.

We can see that empathy has two clearly definable elements—the *recognition* of another's feeling, which is a perception skill, and the *response* to it, which is a communication skill. Let's talk further about achieving an empathic state of mind.

Merely saying, "I'm going to be more empathic," is unlikely to make you more empathic. You have within you forces you can summon that will increase your empathy. You also have within you equally powerful forces that inhibit empathy. Let's examine these two sets of forces:

These forces can promote empathy:

1. *Concentration.*   Just because your eyes are open does not mean that you see; just because your ears are clear does not mean that you hear. Increasing empathy requires that you use your powers of concentration, of selective perception. As Max recounts his frustration at being unable to remember material he had worked on during his study period, your senses are being attacked by a horde of distracting thoughts and feelings. But you have the power to concentrate your attention not on the pain in your knee, not on the letter you must mail before noon, not on the sound of the rain against the window, but *on what Max is saying.*

2. *Active caring.*   Each person who takes time to talk with you is important. If you will remind yourself that this other person's importance is genuine, you will be likely to care about what is happening to that person. If you care, really care, you will facilitate your ability to empathize.

These forces can inhibit empathy:

1. *False biological needs.*   The psychologist Abraham Maslow said that biological needs take priority over all other needs.[4] For example, if you were starving, the need for food would be so overpowering that it would have to be satisfied before you could think about anything else. A simple hunger pang is far from starvation, yet many people are so conditioned

The psychologist Abraham Maslow said that biological needs take priority over all other needs.

---

[4]Abraham H. Maslow, *Motivation and Personality* (New York: Harper & Row, 1954), pp. 80–92.

to reacting strongly to pangs of hunger, thirst, and other mild biological needs that they give them an exaggerated importance. People have allowed themselves to respond to such pangs even if they are not signs of a deep need. However, you have the power to tune out these kinds of mild false biological needs if you want to.

2. *False trauma.*   In addition to false biological needs, people may also experience false trauma. (A trauma can be caused by a severe physical wound or a strong emotional shock.) Now don't misunderstand. People do experience real trauma: accidents happen, tragic events occur, difficult emotional problems may hammer at them. Under these circumstances, people may have every reason to be strongly "I" oriented. But for every real trauma that captures every ounce of their energies and attention, there are many false traumas that compete for attention. A snub from a friend, anxiety over an upcoming test, fear of failing to meet a deadline for a paper—these do not demand all the attention they often get. Think about it: if people worried about *every* real or imagined negative experience, they would exhaust themselves. Most of these experiences can be profitably set aside when attention is needed elsewhere. If a friend is taking the time to tell you something important, set aside those false traumas and listen! You can get back to your real or imagined pains at your leisure.

3. *Fear of weakness.*   Everybody has feelings, and the willingness to show feelings is not unmanly or unwomanly or "un" anything. If we hurt, we should feel free to show it. If we empathize with another person's pain, we should feel free to show that, too. Nevertheless, many people, both men and women, are guided by the belief that any demonstration of feelings—besides cheering at a football game—reveals weakness. Feelings should be somehow covered up as if they didn't exist. If your belief that showing empathy is a sign of weakness is keeping you from empathizing, we hope that you will take time to examine that belief. If you consider your own feelings for a moment, you can see the importance of empathy. How do you feel when someone you care about shows that he understands when you've been hurt, frightened, angered, pleased, or amazed? People want and need *the same* expression of empathy from you that you want and need from them.

Now let's consider a specific plan of action that you can use to heighten your skill at empathizing.

1. *Analyze the basis for your perceptions.*   The relative inaccuracy of your perceptions may well be based upon drawing conclusions from too few clues. In Chapter 2, we spoke of some of the consequences of selective perception. Perhaps you are selecting too narrowly, or perhaps you are seeing only what you want to see. Furthermore, you may be basing your perceptions on verbal clues alone. Try to take into account both the verbal

and the nonverbal clues people are sending. Your reading of Chapter 4 on nonverbal communication should have helped you considerably in sharpening your recognition of the nonverbal elements.

2. *Analyze the methods of others.*   If you will observe the behavior of your friends and acquaintances, you will notice that some are particularly skillful in accurate recognition of others' states of mind. Observe skilled persons closely. What are they doing to help themselves to be more perceptive? Through careful observation of empathic persons, you may pick up some helpful clues.

3. *Practice.*   Part of improving your skill depends upon your making a conscious effort. When you meet another person, it is worth a few moments to ask yourself, "What state of mind do I believe the person is in right now?" and "What are the clues the person is giving that I am using to draw this conclusion?" Asking these questions will help you focus at least some of your attention on others instead of keeping your thoughts mostly on yourself. As you gain skill in making these assessments quickly, you may find yourself much more in tune with the moods, feelings, and attitudes of those with whom you wish to communicate. As a result of such practice, you may be able to maintain or even to create a more positive communication climate.

The procedure for empathizing can be summarized as follows:

1. *Listen to what the person is saying (consider both words and nonverbal behavior).*

2. *Try to recall or to imagine what you would feel like under similar circumstances.*

3. *Say something that indicates your sensitivity to those feelings.*

How would you put the third item into practice? In Chapter 7, we will explore several specific response skills that are manifestations of empathy. In that chapter you will learn to listen empathically, to paraphrase, and to give helpful response.

Communication Session

Reflection

Think of the last time you fully empathized with another person. Did you both recognize and respond? What was the outcome?

Practice

Consider how much you empathize with a person close to you.[5]

1. Choose your spouse, your brother or sister, or a close friend to complete this exercise with you.
2. Select a personality trait like self-confidence, leadership ability, or sense of humor.
3. Circle a number from 1 (low) to 5 (high) to rate each statement. You complete A, B, C, and D; your partner completes E, F, G, and H.

Partner 1: On the personality trait of _____ :

A. I rate myself	1 2 3 4 5
B. I rate my partner	1 2 3 4 5
C. I think my partner would rate himself/herself	1 2 3 4 5
D. I think my partner would rate me	1 2 3 4 5

Partner 2: On the same personality trait of _____ :

E. I rate myself	1 2 3 4 5
F. I rate my partner	1 2 3 4 5
G. I think my partner would rate himself/herself	1 2 3 4 5
H. I think my partner would rate me	1 2 3 4 5

The measure of your empathic ability is determined by calculating how closely your predictions of your partner's ratings (C and D) correspond with your partner's actual ratings (E and F); and, of course, your partner's empathic ability is determined by calculating how closely his or her predictions of your ratings (G and H) correspond with your actual ratings (A and B).

Try this test with three of four other people whom you consider close to you. Is it easier to empathize more with some than with others? Why?

Openness

Openness exists in interpersonal communication to the extent that the people involved feel comfortable sharing their true thoughts and feelings. Individuals vary in their attitudes about how much openness is desirable. As a result, individuals behave in certain ways that communicate their attitude about openness. Although there is considerable agreement that some openness leads to a positive communication climate, there is

---

[5]This self–other rating is adapted from a test developed by Rosalind F. Dymond, "A Scale for the Measurement of Empathic Ability," *Journal of Consulting Psychology*, Vol. 13 (April 1949), pp. 127–133.

little evidence about the amount of openness that encourages effective interaction. Although a lack of openness will not lead to a positive communication climate and may well result in a negative climate, too much openness may destroy a positive climate. Paul Cozby, in his review of self-disclosure literature, says that we should be very careful about any attitude that calls for people to lose their "freedom to have private thoughts because full disclosure is demanded by others. . . ."[6]

We strongly disagree with those authors who demand total openness as a condition of good interpersonal communication. On the other hand, we recognize the importance of some degree of openness in order to maintain a positive communication climate. In this section we will discuss workable guidelines for your use of two very important openness skills: self-disclosure and receptiveness to feedback.

Because a person's willingness to be open with another and the amount of openness that is desirable in a given situation are dependent on the amount of trust between the two individuals, let's lay the groundwork for the development of openness skills with a discussion of trust.

Trust

What does it mean to *trust*? The word is frequently used, but definitions of it vary widely. We relate trust to risk. As Richard Reichert has said, trust is an "ability to risk yourself, to put yourself in the hands of another, to put yourself at the service of another."[7] Trust almost always involves some risk. In effect, trust is a kind of prediction—a prediction that if you "put yourself in the hands of another" the result will be to your advantage. Yet it may not be advantageous. By trusting someone, you are risking a negative result.

Under what circumstances are you willing to trust others, to let others control what happens to you? We'll consider three of the basic elements of trust: (1) The nature of the self, (2) the relative importance of what is being entrusted, and (3) your perception of the person, group, or institution that you have decided to trust.

First is the nature of the self who chooses to trust or not to trust. Some people are highly suspicious, and others are foolishly gullible. Somewhere between these extremes is a normal, desirable degree of trust. If we always behave suspiciously, if we have what is called an "unhealthy fear of the unknown," we can reduce ourselves to total inactivity. The act of living requires some trust: trust that the building we live in

---

[6]Paul C. Cozby, "Self-Disclosure: A Literature Review," *Psychological Bulletin*, Vol. 79 (February 1973), p. 88.

[7]Richard Reichert, *Self-Awareness through Group Dynamics* (Dayton, Ohio: Pflaum/Standard, 1970), p. 63.

won't collapse; trust that a person walking toward us means us no harm; trust that the car we drive will not break down. On the other hand, if we blindly believe that everything and everybody is wonderful and good, we open ourselves to certain heartbreak: we do not entrust total strangers with our deepest secrets; we do not park our car with the doors and windows open and the key in the ignition; we do not trust every politician to make decisions that are in the majority interest. Most people fall between the two extremes of exaggerated distrustfulness and total gullibility. Assuming that you, too, are somewhere between these two extremes, then when and how much trust you will extend probably depends on the next two elements.

The second element is the relative importance of the object, idea, or feeling being entrusted. Consider objects for a moment. Jack owes Sam a dollar. Tom, a person Jack knows little about, sits next to Jack in chemistry class. He will be seeing Sam in Spanish class later that day and offers to deliver the dollar. Jack is a normally trusting person, but whether or not he will entrust Tom with the dollar depends on how important a dollar is to him. The greater the importance of a dollar to him, the less likely Jack will be to trust Tom with it. Suppose Jack will trust Tom to deliver one dollar. At what dollar amount would Jack refuse Tom's offer? Again, the answer depends on how important money is to Jack. A dollar lost might not be significant; but the risk of losing five, ten, or more dollars might be too great for Jack to entrust the money to anyone.

Let's change the example from money to information but continue with the same characters. We've said that Tom and Jack are virtual strangers. Would Jack be likely to tell Tom that he prefers a pencil to a pen for taking notes? Why not—what would Jack have to lose by revealing this information? A preference in writing implements is not important. Would Jack reveal that he doesn't like lobster? Probably—again the information is insignificant. But would Jack tell Tom that he is an ex-convict and an alcoholic? These two facts about himself are highly important to Jack, because they are potentially damaging, and therefore he would be unlikely to reveal them to a stranger. The more important the object, idea, feeling, or information to be entrusted, the more careful a person will be.

The third element is your perception of the person being trusted. Let's return to the example of money. Jack knows little about Tom. His impression of Tom is superficial. A dollar is insignificant to Jack, and, since he has no *negative* information about Tom, he is likely to trust him to deliver the dollar to Sam. As the amount of money increases, however, Jack's need to know something about Tom's trustworthiness is also likely to increase. If Jack learns that Tom has a reputation for being an irresponsible person who volunteers to do things but seldom does them, he may have second thoughts about trusting Tom to deliver even that insignificant dollar. If the amount in question were five or ten dollars, Jack would almost certainly refuse to trust Tom.

Again, let's change the example from money to information. If Jack is alcoholic, will he reveal this to Tom if he knows that Tom cannot keep a secret? Probably not. Your impression of the person being trusted, an impression often based on what you have heard from others about that person, is an important element in determining whether and how much to trust him.

A person builds trust by doing what is expected of him. If Tom delivers the dollar to Sam, Jack may later entrust him with more important objects or information. If Tom keeps a minor secret, Jack may later disclose a more important secret. If, on the other hand, Tom fails to deliver the dollar when he said he would, or if he reveals a secret he has promised to keep, Jack's trust in him will diminish and perhaps disappear.

Undue suspicion, refusal to trust even when the object or information to be entrusted is unimportant, and failure to trust those who have shown themselves trustworthy can all become barriers to effective communication. One of the goals of interpersonal communication is to surmount these barriers and build more- and better-trusting relationships.

Trust is crucial to interpersonal relationships. Trust should be extended not blindly but on the basis of the importance of the entrusted object or information and on the basis of impression and/or experience with the person. The more often your judgment to trust someone is verified, the more likely you will be to trust in the future.

Self-Disclosure

The first openness skill we will consider is self-disclosure. **Self-disclosure with another means sharing biographical data, personal ideas, and feelings that are unknown to the other person.** The first of these reveals facts about you as an individual. A statement such as, "I was too small to make the team in high school" discloses biographical information; "I don't think the idea of rehabilitation of criminals is working" discloses a personal idea; "I get scared whenever I have to make a speech" discloses feelings. Through such self-disclosures others get to know you and understand you. Biographical disclosures are the easiest to make, for they are, in a manner of speaking, a matter of public record. Disclosures of personal ideas and feelings are at the same time more threatening and more important. They are more threatening because they are not a matter of record—they are truly revealing of you as a person; they are more important because they represent the kinds of statements that enable someone really to know you.

Self-disclosure and interpersonal relationships   Now that we have defined self-disclosure, let's consider the ways in which it is appropriate in interpersonal communication. To begin with, a degree of self-disclosure is necessary in the initiation and development of a relationship because people feel closest to those they know the most about. How many times have you observed something like the following scene played out between two people who have just met for the first time?:

Joan: Today is such a beautiful day—just right for tennis. You can play all day and still feel great.

Jill: Oh, do you play tennis?

Joan: I sure do. I love it.

Jill: I play too. How good are you?

Joan: Well, I've had a few lessons, and I think I do pretty well, but Chris Evert doesn't have to worry about me!

During this conversation on tennis, Jill finds out whether Joan would be a good match and whether they might enjoy playing together. Now, whether they ever do play together may depend on some other factors, but through the mutual self-disclosure Jill and Joan discover a common enthusiasm. Through conversations such as these, friendships are born. Had Jill replied, "Well, I don't care for tennis, but I do like to hike on a day like this," the conversation would have taken a different turn, but still through self-disclosure each would learn information about the other that would have suggested the possibility of some relationship.

Even in a relatively impersonal setting, self-disclosure can help people feel closer to others. For instance, you may feel closer to an instructor who becomes a "real person" to you. Through her lecture examples you get to know about the person's family, about her proficiency in cooking, about the way she sees the world, and about her interests, needs, and desires. The simple truth is that it is hard to like anyone about whom you know nothing.

In ongoing relationships self-disclosure achieves a different purpose. It is through your communication and particularly your disclosure of your feelings that *you teach others how to treat you.* The way you define yourself through your communication teaches others how they should act, react to, and communicate with you. For instance, if through your communication and your behavior it becomes apparent that you love to cook, then those around you will talk with you about cooking and seek to interact with you in subjects related to food. If you hide your love of cooking, people will not know your feelings and may not talk with you about food, cooking, restaurants, or similar subjects. Have you ever heard something like this complaint: "I wonder why they don't ask me to go to that new French restaurant that just opened"? The person who makes such a statement may suspect that people dislike him, when actually it may be that they did not realize he was interested in fine foods.

The nature and degree of self-disclosure that you permit yourself are closely related to the degree of intimacy you share with that other person. Our relationships include people we recognize but do not interact with as well as people we are intimate with. The more intimate the relationship, the greater the self-disclosure. But although there are any number of persons you may recognize but interact very little with, there are few with whom you are intimate and share some of your deepest secrets.

More important than the correlation between the amount of self-disclosure and the degree of intimacy is the stimulative effect of self-disclosure on the growth of a relationship. Growth is the increase of intensity of a relationship, based at least in part on the degree of self-disclosure. When you decide you really like what you know about another person and believe that the other person likes what he knows about you, you tend to *intensify* the degree of self-disclosure by revealing more intimate information about yourself. Now, here is where the nature of *risk* becomes important. You may think: "If I reveal my fear of flying to Frank, who goes in for hang-gliding as a hobby, Frank may not continue to like me." The problem is that if you do not reveal risky information, Frank will not understand and may misinterpret your behavior, and a relationship that might have grown to friendship or even intimacy if you had risked self-disclosure may never develop. The risk you think you are avoiding by not disclosing becomes a two-edged sword. You may be cut by self-disclosure, but you may also be cut by keeping quiet.

Whether or not you choose to disclose, *you must be prepared to accept the consequences of your communication behavior.* If you are not willing to face the risk of rejection, you should not disclose. However, if you refuse to disclose anything about yourself, others probably will do likewise. If disclosure does not take place, relationships cannot grow. If Charles finds himself missing the close relationships with women he admires, his failure to develop such relationships could be a consequence of choosing not to disclose information about himself. At least in part, Charles must bear the responsibility for lack of close relationships.

Guidelines for self-disclosure   If you are not used to disclosing information about yourself, doing it is not easy. The advice to "go and self-disclose—but not too much," is not very meaningful. Let's consider some useful guidelines in determining appropriate self-disclosure. As you read these guidelines, keep in mind that the goal of self-disclosure is "to be perceived by the other as the one I know myself to be."[8]

1. *Self-disclosure should come when you believe the disclosure represents an acceptable risk.*   There is always some risk involved in disclosing. But if you

---

[8] Sidney M. Jourard, *Healthy Personality* (New York: Macmillan Publishing Company, 1974), p. 181.

trust another person, you will perceive the disclosure as "safe." Incidentally, this guideline explains why some people engage in self-disclosure to bartenders or people they meet in travel. The disclosures they make are perceived as *safe* (representing reasonable risk) because the person either does not know them or is in no position to use the information against them. It seems to us very sad that some people do not trust their husbands, wives, or other members of the family enough to make these disclosures.

2. *Self-disclosure should move gradually to deeper levels.* Since receiving self-disclosure can be as threatening as giving it, most people become very uncomfortable when the level of disclosure exceeds their expectations. As a relationship develops, the depth of disclosure increases as well.

3. *Intimate or personal self-disclosure is most appropriate in an ongoing relationship.* Disclosures about deep feelings, fears, loves, and so forth are most appropriate in an established relationship. When someone discloses deep secrets to an acquaintance, he is engaging in potentially threatening behavior. If disclosure is made before a bond of trust is established, the person making the disclosure may be risking a great deal. Moreover, some people are embarrassed by and sometimes hostile toward others who try to saddle them with personal information in an effort to enforce a relationship where none exists.

4. *Intimate self-disclosure should continue only if it is reciprocated.* When a person discloses, he expects disclosure in return. When it is apparent that self-disclosure will not be returned, you should limit the amount of disclosure you make.

5. *Consider the reaction of the other person before you disclose.* Some persons are not capable of handling disclosures that alter the nature of their perception of a friend. If Joe has a friend who is strongly opposed to premarital affairs, it may not be in the best interest of Joe's relationship with this friend to reveal that he is having such an affair.

Communication Session

Reflection

Think of one secret about yourself. How many people know it? How do you decide whom to tell? What have been some of the consequences (good and bad) that have resulted from sharing that secret?

Practice

Working alone, label each of the statements below L (low risk), meaning you believe it is appropriate to disclose this information to almost any person; M (moderate risk), meaning you believe it is appropriate to disclose this information to persons you know pretty well and have already established a friendship with; H (high risk), meaning you would disclose such information only to the few friends you have great trust in or to your most intimate friends; or X, meaning you would disclose it to no one.

_____ 1. Your hobbies, how you like best to spend your spare time.

_____ 2. Your preferences and dislikes in music.

_____ 3. Your educational background and your feelings about it.

_____ 4. Your personal views on politics, the presidency, and foreign and domestic policy.

_____ 5. Your personal religious views and the nature of your religious participation.

_____ 6. Habits and reactions of yours that bother you at the moment.

_____ 7. Characteristics of yours that give you pride and satisfaction.

_____ 8. The unhappiest moments in your life in detail.

_____ 9. The occasions in your life when you were happiest—in detail.

_____ 10. The actions you have most regretted taking in your life and why.

_____ 11. The main unfulfilled wishes and dreams in your life.

_____ 12. Your guiltiest secrets.

_____ 13. Your views on the way a husband and wife should live their marriage.

_____ 14. What to do, if anything, to stay fit.

_____ 15. The aspects of your body you are most pleased with.

_____ 16. The features of your appearance you are most displeased with and wish to change.

_____ 17. The person in your life whom you most resent and the reasons why.

_____ 18. Your favorite forms of erotic play and sexual lovemaking.

_____ 19. The people with whom you have been sexually intimate, and the circumstances of your relationship with each.

Discussion (optional)

Working in groups of five to seven, discuss your labeling of the statements. You are not required to make any of the disclosures, only to discuss circumstances, if any, under which you are likely to make them. The purpose of discussion is to see how people differ in what they view as acceptable disclosures.

Receptiveness to Feedback

Another factor contributing to effective communication is receptiveness to feedback. Feedback is the verbal and nonverbal response to you and your communication. You tell a joke and someone laughs—that's feedback; you ask various friends what they think of your new hair style, and they say they like it—that's feedback; you lean close to that someone you care for and she pulls away from you—that's feedback. Feedback is sometimes open and obvious, such as a statement by Jan that she likes your taste in clothes or a groan from Tom when you tell a story; at other times feedback is subtle, as in a pulling back, a slight frown, or a slight shift in position. It is through feedback, especially the type of feedback we refer to as "constructive criticism," that we learn who and what we are.

Our degree of sensitivity and openness to constructive criticism feedback to a large extent determines our effectiveness in our relationships with others. Let's take an obvious example: If after a lunch at an Italian restaurant that features garlic bread with the pasta you find your friends shying away from close contact with you, you may become aware that your garlic breath is offending them. You then can decide what you want to do about the situation. If you are insensitive at that particular time, you may not catch the cues that are being sent—or if you are generally not open to feedback, not willing to acknowledge the cues, you will not profit from the feedback.

Now, feedback of itself does not require alteration of behavior, but sensitivity and openness to feedback make possible a conscious, rational choice about whether or not you will respond to that feedback.

Why are people so inclined to be closed to feedback? For a very simple reason—any implied criticism can be threatening. Because few people like to be criticized, the first tendency for most is to become defensive. For instance, when a friend shies away from your garlic breath, you may see that as a putdown of you as a person, and it may make you angry. Everyone has a vested interest in himself. If a person is reasonably normal in behavior (and most people are), she thinks pretty highly of herself and is protective of that self. Still, everyone can be a better person and a more effective communicator. Many of the cues that come your way give insights into minor weaknesses that can be corrected and strengths that can be maintained.

In Chapter 7 we will consider the skills required to *give* useful feedback. For now, let's look at ways you can demonstrate your receptiveness to feedback. **By receptiveness, we mean creating a climate in which others feel comfortable in giving you feedback.** How can you create such a climate? Although you will probably get feedback even when you don't ask for it, when you want feedback you can so indicate through several verbal and nonverbal cues:

1. *Ask for feedback only when you are sincerely interested in an honest response.* For instance, if you ask a friend, "How do you like this coat?" but you really only want the friend to agree with *your* appraisal, you are not being honest. Once others realize that your request for feedback is not really honest, that all you really want to hear is a compliment, valuable feedback will not be forthcoming.

2. *Try to avoid contradiction between your verbal and your nonverbal cues.* For instance, if you say, "How do you like my paper?" but your voice tone indicates that you do not really want to know, the other person may be reluctant to be honest with you.

3. *Give reinforcement to those who take your requests for feedback as honest requests.* For instance, if you ask a friend how he or she likes your spaghetti and get the response: "The pasta seemed a little overcooked," and you get annoyed and say, "Well, if you can do any better you can fix dinner next time," your friend will learn not to give you feedback even when you ask for it. Instead, reward the person for the feedback. Perhaps you could say, "Thanks for telling me—I'll know not to cook it quite so long next time." In this way you encourage honest feedback.

4. *Outline the kind of feedback you are seeking.* Instead of asking very general questions about ideas, feelings, or behavior, phrase your questions specifically. Instead of saying, "Marge, is there anything you don't like about me?" (which the other person is likely to consider a loaded question), you might say, "Marge, when I'm being critical do I get a cutting or hostile tone to my voice?" Now Marge can speak to the specific behavior in question.

5. *Think of feedback as being in your best interest.* No one likes to be criticized, but it is often through valid criticism that we learn to grow. When you get negative feedback (even when you expected positive), you should not look upon it as destructive to you personally but as a statement that reveals something about yourself that you did not know. Whether you will *do* anything about the feedback is up to you—but you cannot make such a decision about altering negative behavior if you do not know that negative behavior exists.

6. *Check out what you have heard.* Don't jump to conclusions about the meaning of feedback. When a person says something about your behavior, make sure you understand exactly what is meant. Consider the following conversation:

Jack: Marge, when I'm being critical do I have a cutting tone to my voice?

Marge: I don't know—it may be a little sharp.

Jack: Do you mean that when I criticize people, they are bothered by the sound of my voice?

Marge: I can see where they would be. You do get a funny sound to your voice.

Her answer to the second question further clarifies Marge's perception.

Communication Session

Reflection

1. Are people inclined to give you feedback? Under what circumstances?
2. What are some of your personal ways of encouraging or turning off feedback? Are they effective?

Practice

1. Write down one to three specific attitudes or behaviors of yours that you would like feedback on. For instance:

   Does the way I dress make me look younger than I am?

   Do you think I talk too much at meetings?

   Did my analysis of Paul's plan help the discussion?

   Do I do anything to give the impression of being superior to my friends and acquaintances?

2. Ask a close friend for feedback on one or more of the attitudes or behaviors you have listed. Note how you react to this feedback.

Discussion

1. In your discussion group, consider how each of you identifies another person's openness to feedback. What does that person say and/or do?
2. How does each of you know when someone does not want feedback? What verbal or nonverbal cues does the other person emit?

Describing

An important skill in developing and maintaining a positive communication climate is **describing, which is putting sensory data into words.** Although the definition of describing is familiar, the act of describing can be difficult. Why? Because when you think you are describing, you may in fact be evaluating or judging.

For example, as Molly leaves a student senate meeting, she runs into a friend and says, "I just came from the dullest meeting!" As Arnold describes the basketball game he saw the night before, he says, "Grover kept making ridiculous passes!" After Vince eats his fifth enchilada, he turns to Margo and says, "I'm going to die." In each of these examples, describing was the best way to communicate, yet in each example the statements are evaluative or judgmental, not purely descriptive. Calling a meeting "dull" does not describe what did or did not happen; calling passes "ridiculous" does not describe what the passes were actually like; and saying, "I'm going to die" does not accurately describe the feeling of having eaten too much. If, however, Molly had said, "I've just come from a two-and-one-half-hour meeting. We heard four reports, none of which was under fifteen minutes, and we debated for an hour on a topic that ended up passing unanimously," she would have described a meeting that might well be evaluated as dull.

What's wrong with evaluating? The first problem with evaluating is that an evaluation does not inform; **an evaluative response places a value judgment on what has been said or done.** Misunderstandings are often the result of a shortage of information. Before an evaluation can be understood, a person must have the data on which it was based. In conversation, however, people are inclined to skip over the information. At the basketball game, Arnold watched Grover try to pass the ball into crowds of players under the basket, resulting in interceptions; he watched Grover try behind-the-back passes that went out of bounds; and, worst of all, he watched Grover make these passes when he had a good open shot. Arnold has all this information, but when he talks about the game the next day, he says, "Grover kept making ridiculous passes!" Nick, the person Arnold is talking to, wasn't at the game—he has no mental picture of the passes. He has no data he can use to judge the accuracy of Arnold's remark, and the remark itself doesn't really tell him anything. Had Arnold said, "Grover kept trying to pass into crowds, throw behind-the-back passes that went out of bounds, and pass off when he had the best open shot," Nick would have understood what happened and been able to understand Arnold's evaluation of Grover's game.

The second problem with evaluation is its potential for creating a negative climate. When you make an evaluation in the presence of another person, that person may become defensive, especially if the

evaluation is personal, negative, or contrary to the other person's opinion. For instance, Henry and Susan see a musical comedy. Henry is thinking, "That was a really enjoyable show—the songs were great, the sets were good, and every major part was well acted." Suddenly Susan turns to him and says, "What a miserable excuse for a professional production!" Her statement is almost sure to draw a defensive reaction from Henry because it is both negative and contrary to his opinion. Henry may sharply contradict Susan, or he may withdraw in anger from further communication with her. In either case the climate for effective communication between them is likely to be spoiled—at least for the moment.

There are two major kinds of description: (1) descriptions of behavior—"Did you know your eyes sparkle when you're happy?" and (2) descriptions of feelings—"When you look at me like that I feel warm inside." Describing behavior will be discussed as a listening and response skill on page 162; describing feelings will be discussed as a message formation skill on page 130.

Provisionalism

 Provisionalism is the skill of phrasing ideas tentatively rather than dogmatically. There are few subjects on which any individual knows everything there is to know; likewise, there are few ideas so firmly accepted by everyone that some possibility of another way of looking at a subject can be ruled out. When you close and lock your mind about any subject, when you state something inflexibly as if all possible knowledge had been considered and as if you are so wise in your interpretation that no other view is possible, you are being dogmatic. On the other hand, if in your statements you recognize the possibility that more information may be forthcoming or an opposite view may be held, you are being provisional.

Dogmatic statements are likely to create a defensive rather than a positive climate. Dogmatic people are often viewed as "know-it-alls." Provisional statements, on the other hand, help to create or to maintain the positive communication climate. How? By acknowledging that the other person has a viewpoint and letting it be heard even if it is not accepted.

Consider a situation in which two newlyweds are buying a television set. As they approach the subject of whether to pay cash or to finance it, the husband looks at the wife and says, "There's only one way to do it —and that's to pay cash." Or consider a situation where a man is trying to sew a button on his shirt. His mother watches him for a minute and then says, "Give me that—there's only one way to sew a button on so that it will stay." In each case the dogmatic statement is likely to cause a negative communication atmosphere. The wife may experience irritation, even anger, because her viewpoint has not even been asked for, and the son may react with belligerent stubbornness because he believes his way is as good as any other.

How is provisionalism demonstrated in communication? One way is by recognizing that, except for statements of fact, there are many possible opinions on any subject, and yours is not necessarily the same as one held by someone else. Be willing to state that your opinion is your view and not some universal, absolute principle established at the beginning of time. Instead of saying, "There's only one way to do it—and that's to pay cash," the husband might have said, "I was brought up to believe that paying cash will save me money." Notice that this statement allows for flexibility of action and/or belief. It does not close the door to discussion. Instead of saying, "There's only one right way to sew on a button," the mother could have said, "You probably have an idea of how to sew on that button, but I know a way I'd like to share with you that really helps a button to stay put."

Another way of showing provisionalism is by stating that something that seems to be true under these circumstances may not be entirely true or may not be true under all circumstances. Again, the husband could have said, "I've been brought up to believe that I can always save money by paying cash—I don't know whether that would be true in this set of circumstances." Likewise, the mother could have said, "I know there are several ways to sew on a button, but let me show you the way that has always worked for me in the past, although it may not work better on this particular garment."

Speaking provisionally may seem less dramatic than describing seems. Perhaps it is. But remember that a good communication climate is all too easy to destroy. Once the other person gets on edge or feels those nape hairs begin to rise, it might take a while to clear the air. With just a little care in phrasing your statements, you can prevent a negative climate from developing and build or maintain a positive one.

The procedure for provisionalism? Keep it in mind:

1. *Consider what you are about to say.*

2. *Determine whether it contains a wording that shows an attitude of finality, positiveness, or allness of concept.*

3. *If it does, add a qualifying statement that recognizes (a) the statement is your opinion and (b) the statement may not necessarily be entirely true or true under this set of circumstances.*

Equality

How do you feel when someone says something that you *perceive* as meaning that she knows more, is a better person, or in some way is speaking as a superior? Most people react uncomfortably to such statements.

George Orwell needled the superiority attitude in *Animal Farm:* "All animals are equal, but some animals are more equal than others." The implication was that some animals were to be treated as superior, with special privileges. Some persons believe that their positions make them superior to those around them. The head of the department or the oldest member of the family may think that he is basically more intelligent, wiser, quicker, more mentally alert because of his age and position—and this may be true. However, whatever the basis for the assumption of superiority, projecting it often results in a negative rather than a positive communication climate. This is particularly true when others involved are not at all convinced of that superiority.

A positive communication climate may be achieved by projecting an attitude of equality rather than an attitude of superiority. **Equality means being on the same level, or seeing others as worthwhile as one's self.** It is usually shown by the exclusion of any words or nonverbal signs that might indicate the opposite.

One way to alter statements that project delusions of personal superiority is to make statements issue-related. Instead of saying, "Listen, I know that LLG is the top stock to buy, I'm an expert in these kinds of things," try something like "LLG looks like a good stock to buy; it has paid solid dividends exceeding bank interest rates for the last eight years."

A second way is to be very conscious of sound of voice, facial expressions, dress, and manners. In words and actions, you need to show that you are a person—no better and no worse than others. By being willing to listen to others' ideas, by pitching in and working, by really hearing what is being said, and by respecting what others say, you show the attitude of equality.

In summary, then, the procedure for showing equality is as follows:

1. *Consider what you are about to say.*

2. *Consider whether it contains words or phrases that indicate or imply that you are in some way superior to the person or persons you are speaking to.*

3. *If there are signs of superiority, recast the sentence to change the tone.*

Spontaneity

We assume that, when one person raises an issue for discussion, the person bringing up the subject is communicating honestly and openly. Yet all too often the agenda for a communication event really is not what it may seem to be. What is an agenda? It is the subject matter to be discussed, the purpose for the communication. For instance, if the boss calls Sanders in to talk about his progress on the Morris account, the discussion of that account is the reason for the meeting—it is the agenda. For a family deciding whether to send the children to camp, making the decision is the agenda, the subject of the conversation. In normal conversation, the agenda is often made up as participants go along. It is usually flexible, and the conversation leads where it will. In more formal settings, an agenda arises from the situation at hand, and people meet to accomplish what is on the agenda.

What then is a hidden agenda? A *hidden agenda* is a reason or motive for a communication event that is not disclosed to other participants. For instance, if the account executive called Sanders in to talk about the Morris account but really wanted to find out why Sanders had seemed so depressed lately, trying to discover the reason for the depression would be the executive's hidden agenda. In a meeting with many participants, each may have a hidden agenda that controls his behavior. For instance, if an office group meets to discuss a gift for their supervisor who is being transferred, Madge may not care about the gift—her agenda may be her willingness to go along with anything; Warren may have only thirty minutes on his parking meter, so his agenda is to hurry the meeting along; Audrey may harbor a secret passion for the supervisor, so her hidden agenda may be to try to promote an exquisitely personal gift that will somehow show that she cares. A hidden agenda, then, is any strategy that is unknown to one or more of the parties in the conversation but that determines the nature or direction of the behavior of the individual.

Many people use the hidden agenda as a strategy to play psychological games with other people. A game is nothing more than one person's attempt to manipulate another person's behavior until the manipulator gets some payoff, usually a predictable behavior. Art knows that Madge gets angry when he turns off the television without asking her—so, he turns it off and acts amazed when Madge loses her temper. Rachel knows that Steve is likely to become uncomfortable when his former girl friend, Doris, is mentioned. So, in his presence Rachel "innocently" asks, "Say, has anyone seen Doris lately?" In both cases, the person's hidden agenda was to create a painful experience. If the behavior gets the desired response, the person "wins." And it is this win-lose element that makes such statements games.

Are hidden agendas always barriers to communication? Usually, if not always. Although as a matter of tact or propriety you may sometimes stipulate one agenda when in reality you support another one, such deception all too often degenerates into manipulation. If Max is suspected of cheating on a test, the instructor may call him into the office supposedly to talk about the subject of his next report but really with the intention of trying to get indirectly at the subject of cheating. In this instance, the hidden agenda may appear to be a proper procedure; but in terms of interpersonal relations, it includes elements of manipulation. Since the hidden agenda often is beneficial only to the person holding it, it can be detrimental to other persons involved or to the subject being discussed.

The base for good interpersonal communication is a willingness of all parties to be open with each other. Disclosures of true feelings, attitudes, and beliefs are fundamental to good working relations among people. When hidden agendas are discovered, the fragile bond of trust can be frayed or perhaps even broken; and, once trust is gone, the chance for good interpersonal relations is gone. So although hidden agendas may appear expedient, we do better to avoid them.

How can we avoid the problems created by a hidden agenda?

1. *Through direct confrontation.* "Bill, you called me in here to talk about the Morris account. Is that really what you had in mind?" Or, "Art, you know I get angry when you turn off the TV without asking—are you trying to hurt me?" When the agenda is open, it can be handled. Often a direct confrontation will bring the subject into the open. Perhaps the subject is hard to talk about, delicate, risky—it does not matter. Get it out in the open.

2. *Through openness on the part of the initiator.* "Max, I called you in because I'm really concerned about your last test. My perception is that you cheated. Am I correct?" Openness leads to discussion of issues. Now instead of dealing in implication and innuendo, those involved know the issue and can talk about it.

Communication Session

Reflection

Think of the last time you met with a group of people. Did you have a hidden agenda? How did it affect your communication?

Practice

Give each of three of four people in a group a hidden agenda. Have the group then discuss a topic such as the nature of the gift for another group member's birthday. Note the way the hidden agendas are introduced. See whether the people involved can deal with them.

Discussion

In groups of four to six, discuss how you feel when you discover that you have been following someone's hidden agenda. How do you deal with those feelings?

Nonverbal Recommendations

Our emphasis in this chapter has been on statements that will help develop or maintain a positive communication climate. Now we would like to draw your attention to some nonverbal elements that can also be of help. You can probably use everything we discussed in Chapter 4, The Nonverbal Base of Communication, to your advantage. Let's stress just three points:

1. *The environment.*   Try to reduce or eliminate noise. It's hard to develop a good climate when a radio, a television, or a stereo is blaring or when people are chattering in the background. You should also be sure that the seating arrangement in the room has a positive effect. Two people can be more relaxed seated than standing, but they should avoid sitting across from each other at a table, which can create an adversary relationship. Be sure the lighting, temperature, and ventilation contribute to rather than distract from the conversation.

2. *Bodily actions.*   If the topic you will be discussing is important to you, you are likely to be tense. Your anxiety is likely to show in your posture, gestures, and body movements. Monitor your behavior periodically. Are you standing or sitting with arms folded, hands clenched, or with a rigid posture? Any of these may be a sign of a defensive attitude that is likely to hurt the climate.

3. *Facial expression and tone of voice.*   One of the best ways to approach another person is with a warm, friendly attitude, a pleasant tone of voice, and a smile. You can do a lot of things wrong, but a sincere smile can do a lot to maintain a positive atmosphere. Remember the line in the western where the hero, just after the villain has cursed him, looks the villain in the eye and says, "Smile when you say that, partner"? The power of a sincere smile is tremendous.

We recently tested the value of the warm approach. One hundred and seventy-one students were given the following questionnaire: "You are sitting at your desk with your fist clenched and a scowl on your face. A friend enters the room. Which of the following statements is most likely to get you to talk with your friend about what is bothering you?"
Read the following five choices and see which you would pick:

1. *"From the way you're acting I get the feeling that you are really upset about something. Am I right?"*

2. *"What in the world is bugging you? You look like you could chew nails."*

3. *"Hey—let's go get something to drink—you look like you could really use one. Then we can talk."*

4. *"Out with it! What's eating you?"*

5. *"Hey—" (said with a smile) "don't hit me—I come unarmed! What's happening?"*

As we expected, only a small number selected choices 2 and 4. The question, choice 2, is rather harshly phrased, and the demand, choice 4, is even worse. From a verbal standpoint choice 1 is a good one. Later we'll define this response as a perception check—a valuable response skill. Yet only thirty-four students, roughly 20 percent, selected it. The two that the students liked best, choices 3 and 5, are both friendly in tone. Choice 3 is a type of supportive statement—it shows concern; choice 5 is basically humorous—it says, "I'm on your side—let's talk." Fifty-three students chose 3 and fifty-one chose 5. (Six students made no choice.) Which one did you pick? If you chose either 3 or 5, you know something about establishing a positive climate.

It's hard for a person to get angry, be hostile, or become defensive in the face of a person who is smiling. Not a sneer, not a smirk, not a put-down, but a warm, friendly smile. Try it!

Summary

A positive communication climate results from a positive attitude and behaviors that communicate this attitude. Some of the major behaviors for developing a positive climate are empathy, openness, describing, provisionalism, equality, and spontaneity.

Empathizing is being able to detect and identify the immediate affective state of another and being able to respond in an appropriate manner. Empathy is promoted by concentrating on the other person's words and nonverbal reactions and by caring about that person. To ensure being able to empathize, you will have to guard against concentrating too much on your own needs and feelings.

Openness is a willingness to share thoughts and feelings. The amount of openness will depend upon the amount of trust in an interpersonal communication. Trust involves taking risks. The elements of trust are the nature of the self, the relative importance of what is risked, and the impression given by the person, group, or institution trusted.

The major aspects of openness are self-disclosure and receptiveness to feedback. Self-disclosure is the sharing of ideas and feelings. Self-disclosure is necessary to help you teach others how to treat you. The guidelines for self-disclosure include willingness to accept risk, moving gradually to deeper levels of disclosure, and the need for reciprocal behavior.

Receptiveness to feedback means acting in a way that will encourage others to give feedback. You should ask for feedback when you want it, you should avoid giving contradictory reactions to feedback, you should react positively to those who give you feedback, and you should check out what you've heard to make sure you understand.

Describing is putting sensory data into words. People are inclined to evaluate when they should first describe. Two important describing skills that will be discussed later are describing behavior and describing feelings.

Provisionalism is phrasing ideas tentatively rather than dogmatically; equality means speaking on the same status level; spontaneity means revealing what you plan to do and how in a way that allows for participation by the other person. All three of these skills are effective in maintaining a positive atmosphere.

In addition to what are primarily verbal skills, you should also pay attention to the nonverbal elements in a communication climate. You can control the environment by reducing or eliminating noise and making careful seating arrangements; you can avoid such defensive, provoking bodily actions as clenched hands, folded arms, and rigid posture. And, perhaps most important, you can approach the discussion in a warm, friendly manner and with a smile.

Suggested Readings

Jack R. Gibb. "Defensive Communication." *Journal of Communication*, Vol. II (September 1961). This landmark article provides an excellent analysis of communication climates.

Sidney M. Jourard. *The Transparent Self*, rev. ed. New York: D. Van Nostrand Reinhold Co., 1971. Jourard's book is basic reading in the field of self-disclosure.

W. Barnett Pearce and **Stewart M. Sharp.** "Self-disclosing Communication." *Journal of Communication*, Vol. 23 (December 1973), pp. 409–425. Not only does this article provide an excellent overview of the subject, but also it contains a good review of the research.

Carl R. Rogers and **F. J. Roethlisberger.** "Barriers and Gateways to Communication." *Harvard Business Review*, Vol. 30 (July–August 1952). Although the article is more than twenty-five years old, it still provides valuable insight into dealing with barriers.

Chapter 6
Message Formation Skills

1. *Discuss the consequences of not dating or indexing statements.*
2. *Date and index statements as necessary.*
3. *Use accurate, specific, and concrete words in place of inaccurate, general, and abstract words.*
4. *Discuss the abuse of vocal interferences, "you know," and empty expletives.*
5. *Devise a plan to rid yourself of your nonfluencies.*
6. *Define crediting and discuss its purpose.*
7. *Credit statements of self and others.*
8. *Explain the importance of description of feelings statements.*
9. *Describe your feelings to others.*
10. *Define assertiveness.*
11. *Contrast assertive behavior with passive and aggressive behavior.*
12. *Explain how the use of transfer stations and information overload detract from communication effectiveness.*

Mark and Lillian are walking to their car from the restaurant where they have just eaten. As they pass a store window, Lillian spots a scarf that she thinks will go well with her new blouse. She says to Mark . . .

Gordon is reading a letter that explains why his uncle won't be able to hire him for the summer job he has had for the past several years. The totally unexpected news so late in the year is devastating to Gordon. He turns to his roommate Phil and says . . .

Jan has just bought herself a new car—well, a new old car. She approaches a group of her friends bursting with excitement to tell somebody about her purchase. She says . . .

These anecdotes are similar in at least one respect: each is a prelude to a conversation. Will Lillian, Gordon, and Jan be able to get their ideas and feelings across? The effectiveness of their communication will depend in part on how they form their messages. This chapter focuses on a number of important skills in message formation. The first five (dating, indexing, accuracy, use of specific and concrete words, and fluency) are language skills that will help you sharpen your ideas; the next two (crediting and describing feelings) will help you better communicate your feelings. In the final part of the chapter we'll look at assertiveness and then examine two barriers to successful message formation.

Dating

A simple yet effective way to clarify meaning is called *dating*. **Dating** **means including in your statements a specific time reference that indicates at what point in the past a given fact was true.** The statement, "We thought the prices in Nassau were reasonable; *at least they were in 1976*," is an example of dating. Even though all things are subject to change, it seems characteristic of human behavior to see some elements of our world as static. There seems to be some satisfaction in believing that a person, an idea, a movement can be "pegged." Yet our impressions of people, things, and ideas that we use in our communication were formed sometime in the past—perhaps only a few minutes ago, perhaps many years ago. When we talk about those people, things, or ideas, we tend to use language that explains these things as they were and not necessarily as they are. Yet, if we stop to think about it, we become aware that such places as Myrtle Beach, Disneyland, or the Wilderness Trail are not the same this year as they were last year; standards of television censorship today are not the same as they were in the 1960s; the car you drive is not the same as it was when you bought it; and neither your father, your mother, nor you yourself are quite the same as you were five years ago or even last week, for that matter! Everything ages, grows, learns, wears out—in effect, everything changes. Some changes may be nearly imperceptible, but some changes are so great as to make the person, idea, or thing nearly unrecognizable. Whatever you are talking about, you should actually or mentally indicate the date when your view of that phenomenon was true. Consider this conversation:

> **Max:** I'm being transferred to Henderson City. Do you know anything about the place?
>
> **Ted:** Well, *six years ago when I was there* a lot of folks were unemployed, and it was a pretty grim city.

Ted could have said, "Henderson City's a loser—the economy is very depressed." By dating his statement, Ted allows for the possibility of change.

Dating statements is a simple, two-step process:

1. *Before you make a statement about an object, a person, or a place, consider* when *the statement you are about to make was true and if it is still likely to be true.*

2. *If your statement is not based on current information, tell your listener(s)* when *the statement was true.*

The statement you then make will be similar to these:

"When we were in Palm Springs two years ago, it was really popular with the college crowd."

"Powell brings great enthusiasm to her teaching—at least she did last quarter in communication theory."

"Four years ago the Death Ride was rated the most exciting roller coaster in the country."

"You think Mary is depressed? She seemed her regular high-spirited self when I talked with her the day before yesterday."

Because you have no power to prevent change, you should recognize the reality of change by dating the statements you make.

Indexing

Indexing is a companion skill to dating. Dating accounts for differences caused by the passing of time. Indexing accounts for the innate differences among people, objects, or places. **Indexing is the mental or verbal practice of accounting for individual differences.** It is especially useful to help a person cope with the tendency to make decisions based on faulty generalization.

The ability to generalize is one of the great powers of the human mind. Generalization allows us to use what we have learned from one experience and apply it to another experience. When George tells Glenda that he caught five beautiful bass near a fallen tree on the eastern shore of Eagle Lake, a spot that seems to attract bass, Glenda is likely to look for a similar place to fish. When Sam notices that his girl friend seems to enjoy the fragrance of the new cologne he is wearing, he is likely to wear it again when they are together. When Marie learns that three of her fellow teachers have been promoted for excellence in teaching, she is likely to try to improve her teaching. Glenda, Sam, and Marie have used what they learned from one experience and applied it to another. They have generalized.

Yet, misuse of this power can cause at least two serious communication problems. One is the tendency to take the characteristics of a class of people or objects and assign them to all the individual members within that class. For instance, just because women (a class) have less strength in general than men (a class) does not mean that Barbara (a member of a class) is weaker than Max (a member of a class); just because a university is ranked among the top twenty in the nation does not mean that every department in that university is so ranked. This particular generalization problem is called *allness*.

A second problem is the tendency to transfer a characteristic of one person (or object) to another person (or object) just because the other person (or object) is within the same class. For instance, just because Klaus, a German, is industrious does not mean either that all Germans are industrious or that Fritz, who is also German, is industrious. Likewise, just because one Chevrolet goes 50,000 miles without a brake job does not mean that all Chevrolets can.

Now that we've considered the need for indexing, accounting for individual differences, let's see how the skill is applied. Consider a conversation about actors. Actors as a group may have many characteristics in common, but to assume that all actors have the same characteristics would be to make a false generalization. In a conversation about actors, then, we could show the potential for differences among them by mentally indexing—by assigning numbers to each member of the class. In our conversation then we would think of Jerry as actor[1], different from Doris as actor[2], different from Jack as actor[3], and so forth. Or if we were talking about Catholics, Susan (Catholic[1]) is different from Mary (Catholic[2]), who is different from Patrick (Catholic[3]). How do we do this in conversation? Consider the following dialogue:

> **Bill:** I'm really ticked: I've got a graduate assistant as my teacher in speech class. The last time I had a graduate assistant in class it was a real waste.

> **Art:** I know graduate assistants as a group are not the most experienced teachers, *but your teacher is not the same one you had before.* I would at least give him a chance.

Bill was generalizing from his one experience—he was making an "all" statement: "all graduate assistants are poor teachers." Art used an indexing statement ("this one is different from the other"—that is, graduate student[1] is not the same as graduate student[2]) to try to get Bill to see the possibility for individual differences. Let's try one more. Greg says, "I'm worried about Joan's ability to read. I had her brother Charley in class two years ago and he was a problem." As he thinks about what he has said, he adds, "I should keep in mind, though, that Joan and Charley are different even though they are members of the same family."

Let's review the procedure for indexing statements:

1. *Before you make a statement about an object, person, or place, consider whether your statement is about that* specific *object, person, or place or whether it is a generalization about a class to which the object, person, or place belongs.*

2. *If your statement is not based on specific knowledge, inform your listener of that fact.*

Here are some examples of indexing in conversation:

"I think this house is probably well built—Conway, the builder, has a reputation for solid construction. This house may be an exception, *though, so I'm going to look it over pretty well."*

"Breakfast cereals are almost all sugar—they're just not good for a kid's teeth. Well, at least most of them aren't. Heap O' Wheat could be an exception, *but you'd better check the list of ingredients."*

"Listen, I know Professor Barker was a poor teacher in business fundamentals, but organizational behavior is his specialty—we'd better see what he is like in that course *before we decide to take a different class."*

As a human you cannot avoid generalizing, but indexing your statements can help you avoid the problems that generalization sometimes creates.

Communication Session

Reflection

Have you ever had communication difficulties because of a lack of dating and indexing skills? What was the history of the incident?

Practice

Working in groups of three to six, have two persons discuss topics like the ones below. The rest of the group should observe when dating and indexing are being used, how well they are being used, and when they should have been used. Each person in the group should have an opportunity to practice.

Cars	*Equal opportunity laws*
Food preferences	*Minority groups in college*
Politicians	*College course requirements*
Job interviewers	*Wedding rituals*

Discussion

Are dating and indexing hard for you to do? Why?

Accuracy

You will recall from our discussion of language in Chapter 3 that meanings are in people. We can try to pick the word that best stands for the thought or feeling we are trying to communicate, but for no two people will a given word evoke exactly the same thoughts and feelings. When Carl tells Joan that he saw Mack *sprinting* to catch a bus, both Carl and Joan will have a mental image of *sprinting*, but the images will differ. Not only will their denotations (dictionary meaning) for *sprinting* differ, but their connotations will as well. In this instance, the differences are relatively minor and unimportant. They do not significantly interfere with communication.

There is a great gulf, however, between minor differences in connotation and denotation and truly major differences. Consider the following three sentences:

1. *Carl tells Joan that Mack was* sprinting.

2. *Carl tells Joan that Mack was* trotting.

3. *Carl tells Joan that Mack was* walking.

However Joan interprets the word *sprinting,* her image will be much different from her image of *trotting* or *walking.*

None of these words is rare, unusual, difficult, or understood only by a person with a large vocabulary. Any adult should have a reasonably good grasp of the meaning of these words. Each describes forward movement of some kind, but which is most accurate in the context? What was Mack doing? If Mack was running as fast as he could in the twenty-five-yard distance between him and the bus, *sprinting* is accurate. Neither *trotting* nor *walking* would be.

Accuracy means selecting the words to represent thoughts and feelings that are recognized by others in our culture as symbolizing those thoughts and feelings. Let's look at three sets of sentences. Notice the differences in meaning in each of these pairs of statements:

Gail says that Mary is an average *student. She studies about* an hour *a day. She gets* C's.

Gail says that Mary is an exceptional *student. She studies* three hours *a day. Her grades are* nearly straight A's.

They bought twin *beds for the boys. They're doing the room in* early American.

They bought bunk *beds for the boys. They're doing the room in* Danish modern.

They'll be coming in a pickup truck.

They'll be coming in a van.

Each of the statements is carefully phrased, and each could be a true statement, although the meanings in each pair are different. The point, however, is not which is true—there's no way of knowing—but that the differences in meaning are a result of a precise, accurate use of words.

When William Pitt "the Elder" (Prime Minister of England in the 1770s, and regarded by some as one of England's greatest orators) was a teenager, he gained an understanding and appreciation of language by twice reading in its entirety a famous dictionary of his day. Dictionary reading is still a good way to sharpen your understanding of words. You should also be familiar with books of synonyms such as *Roget's International Thesaurus.* A study of synonyms helps you to develop a flexible vocabulary.

You can improve the accuracy of your word choice by following these three steps:

1. *Before you speak, ask yourself if the word you are about to say is the best representation of your thought or feeling.*

2. *Make your statement.*

3. *If you have inadvertently used the wrong word, call attention to the misuse and correct it.*

The following three quotations show how accuracy can be achieved during the actual process of speaking. The first speaker finds the word he wants while the sentence is being spoken; the next two pause and correct themselves in the interests of accuracy.

"I think that many of Mark's statements are very [split-second pause while thinking: I want the word that means know-it-all] dogmatic."

"Well, she was driving one of those vans—no, I'm sorry, I don't mean van. She was driving one of those new extra-large station wagons."

"He looked really nice. He was wearing his new blue . . . I want the word for that special kind of jacket . . . I've got it . . . he was wearing his new blue blazer."

Using Specific and Concrete Words

Accuracy helps meaning by giving the best or most correct image; specificity and concreteness help to focus on the image. Specificity and concreteness go hand in hand in sharpening meaning by reducing choice on the part of the listener. When you are not careful, you may use words that are more general and abstract than they should be, words that allow the listener the choice of many possible images rather than a single intended image. The more the listener is called upon to provide his own image, the more likelihood the meaning he sees will be different from the meaning you intended.

"General" means an entire category; "specific" means one item within the category. When someone says "car" to you, what do you see? It may be any of a number of four-wheeled vehicles used primarily to transport people. In your mind you may see a large car or a small one, a sedan or a coupe, a Buick or a Datsun. If someone says "new Aspen," the number of choices you can picture is reduced. If the person says, "new blue Aspen station wagon," the likelihood that you and the sender will picture the same image is considerably better.

Whereas *"general* versus *specific"* deals with object language, *"abstract* versus *concrete"* deals with ideas or values. Concrete language turns an abstract idea or value into clearly pictured behavior. When people say they are "loyal," for instance, you may think of the dictionary definition of faithful to an idea, person, company, and so on. However, what "loyal" means in a particular situation is hard to say. What is an act of loyalty to Jim may not be an act of loyalty to you. To avoid ambiguity and confusion, a person might say, "They always buy the products made by their employer." Now the receiver would have a concrete picture of the loyal behavior of a group of employees.

Semanticists speak of levels of abstraction. In some instances you can take an idea from a general abstract level and move it to a specific concrete level through a series of stages. Earlier we talked about cars. We could write down a sequence that moved from the abstract term *vehicle* to motor vehicles, to passenger cars, to station wagons, to Aspen wagons, to the very concrete specific of my blue Aspen station wagon. Or, follow another sequence: She likes to have fun; she's a sports enthusiast; she enjoys ball games; she likes to participate in ball games; she plays paddleball every lunch period.

When you select a general or abstract word to encode your message, you are inviting confusion. The receiver may have to go through numerous paraphrases to help sharpen the meaning of the message you were trying to send. On the other hand, if you select specific or concrete words to encode your message, there is a much greater likelihood that the receiver will share your meaning with little additional effort. In summary, then, **speaking in specific and concrete words means using words that indicate a single item within a category or a single representation of an abstract value.**

You can increase the specificity and concreteness of your messages in the following way:

1. *Before you speak, ask yourself if the word or phrase you are about to speak is specific and concrete enough to carry the meaning you intend.*

2. *Make your statement.*

3. *If you have inadvertently used a more general or abstract word than you should have, correct it by using a specific, concrete word.*

As you can see, the procedure for developing specificity and concreteness in language selection is similar to the procedure for developing accuracy.

In the following three sentences the attempts to make language more concrete and specific take the same form as the attempts to make language more accurate. The difference is that in order to make language more specific you must first be able to identify language that is general and abstract. Otherwise you will be unable to correct yourself.

> *"Gail, would you please bring up all the stuff . . . that is, would you please bring the bag of groceries and my briefcase—you can leave the rest of the items in the car."*

> *"I think Carson is a good person to take a course from because he is fair; that is, he treats everyone as equals."*

> *"Mother, just everybody is getting her hair done this way . . . well, what I mean is that five girls in my dormitory have gotten their hair done this way this month alone."*

Fluency

The more accurate, specific, and concrete we make our speech, the more effective our communication will be. Some people, however, continue to have communication problems no matter how clear their messages. These are people who clutter their sentences with nonfluencies. *Nonfluencies* are speech sounds that add no substantive content to the message. **Good speaking must be fluent, smooth and uncluttered. It avoids such common nonfluencies as vocal interferences, "you know," and empty expletives.**

Vocal interferences are the "uh's," the "er's," the "well's," and the "OK's" that are so hard to eliminate from our speech. They are often caused by a fear of momentary silence. In some instances, this fear of silence is real. Americans have been taught that it is impolite to interrupt another person until the flow of sound stops. A problem occurs for the speaker when he pauses for the right word or idea. The split second it takes for him to come up with the word may be perceived by others as "dead air time." For fear that another person may perceive the pause as a full stop, the person often fills that dead air time with sound. More often than not, the sound has no meaning. For some, the customary filler sounds are "uh" or "er"; for others, they may be "well uh" or "um." Although the fear of being interrupted may be real (some people will interrupt at any pause), the intrusion of fillers is a high price to pay for occasional interruption.

Equally prevalent, and perhaps even more irritating than the vocal interferences, is the incessant use of "you know." The "you know" habit may begin with a teenager seeking to find out whether what he is sending is already known by a receiver. For some, "you know" may be a source of identification; the sender seeks to show that sender and receiver share common knowledge. We believe that for most people, however, the adulteration of sentences with "you know" is just a bad habit, especially when "you know" simply fills time and serves absolutely no communication purpose.

For the most part, excessive use of "you know" is an irritant that may force listeners to be poor listeners in self-defense. It has been our experience that no matter how irritating the use of "you know" may be, the listener is unlikely to acknowledge irritation. Seldom if ever does anyone say openly to another person anything like, "Your use of 'you know' at every break in thought really causes me great difficulty in listening to you and concentrating on your ideas." Yet passages like the following are quite common:

> *You know, the way things are going now, you know, I doubt that, uh, I doubt that we're ever going to get things, you know, straightened out.*

In addition to one "uh" and one repetition, that sentence contains three "you knows." We wish such uses were exaggerations. Unfortunately, they are not. Perhaps you should start pointing out this irritant in others' speech; most important, you should monitor your own speech for such use and do what you can to eliminate it. How should you proceed? We'll offer a workable plan after we have considered the third common nonfluency.

To some, especially in informal and relatively intimate situations, a third nonfluency becomes nearly as prevalent as the first two discussed; this nonfluency is the empty expletive. Students of language are aware that language usage has become increasingly more permissive during the last ten years. At one time certain four-letter words were seen only on walls or spoken only by "coarse," "vulgar," or "crude" persons, but now even some highly educated individuals apparently have some special affection for one or more of these all-too-common words. It is not, however, use of four-letter words that mars communication, it is the use of the expletive as a nonfluency—the use of the expletive indiscriminately with no apparent meaning.

Perhaps you have a friend or acquaintance for whom some pet expletive has lost all meaning other than to fill space between words or take the place of other, more precise words. When the expletive is used, not to convey thought but to fill space, it becomes a nonfluency.

For purposes of illustration, let's invent a new expletive—one that can stand for any that you enjoy or resent. This new word is *trid*. Now, if on some dim morning you are jolted from sleep by the alarm, fumble out of bed, and in a rush to the john stub your toe on the dresser, shouting "Oh, trid!" may have a therapeutic effect and certainly does express the pain and anguish you are experiencing. Perhaps even saying that the last test was a lot of trid is expressive. What we are talking about is the use of expletive as noun, verb, adjective, or adverb indiscriminately with no apparent meaning. For instance:

> *Oh, trid. That was one tridding test. If I ever catch that tridder outside of the tridding class you can bet your tridding butt that I'll have something to say to that tridder.*

Expletives may add a certain earthiness or even a certain sense of intimacy to a conversation—but at some point the usage reaches a point of diminishing returns, and with most of us that point is reached far too often. When the expletive is used not to convey thought but to fill space, it becomes a nonfluency.

Now, in any minute of conversation, most of us may use one or more nonfluencies; few of us can completely avoid their use. However, with some practice, you can limit their occurrence in your speech and thus become much more fluent. Remember, although they may not be willing to tell you about it, most people are distracted or irritated by nonfluencies. If you are not being listened to the way you think you should be, it could be that people are tuning you out because listening to you carefully is actually painful! What do you do? We offer the following three-step method:

1. *Become aware of usage.*   In self-defense, perhaps, your ear seldom hears your own nonfluencies. You may believe that you never use them when in fact they may be a major part of your sending style. There are two ways of learning to be aware. One way is to tape-record yourself talking for several minutes, and then listen to the recording. Turn the recorder on and talk about the football game you saw yesterday or the test you took or any of the kinds of things you are likely to talk about with a close friend. When you play it back, your ear will begin to pick up your nonfluencies. A second way is harder, but we believe it brings about quicker benefits. Have a close friend listen to you and raise his hand or drop a penny into a tin can every time you say "uh" or "you know" or use an empty expletive. You may find the experience nerve-racking, but soon your ear will start to pick them up as fast as the listener's.

2. *In practice sessions see how long you can go without using a nonfluency.* Start out by trying to talk for fifteen seconds. Continue to increase the time until you can get to two minutes. In these practices, meaning may

suffer. You may spend a disproportionate amount of time avoiding non-fluencies. Still, it is good practice.

3. *In regular conversation mentally note your usages.*   You will be making real headway when in the heat of conversation you can *recognize* your nonfluencies. When you reach this stage, you will find yourself beginning to avoid their use.

It is hard work—but it is worth it. Conversation would be a lot more pleasant if everyone would work to reduce nonfluencies by just 50 percent.

Communication Session

Reflection

Which of the language skills mentioned so far (accuracy in symbol selection, use of specific and concrete symbols, or fluency) causes you the greatest difficulty? Why?

Practice

1. For each word listed below, try to find three words or three phrases that are more specific, more concrete, or that are synonyms.

bread	*school*
happiness	*bad*
pretty	*unclear*
red	*rock*
chair	*coat*

2. Working in groups of three, have two members of the group discuss some topic of common interest. The third person should stop either person if he or she uses a general or an abstract word in any statement. When stopped, the person should substitute a specific or concrete statement for the general or abstract. The observer will have to be on his toes—we are so used to general-abstract language that sometimes we do not even notice it.

3. Working with groups of four to six persons, each person should try to talk continuously for two minutes. When it is your turn, you can select your own topic—talk about such matters as a movie you saw recently, the success of your school team, difficulties you are having with a particular course, and so forth. Whenever you use a nonfluency, one of the members of the group will drop a penny into a tin can. At the end of your two minutes, the pennies will be counted. Give

everyone in the group two chances. See who can contribute the fewest pennies. The "penny in the tin can" device can also be used in the specific-concrete practice above.

Discussion

In groups of four to six persons, discuss the following:

1. Why is it easier to be general and abstract than to be specific and concrete?
2. Why are people unlikely to express their displeasure at others' nonfluencies?
3. What do you consider to be the most irritating nonfluencies? Why do they bother you?

Crediting

Crediting means identifying the source of a particular idea, statement, or feeling. In a term paper, you give credit to those from whom you have taken words verbatim or paraphrased, thus giving credit to the original source and avoiding plagiarism. In interpersonal communication, you credit for two similar reasons: you credit the person whose ideas you are using to confirm the individual; and you credit your own feelings to differentiate them from the feelings of others. There are two skills that will help you reach these two goals; let's examine each of these two skills separately.

Crediting Others

As we have mentioned many times before, one of the goals of interpersonal communication is to build and maintain relationships. People get along better with others when they believe that they are recognized as individual persons—when others recognize their personal worth. Yet as senders of information we often act (usually inadvertently) to chip away at the very relationships we are trying to build or to maintain. **Crediting others means verbally identifying the person whose ideas you are using.** Consider the following illustration. Bart and Mike are discussing ways of making money, and Mike suggests buying a valuable item (a television set, a canoe, or whatever) at discount and then selling raffle tickets. Bart expresses his interest in the idea. The next day at a meeting of the entire fund-raising committee of seven members, Bart says, "What about buying a television at discount and selling raffle tickets? We could probably make a couple of hundred dollars!" The group responds immediately with such comments as "Great idea!" and "Let's do it!" At this point, what is Mike, the originator of the idea, likely to be feeling? If he says, "That was my idea," the group may think less of him for quibbling over whose idea it was. If he says nothing, he is likely to feel resentful toward

Bart. In this instance, it was Bart's *responsibility* to give credit to Mike for originating the idea.

Is this important? Of course it is. Think of the times you were hurt because an idea of yours was not credited. Giving credit to others is an essential skill of interpersonal communication. Had Bart just said, "Mike had a great idea—what about buying a television at discount and selling raffle tickets?" the group's reactions would probably have been the same, but Mike would have felt much better because his idea would had been properly credited.

Crediting Self—Making "I" Statements

When you talk, others assume your statements represent your ideas or feelings. Although people are willing to divulge most of their thoughts, they are often unwilling to divulge or take credit for their personal feelings. Instead of crediting self, they wrap their feelings in impersonal or generalized language or attribute them to unknown or universal sources. **Making "I" statements means identifying yourself as the source of a particular idea or feeling.** Some people refer to this skill as *owning feelings*. Consider the following paired statements:

"The Dodgers are a great team."

"I believe the Dodgers are a great team."

"Nobody likes to be laughed at."

"I don't like to be laughed at."

"Nobody's going to take the word of a kid against an adult."

"I'm not going to take the word of a kid against an adult."

Each of these examples contrasts a generalized or impersonal account with an "I" statement. Note, as in the first example above, an "I" statement can be any statement that has a first person pronoun such as "I," "my," "me," or "mine." For purposes of accuracy of information and for purposes of helping the listener to understand fully the nature of the message, it is essential to credit self by making "I" statements. Why are people so reluctant to do so? Saying "Everybody knows the Dodgers have the best team" means that if the listener doubts the statement he is bucking the collective evaluation of millions of Americans. Of course, not everybody knows the Dodgers are best; in this instance, the statement really means that one person holds the belief. Yet, because a person may think that his feelings or beliefs will not carry much power, he may feel the need to use unknown or universal sources for those ideas or beliefs. Similarly, people use collective statements such as "everybody agrees" and "anyone with any sense" to escape responsibility for their own feelings and thoughts. It seems far more difficult for a person to say, "I don't like Herb" than it is to say, "No one likes Herb."

To avoid misunderstandings and false generalizations, you need to develop the skill of making "I" statements. Everyone has a right to an opinion. If what you are saying is truly your opinion, then let others know, and be adult enough to take responsibility for what you believe or feel. If you don't, you may alienate others who would understand your opinions or feelings even though they differ with you.

Communication Session

Reflection

Are you likely to credit statements of others? of your own? Under what circumstances?

Practice

Write down five opinions, beliefs, or feelings of yours. Check to make sure each is phrased as an "I" statement. If not, correct each one; for example, "~~Nobody likes~~ a sore loser" "I don't like a sore loser."

1.
2.
3.
4.
5.

Describing Feelings

We are all human and we all have feelings. We differ from one another in how we deal with our feelings. We believe that describing feelings is the best way of dealing with feelings.

 Describing feelings means making statements that put emotional states into words. Psychologists say that bottled-up emotions can cause psychological problems, but why is describing feelings better than expressing them in some other way—by screaming or breaking something, for example? In most circumstances describing feelings is the best way to handle them because it gets them out in the open and because it teaches people how to treat you. (You'll recall that we first discussed the value of describing feelings in the section on self-disclosure in Chapter 5.)

Let's begin to explore the importance of describing feelings by asking a question. How many times have you experienced discomfort or anxiety because (1) people borrow your car or your camera because "you don't mind"; (2) people tease you a lot because you "take it so well"; (3) people frequently rely on you to get things done because you do them well "without putting up a fuss"; or other, similar actions based on misperceptions of your feelings?

Do the people who impose on you want to cause you discomfort? Perhaps their thoughtlessness is partly your fault because by not saying anything you have encouraged their behavior. You see, your silence reinforces their actions: because you don't say anything, they think they are treating you as you want to be treated—or at least don't mind being treated. Have you ever heard a person defend his teasing by saying, "Oh, don't worry, she really enjoys it"? If the person being teased has never objected, people assume she doesn't mind. "But," you say, "a person's nonverbal reactions can make it clear that she dislikes something." Unfortunately, some people are insensitive to others; they don't catch the non-verbal clues that can reveal a person's true feelings. You have to take the responsibility for saying what you like and what you don't like.

Describing your feelings frankly is a starting point in educating others about your feelings. You can make such statements as, "Cliff,

Describing your feelings frankly is a starting point
in educating others about your feelings.

when you borrow my best sweater without asking, it makes me angry with you"; or "Rick, I know you think I don't mind it when you tease me about how I talk, but it makes me feel self-conscious about what I say"; or "Maria, I get the feeling that you think it's a compliment to my ability to get things done when you leave me with the dirty work, but in fact I resent being left with those jobs."

Describing your feelings will not necessarily get someone to change his behavior toward you. After all, people behave as they choose. But if you have been candid with someone about your feelings, at least that person now knows what has happened inside you as a result of his behavior. Some understanding has been achieved.

Why don't people describe their feelings more often? Failure or refusal to reveal feelings may be the result of one of the following assumptions: (1) if you describe your true feelings, they will reveal too much about you and you will become vulnerable; (2) a revelation of your feelings will in some way cause harm; and (3) feelings that cause guilt should be repressed. Let's examine the fallacies behind each of these assumptions.

1. *If you describe your true feelings, they will reveal too much about you and you will become vulnerable.*   True, revealing your feelings does involve a certain amount of risk, but you have to take some risks in order to bring change. For instance, Joe likes Doris. He would like to get to know her a lot better—he'd like to ask her to go with him for a drink after class. But Joe fears rejection. What if he asked Doris and she laughed at him or said, "Get lost"? Rejection hurts. But what if Doris wants Joe to ask her for a date? His fear of taking the risk may prevent establishment of a lasting friendship.

2. *You believe that revealing your feelings will in some way cause harm.*   The fact is that failure to reveal is likely to hurt as much as revealing. Isn't it better for people to hear that something they do irritates you than to risk losing your friendship because you can't deal with anyone who does things that irritate you?

3. *You believe that you should repress feelings that make you feel guilty.*   The fact is, you have these feelings whether you think you should or not. Maybe you should not get angry with a loved one; but, if you are angry, the feeling exists and must be dealt with. Unless it comes out in a descriptive statement, it may come out some other time in a more destructive way.

We are often caught up in the communication dilemma, which can be stated as follows: We are not inclined to let a person into our real world of feeling unless he is a close personal friend; yet, we are not likely to have a close personal friend unless we are able to let him into our real world of feeling. At first this looks like an impossible dilemma. But if you examine it carefully, you will see that our perception problem comes with what is meant by "real world of feeling." Most of us think of a total either/or situation. Either we hold everything in or we let everything out. It is true that you would be foolish to be completely open and honest with everyone you happen to meet. Few people wish to hear the innermost feelings of someone they have just met. As a result, most people go to the other extreme—they reveal nothing of themselves even to those with whom they wish to be closest. Improved interpersonal relations come with improved interpersonal communication. And you begin by describing feelings.

Let's examine two alternatives to describing feelings. The first alternative is to acknowledge feelings internally but withhold expressing them. People who behave in this way put a lid on their feelings. Consider the following two examples.

> Dan takes Esther out to dinner on her birthday. As they are looking at the menu, Esther says, "The lobster sure sounds great!" Dan begins to panic as he realizes Esther wants a dinner that is five dollars higher than anything else on the menu. He replies, "Yes, it does sound good."

> Doris is taking lessons from Candy to improve her tennis backhand. Doris is becoming frustrated because she doesn't understand what Candy is telling her. Candy says, "Now that you understand it, you'll see that the backhand is really an easy stroke." Doris replies, "I can see that."

In neither case does withholding feelings help Dan or Doris. From a psychological standpoint withholding feelings is bad. They can't be held forever. When Dan and Doris finally release their feelings, they may direct them against people who did not cause them, or they may direct them against Esther and Candy in a context having nothing to do with the lobster or the tennis lesson.

A second alternative is to express feelings verbally or nonverbally by immediately reacting to something that has been said or done. Consider the following two examples.

> During an exciting part of a movie, Kathy, caught up in the action on the screen, begins to crunch the ice of the soft drink she is sipping. Randy is getting more and more irritated as Kathy crunches. After about five minutes in which most of his attention is being focused on the ice crunching, he looks at her and says, "Damn it, Kathy, cut it out!"

> Mickey is going over his criticism of Al's carpentry in front of the other members of the construction crew. As Mickey enumerates the many mistakes Al has made, Al's resentment of Mickey's public criticism gets stronger and stronger. As he reaches the boiling point, Al shouts, "That was the first time I tried that job—if you wanted an expert to do it, you should have hired one. So get off my back!"

Expressing feelings in this way is probably better than withholding them because the expression provides an immediate outlet. Expressing positive feelings immediately is almost always a good thing to do. The bumper sticker that says, "Have you hugged your kid today?" is a reminder that many people do not take the time to show their love or affection to those close to them. But in the two preceding examples, the outbursts will make it hard to restore rational communication for quite a while. Expressing negative feelings spontaneously benefits the one doing the expressing, but it is usually harmful to communication.

Many people have difficulty in recognizing the difference between describing and expressing feeling, and until they learn the difference, they will have trouble describing their feelings clearly. One of the exercises at the end of this unit gives you a chance to test your ability to tell the difference between describing and expressing.

Despite the importance of being able to describe feelings, doing so is hard for many people. The more personal and the stronger the feeling, the less likely people are to describe it. Let's look at the procedure for describing feelings.

1. *Know what you are feeling. This sounds easier than it sometimes is. When a person experiences a feeling, he will sometimes express it without thinking about it. You must be aware of exactly what it is you are feeling—is it anger? resentment? pity? scorn? hate? happiness? joy? concern? inadequacy?*

2. *Credit your feelings—make an "I" statement.*

3. *Make sure the statement names an emotion.*

4. *Describe the specific cause of the feeling, if you can.*

We need to describe feelings in order to send messages more accurately and to open ourselves up to reach our fullest communication potential. How can we start in a way that will not be too risky for us but will tell others that we want to share a part of ourselves?

A good starting point is with positive feelings. You may not find it difficult to say, "The sun's out today—I feel great." By beginning with a conscious effort to state your positive feelings, you will soon discover that such statements are accepted by others, make you feel better, and help other people learn how to treat you. Success with positive statements will make it easier for you to try to describe your negative feelings. Try to get in the habit of including how you feel with each statement you make. You will discover that a statement such as "The sun isn't out today—I'm feeling a little depressed" is not hard to make. Practice by communicating positive and less threatening negative feelings. As you see how your communication improves, you will be encouraged about describing your feelings more accurately on all levels.

Communication Session

Reflection

Do you describe feelings or do you express them? When? Under what circumstances?

Practice

1. In each of the following sets of statements, place a *D* next to the statements that describe feelings; place an *X* next to the statements that convey feelings by expressing them or by showing the effect of a feeling without actually describing it. Such statements can be called *evaluative.*

   1. ____ a. That was a great movie!

      ____ b. I was really cheered up by the story.

      ____ c. I feel this is worth an Oscar.

   2. ____ a. I feel you're a great writer.

      ____ b. Your writing brings me to tears.

      ____ c. Everyone likes your work.

   3. ____ a. If things don't get better, I'm going to move.

      ____ b. Did you ever see such a hole?

      ____ c. I feel depressed by the dark halls.

   4. ____ a. I'm not adequate as a leader of this group.

      ____ b. I feel inadequate in my efforts to lead the group.

      ____ c. I'm depressed by the effects of my leadership.

   5. ____ a. I'm a winner.

      ____ b. I feel I won because I'm most highly qualified.

      ____ c. I'm on cloud nine after winning that award.

Answers to 1: a. expressive/evaluative; b. descriptive; c is an evaluation dressed in descriptive clothing. Just because the word *feel* is in a statement does not mean the person is truly describing feelings. "This is worth an Oscar," is an evaluation, not a feeling.

Answers to 2: a. expressive/evaluative (there's that word *feel* again); b. descriptive; c. expressive/evaluative.

Answers to 3: a. the result of feelings, but not descriptive of the feelings; b. evaluation in question form; c. descriptive.

Answers to 4: a. expressive/evaluative; b. descriptive (similar to a except that here the feeling is described, not stated as an evaluation); c. descriptive.

Answers to 5: a. evaluative; b. evaluative; c. descriptive.

---

2. For each of the examples on page 133, change the final sentence into a well-phrased description of feelings.

3. Work in groups of four to six. Each person role-plays a situation (for example, your roommate borrowed your car without asking permission; he comes into the room later and, giving you the keys, says, "Thanks for the car") and then tells how he feels about it. Other members of the group paraphrase what he has said until feelings have been described fully. Exercise continues until each member of the group has had practice with describing feelings.

Discussion

1. After completing the practice, the group should discuss how they feel about describing feelings. Is it difficult or easy? Why? How do circumstances affect your attitude toward describing your feelings?

2. Develop a list of contexts and arrange them from "contexts in which I am unlikely to describe feelings" to "contexts in which I would easily describe my feelings." Share your lists in the group. Where are there similarities? Discuss the differences.

Assertiveness

We have saved for last a message formation skill that has been the subject of more recent discussion than nearly any other in this book: assertiveness. The women's movement and affirmative action programs that help minorities and people in subordinate positions to try to get ahead have revealed that large numbers of people are unable to take advantage of opportunities to advance themselves because they lack assertiveness. For this reason, more and more people—especially women—are enrolling in courses, programs, and workshops on asser-

*Assertiveness is the skill of learning to state your ideas
and feelings openly in interpersonally effective ways.*

tiveness training. **Assertiveness is the skill of learning to state your ideas and feelings openly in interpersonally effective ways.** The ability to be assertive is a direct outgrowth of your feelings about your self-worth and importance. As we see it, assertiveness is not a single, individual skill but the mastery of—and willingness to use—several of the skills we've discussed, with special emphasis on *describing feelings*.

We believe that assertiveness is a desirable behavior. When two people act assertively toward each other, the communication channels are opened. They are exchanging vital information about the nature and character of their relationship. Being assertive allows you to share your ideas and feelings in a positive way. It is hard to establish any kind of relationship with someone who refuses to state a position on an issue, and it is difficult to know someone who refuses to disclose his feelings.

People who are not assertive are likely to be either passive or aggressive. Let's first consider *passive* behavior. Many American women are passive because they play the role that society has taught them: women must be soft, warm, and loving; any signs of assertiveness are unwomanly. Fortunately, passive behavior is no longer seen as an ideal way for women to act. Women are flocking to courses on assertiveness training because they have spent the better portion of their lives being passive and now need to learn to assert themselves.

What are some signs of passive behavior? People who are passive are often shy. People who are passive are reluctant to state their opinions, share their feelings, or assume responsibility for their actions. They often give in to the demands of others, even when doing so is inconvenient or against their best interests. They often pay dearly for their passivity. For instance, passive people often fail either to describe or to express the anger they feel; the outcome is often resentment, depression, or sickness.

Another kind of nonassertive behavior is *aggressiveness*. Unfortunately, too many people equate assertiveness with aggressiveness, although the difference between the two is enormous. Assertiveness is stating what you believe to be true for you, taking responsibility for your actions and feelings, but not attacking another individual personally. Aggressiveness, on the other hand, is behavior that is highly defensive. It is judgmental, dogmatic, and often fault-finding.

Let's see how passive, aggressive, and assertive behaviors differ by examining two different situations.

> *Bill has just purchased a new color television set at a local department store. When he uncrates the set at home, he notices a large, deep scratch on the left side of the cabinet.*

If Bill's behavior were *passive*, he would be angry about the scratch, but he would keep the set and say nothing to the store clerk from whom he purchased it. He might complain to his family about the decline of pride in workmanship or about stores that sell damaged goods, but he would say nothing to anyone associated with the store.

If Bill's behavior were *aggressive*, he would be angry about bringing home a damaged set. He might storm back to the store, loudly demand his money back, and accuse the clerk of intentionally selling him damaged merchandise. He would threaten the store with a lawsuit, and he would not stop until he received satisfaction.

If Bill's behavior were *assertive*, he would be angry about bringing home a damaged set. Then he would proceed to assert himself in one of several ways. For example, he might call the store and ask to speak to the clerk from whom he had purchased the set. When the clerk answered, Bill would explain that when he uncrated the set he discovered a large scratch on the cabinet and that he was calling to find out what he had to do to return the damaged set and get a new one.

Both the aggressive and the assertive behavior would probably get Bill a new set. But the assertive behavior would achieve the result at lower emotional costs to both Bill and those with whom he talked.

> *Betty arrives late to a large lecture class. Because all the seats in the front section are occupied, she is forced to sit in the back of the room. She notices two men in front of her talking noisily. She assumes that they will quiet down when Professor Green arrives and begins his lecture. Several minutes into the lecture, however, they are still talking.*

If Betty's behavior were *passive*, she might just sit there boiling inside and feeling powerless to do anything.

If Betty's behavior were *aggressive*, she might tap one of the men on the shoulder and say in a loud voice, "I guess neither of you cares about this lecture, but I'm trying to listen. Will you knock it off?" She might turn to the person sitting next to her and say in a loud voice, "If I were Professor Green I would long ago have thrown out these two creeps in front of us who keep babbling."

If Betty's behavior were *assertive*, she might tap one of the men on the shoulder and say, "Excuse me, but I'm having a hard time hearing Professor Green."

There is no guarantee that either the aggressive or the assertive behavior will make the men be quiet. In fact, the aggressive behavior may cause them to keep talking just to further irritate Betty (a defensive reaction). The assertive behavior will appeal to those who wish to act rationally. If she achieves nothing with her statement, then she can move to another part of the room. If Professor Green asks her why she is moving, she will tell him politely but firmly.

Many people are not assertive because either they think they are not important or they feel guilty about their emotions. First, everyone is important. It doesn't matter whether you are a poor person with little education, a shop supervisor, the president of the PTA, or the chairperson of the First National Bank—you are important.

Second, as we said earlier, any feeling you have is your feeling and you should not feel guilty about having it.

To be assertive you should:

1. *Identify what you are thinking or feeling.*

2. *State it in the most interpersonally sound way possible.*

Two Barriers to Message Formation

The result of effective message formation is that meaning will be communicated more accurately and thus be more likely to be shared. But message formation skills are not enough; a sender must also avoid two common barriers to communication.

First, a communicator must be sure that his message is going directly to whoever needs the information. When the receiver is one person, no problem occurs. But when the information is needed by many people, senders sometimes find themselves having to use transfer stations. Sending messages through transfer stations means transmitting information from one receiver to another in a chain-link fashion. If Terry needs to get information to Ted, Joan, and Max, she is much better off if she talks to each individually or all three together than if she tells Ted and then asks Ted to "pass it along." Perhaps you've played the party game called Telephone (or Gossip), in which one person whispers a statement to another, who in turn whispers what he "heard" to the next person, and so on until the statement has gone through five or six transmissions. By the time it

Sending messages through transfer stations means transmitting information from one receiver to another in a chain-link fashion.

reaches the last person, the message may be so garbled that it is unintelligible.

In such a chain, each person acts as a transfer station. The original sender may have all the information he needs to communicate a relatively complex idea. When Carl, the sender, encodes the message into words, he has already simplified, limited, and interpreted the original idea. The person who is the first transfer station for the message does not have benefit of the entire background for the idea. He has only the words the first person used. He may not be able to remember all the words; he may not understand all the words; he may let semantic noise interfere with his understanding of the words. Nevertheless, he communicates what he now perceives as the message to the next person, who communicates what she perceives. As the message moves on down the line, each transfer station affords another opportunity for selection and interpretation. If there are enough transfer stations (and it does not take many), the message can be distorted beyond recognition. Unscrupulous persons have used the technique to spread rumors for as long as people have used speech. Rumors are statements that are passed from person to person and usually embellished along the way, becoming bigger, bolder, bloodier all the time. (It is interesting that messages with many facts are not only distorted in transmission but also shortened; messages that are storylike usually get embellished—certainly they are distorted, but instead of becoming shorter, they often become longer.)

The best way to avoid this barrier is to create a face-to-face communication setting with all those who must have the information. Even under the best of circumstances, pass-it-along, transfer-station transmission distorts messages—the problem is how to minimize the distortion.

Second, a sender must consider the quantity of information he is trying to communicate. Too much information, too great a density of information, or too fast a rate of information transmission can result in a barrier known as information overload.

Because you are a human being and not a high-speed computer, there is a limit to the amount of information you can process at any given time. You have probably had the experience of trying to get directions to a particular place in an unfamiliar area. When you think you are at last in the right area, you stop a pedestrian and ask, "How do you get to the stadium from here?" If the person says, "Go three blocks north, turn to the right, and it's down a block or two on the left-hand side," you can probably process the information easily enough and get to your destination with little difficulty. But have you ever had something like the following experience? The local character says to you, "Well, let's see, go three blocks north, turn right, go five blocks until you come to a Texaco station, turn left until you hit the third stop sign, turn left again . . ." If you are like most people, you will probably go part of the way and then seek new directions. Regardless of how well you listen, you can be overloaded with details of information.

You can use selective perception, accepting only the input you want to perceive or are used to perceiving, to cope with the barrier created by overload. In practice, there should be a basis for the selection—perhaps a criterion that you can apply consciously to the volume of material. As the sender of information you can protect against information overload by limiting the details of the message, by grouping ideas, and by emphasizing the key points verbally or nonverbally. Of course, the more information you elect to send, the greater the likelihood for overload.

Summary

In this chapter we looked at message formation skills. The four language skills of dating, indexing, accuracy in word choice, and use of specific and concrete words are directed at sharpening the meaning of the message. Increased fluency helps the listener concentrate on the content of the message rather than the "uh's," "um's," "you know's," and empty expletives that pepper some people's speech.

Crediting clarifies the source of ideas and contributes to the good feelings of the people being credited. Describing feelings, one of the most important as well as one of the most difficult of skills, helps teach people how to treat us. Although expressing feelings is good psychologically for the person doing the expressing, describing feelings is a more interpersonally sound way of handling feelings.

Assertiveness is the skill of stating your ideas and feelings openly in interpersonally effective ways. Passive people are often unhappy as a result of not stating what they think and feel; aggressive people get their ideas and feelings heard, but may create more problems for themselves because of their aggressiveness.

Any speaker must be aware of the potential problem of transmitting information from person to person in a chain-link fashion and of presenting so much information at one time that the listener is overloaded.

Suggested Readings

John C. Condon, Jr. *Semantics and Communication,* 2d ed. New York: Macmillan Publishing Co., 1975. This short paperback provides an excellent explanation of semantics.

William V. Haney. *Communication and Organizational Behavior: Text and Cases,* 3d ed. Homewood, Illinois: Richard D. Irwin, 1973. This is an updated version of a classic work in the field of semantic application. Haney supplements and illustrates his points with easy-to-read case studies. Well worth a careful reading.

David W. Johnson. *Reaching Out: Interpersonal Effectiveness and Self Actualization.* Englewood Cliffs, New Jersey: Prentice-Hall, 1972. See especially pages 90–98 for a discussion of describing feelings.

John L. Wallen. "Developing Effective Interpersonal Communication," in R. Wayne Pace, Brent D. Peterson, and Terrence R. Radcliffe (Eds.), *Communicating Interpersonally—A Reader.* Columbus, Ohio: Charles E. Merrill Publishing Co., 1973. This article has a particularly good section on describing feelings.

Philip G. Zimbardo. *Shyness.* Reading, Massachusetts: Addison-Wesley Publishing Co., 1977. An excellent analysis of shyness and many good ideas about how to cope with it.

Chapter 7
Listening and Response Skills

PAYOFFS *After you have read this chapter, you will be able to:*

1. *Tell the difference between hearing and listening.*
2. *Apply the four-step process for improving listening efficiency.*
3. *Identify and present appropriate supporting, questioning, paraphrasing, and interpreting responses.*
4. *Tell the difference between a paraphrase of content and a paraphrase of feelings.*
5. *Identify and present description of behavior and perception checking responses.*
6. *Name the types of personal feedback.*
7. *Understand the rules for giving personal feedback.*
8. *Give personal feedback in a supportive manner.*
9. *Identify less helpful and inappropriate responses.*

In conversation people respond to each other in many ways. The kind of response—asking questions, changing the subject, arguing, showing understanding, giving opinions—influences the interpersonal relationship of which the conversation is a part. Even when a person feels strongly about a subject, he may be reluctant to respond in a way that will create disharmony. Response choices can heighten or sever the fragile bond of communication.

Responses can be divided into two basic categories: those that are helpful or appropriate and those that are less helpful or inappropriate. Helpful responses are the empathic responses that make communication easier: they confirm a person's right to his thoughts or feelings, and they help to sharpen understanding. Less helpful or inappropriate responses hinder communication. They plant seeds of discontent within a person, about both himself and what he is thinking or feeling, and they ignore or scuttle efforts at understanding. The seven basic helpful responses are supporting, questioning, paraphrasing, interpreting, describing behavior, perception checking, and giving personal feedback. Less helpful or inappropriate responses are interrupting, irrelevant comments, tangential statements, incongruous replies, and unsolicited evaluation.

As we discuss each of the major helpful responses, we'll explain them, give examples, outline the steps in phrasing them, and, when useful, contrast them with typical less helpful or inappropriate responses. The seven helpful responses are not mutually exclusive. For example, as you will see, supportive statements should probably be a part of any helpful response. Likewise, you may find yourself combining paraphrasing with any of the other responses. Moreover, there is not necessarily any one correct way to respond. Part of the behavioral flexibility you are hoping to develop in your interpersonal communication depends on learning to select the response or combination of responses that is best suited to a particular situation.

Because all other response skills begin with and depend on listening, let's begin with that important skill.

Listening

Listening provides us with data to which we can respond. Our eyes see the nonverbal cues that illustrate, clarify, and occasionally countermand the apparent meaning of verbal messages. The principal instrument for recording verbal messages, however, is the ear.

You may already be aware that in your daily communication you spend more time listening than you do speaking, reading, or writing. A recently completed study of college student communication habits shows that college students spend 22 percent of their time speaking, 20 percent reading, 8 percent writing, and 50 percent of their time listening.[1] Yet of these four skills, people tend to be most complacent about their listening. Studies indicate that although most people have the physical capabilities of recording audio impulses, many are not good listeners. Receiving audio stimuli is hearing; **listening means making sense out of what we hear.** Research studies have shown that most of us listen with only 25 to 50 percent efficiency.[2]

Receiving audio stimuli is hearing; listening means making sense out of what we hear.

---

[1]Rudolph Verderber and Ann Elder, "An Analysis of Student Communication Habits," unpublished study, University of Cincinnati, 1976.
[2]Ralph G. Nichols and Leonard A. Stevens, *Are You Listening?* (New York: McGraw-Hill Book Company, 1957), pp. 5–6.

In our analysis of listening, let's first consider those listening factors that are a product of your heredity and environment.

Hearing Acuity

Some people have severe hearing problems. Estimates are that as many as 10 percent of any adult audience have some hearing difficulty. If you know you have a hearing problem, you may now wear a hearing aid, or you may have learned to adjust to the problem, but if you are not aware of the problem, poor hearing alone may limit your listening effectiveness.

If you suspect that you may have a hearing problem, your school probably has facilities for testing your hearing acuity. The test is painless and is usually provided at minimal or no cost to the student.

Vocabulary

Listening and vocabulary are definitely related. If you know the meaning of all the words you receive, you are likely to better understand what is being said and have better retention. However, if you do not know the meaning of some words used by the sender, you will not understand them, and your listening may well be affected. Many "poor students" have average or better intelligence, but are handicapped by a poor vocabulary. If you have a below average vocabulary, you must work that much harder to develop listening skills. Or work to improve your vocabulary.

When Sally uses a word that Paul does not understand, he may sit in silent ignorance rather than take a step toward improving his vocabulary by asking Sally to define the mysterious word. Is Paul's behavior like yours? Perhaps you fear appearing foolish for not understanding the word in the first place. Isn't it even more foolish to respond to something you don't understand? The tendency to respond as if we really understand is illustrated by results of a telephone survey conducted to find out if people were continuing efforts to save energy. Most respondents answered "yes" to questions about turning out unneeded lights, keeping thermostats at 68 degrees, and driving at 55 miles per hour; however, a surprising number also said "yes" to a question about installing a "thermidor" on the family car. Think how foolish these people would feel if they found out they had confirmed that their engines were now equipped with seafood casseroles! You may feel foolish to ask; you are likely to behave more foolishly if you do not ask.

An Ear for Language

If your family is articulate and given to verbalizing, there is a good chance that you have a natural "ear for language," that you have a grasp of good thought structure, and that you have had experience with various kinds and levels of listening. If you have not developed an ear for language at home, then your ear may not be tuned to the difficult kinds of listening that you may encounter at school.

Improving Listening

You may have some listening problems, but you can improve your listening ability. The following suggestions can be put into practice if you are willing to concentrate and practice.

1. *Get ready to listen.*   Listening efficiency increases when the listener follows the apparently elementary practice of really being ready to listen. "Getting ready" involves both mental and physical attitudes. Mentally you need to stop thinking about any of the thousands of miscellaneous thoughts that constantly pass through your mind; all your attention should be directed to the sender and to what is being said. In effect, the sender is in competition with all these miscellaneous thoughts and feelings. Some of them may be more pleasant to tune into. Anticipation of an exciting evening; thoughts about a game, a test, or what's for dinner; and recreating in your memory scenes from a memorable movie or television show may offer more attractive pleasures than listening to factual data, yet attention paid to such competing thoughts and feelings is one of the leading causes of poor listening.

You need to stand or sit in a way that will help you listen. Since physical alertness encourages mental alertness, you may find that how you stand or how you sit affects how messages are received. You may also find it helpful to look the speaker in the eye as he or she talks with you. A visual bond between sender and receiver helps form a mental bond.

2. *Make the shift from speaker to listener a complete one.*   In a classroom setting in which you are planning to be a listener, it is relatively easy to get ready to listen. In conversation, however, you switch roles from speaker to listener and back to speaker again quite frequently. If as listener you spend your time preparing your next contribution (that is, thinking about how to say something clever or trying to recall some fact you can use to make your point), your listening efficiency will take a nose dive. We have all experienced situations in which two persons talked right past each other under the guise of "holding a conversation." In comedy routines such situations are often hilarious. In real life, the results of such "communication" are often pathetic—each of two participants broadcasting with no one receiving! The next time you are conversing, check yourself—are you "preparing speeches" instead of listening? Perhaps putting the sender's ideas in your own words will help you stay tuned in.

Although making the shift from speaker to listener may be difficult to put into practice consistently, it is especially important.

3. *Listen actively.* Because you think faster than most people talk, you can use your thinking capacities to make you a better listener. As noted in points 1 and 2, if you let your mind wander or if you prepare replies while you are supposed to be listening, your efficiency will go down. On the other hand, if you mentally or actually paraphrase, question, interpret—use the skills discussed in this chapter—you may be able to raise your listening efficiency. Many of the skills we will discuss are called "active listening" skills. Too often people think of the listening experience as a passive activity in which what they remember is largely a matter of chance. In reality, good listening is hard work that requires concentration and a willingness to mull over and at times verbalize what is said.

4. *Withhold evaluation.* By this we mean that you need to control your emotional responses to a speaker's content. Are there any words or ideas that are red flags for you, words whose mere utterance causes you to lose any desire to listen to the speaker? Do you react to such terms as "chauvinist," "libber," "gay," "Democrat," "Republican," "Communist," "Catholic," "Jew," "atheist," "Jesus freak," "black," "white," "Chicano"? Would any of these words turn you off? Often, poor listeners (and occasionally even good listeners) are given an emotional jolt by a speaker invading an area of personal sensitivity. At this point all you can do is to be wary. When the speaker trips the switch to your emotional reaction—let a warning light go on before you go off. Instead of tuning out or getting ready to fight, work that much harder at being objective. Can you do it? If you can, you will improve your listening.

In the above list, we have been concerned primarily with what you can do to improve your listening skills related to comprehension and retention of information. Before we explore the remaining response skills, let's test your listening.

Communication Session

Reflection

Under what circumstances do you really listen? Can you tell when you are really listening and when you are not?

Practice

Ask someone to read the following information to you once, at a normal rate of speech. Then give yourself the test that follows. Although the temptation is great to read this item to yourself—try not to—you will miss both the fun and the value of the exercise if you do.

Today is your first day on an office job. A fellow worker gives you the following information:

> *Since you are new to the job, I'd like to fill you in on a few details. The boss probably told you that typing and distribution of mail were your most important duties. Well, they may be, but let me tell you, answering the phone is going to take most of your time. Now about the typing. Goodwin will give the most, but much of what he gives you may have nothing to do with the department—I'd be careful about spending all my time doing his private work. Mason doesn't give much, but you'd better get it right—she's really a stickler. I've always asked to have tests at least two days in advance. Paulson is always dropping stuff on the desk at the last minute.*

> *The mail situation sounds tricky, but you'll get used to it. Mail comes twice a day—at 10 A.M. and at 2 P.M. You've got to take the mail that's been left on the desk to Charles Hall for pickup. If you really have some rush stuff, take it right to the campus post office in Harper Hall. It's a little longer walk, but for really rush stuff, it's better. When you pick up at McDaniel Hall, sort it. You'll have to make sure that only mail for the people up here gets delivered here. If there is any that doesn't belong here, bundle it back up and mark it for return to the campus post office.*

> *Now, about your breaks. You get 10 minutes in the morning, 40 minutes at noon, and 15 minutes in the afternoon. If you're smart, you'll leave before the 10:30 classes let out. That's usually a pretty crush time. Three of the teachers are supposed to have office hours then, and if they don't keep them, the students will be on your back. If you take your lunch at 11:45, you'll be back before the main crew goes.*

> *Oh, one more thing. You are supposed to call Jeno at 8:15 every morning to wake him. If you forget, he gets very testy. Well, good luck.*

Answer true or false:

_____ 1. Mail that does not belong in this office should be taken to Harper Hall.

_____ 2. Mail comes twice a day.

_____ 3. You should be back from lunch by 12:30.

_____ 4. Paulson is good about dropping work off early.

_____ 5. Mason gives the most work.

_____ 6. Goodwin gives work that has little to do with the department.

_____ 7. Your main jobs according to the boss are typing and answering the telephone.

_____ 8. Mail should be taken to McDaniel Hall.

_____ 9. The post office is in Harper Hall.

_____ 10. You get a 15-minute morning break.

_____ 11. Call Jeno every morning at 8:45.

_____ 12. You don't have to type tests.

Answers: 1. F; 2. T; 3. T; 4. F; 5. F; 6. T; 7. F; 8. F; 9. T; 10. F; 11. F; 12. F

Supporting

Supporting someone is saying something that soothes, approves, reduces tension, or pacifies. A supportive statement is a major empathic statement. It shows that you can empathize with someone's *feelings.* The feeling you are supporting may be positive (joy, elation, pride, satisfaction) or negative (sadness, anger, sorrow, disappointment). The feeling may be intense, so much so that it almost short-circuits the thinking process, or it may be mild. Whatever the direction or intensity of the feeling, the supportive statement shows (1) that you care about the person and what happens to him; (2) that you can empathize with that feeling, and (3) that you acknowledge the person's right to the description or expression of that feeling. Whether a person "should" be having the feeling is not your concern.

If the feeling is positive, a supportive statement is your attempt to share in the feeling and help sustain it. People like to treasure their good feelings; they don't want them dashed by inappropriate words. If the feeling is negative, the supportive statement is your attempt to help the person work through the feeling without intensifying it or in some other way becoming more uncomfortable or unhappy. When a person's feeling is highly negative, it may take that person a few seconds, a few minutes, or even a few hours to calm down and think rationally. When a person expresses a highly negative emotion, you want to say something that will help defuse the emotion so the person can begin to return to normal.

Here are two sets of helpful, supportive phrases paired with responses that are either less than helpful or totally inappropriate. The first examples are responses to a positive emotion.

> *Julie hangs up the phone, turns to Gloria, and says, "That was Paul. He asked me to go to the Homecoming Dance. I never thought he even noticed me!"*

Supportive responses:

1. *"Julie," Gloria says enthusiastically, "you must feel terrific!" (This*

Less helpful or inappropriate responses:

1. *"That's not any big deal—I hear Paul has gone out with nearly every*

statement supports Julie's positive feeling.)

2. *"Julie, I'm so happy for you—you really seem excited." (Shows that Gloria wants to share in the positive feeling.)*
3. *"I can see why you're so happy—Paul's one of the cutest guys around." (Support through confirmation of Paul's value.)*

girl in class." (Inappropriate because it detracts from the value that Julie places on the call; it will probably irritate Julie rather than please her.)
2. *"Take it easy, Julie, you might be disappointed yet." (Julie is happy, why be negative for no apparent reason?)*
3. *"That's nice. By the way, did I tell you I was able to get tickets for the jazz concert?" (By changing the subject, Gloria refuses to acknowledge Julie's good feeling.)*

The second set of responses are examples of how and how not to deal with another person's negative feelings.

Julie hangs up the phone in tears and says, "That was Paul—he called to break our date, but he wouldn't even tell me why!"

Supportive responses:

1. *"That's terrible. I can see he's really hurt your feelings!" (Recognition of Julie's hurt.)*

2. *"Breaking a date is bad enough, but not even telling why . . ." (Empathizing with Julie.)*

3. *"He did what? Oh, Julie, that hurts!" (Empathizing with the pain.) "Anything I can do for you?"*

Less helpful or inappropriate responses:

1. *"Grow up, Julie. That won't be the last time something like that happens." (Maybe Julie should grow up, but this is not the time to tell her so. Now is the time to acknowledge the hurt.)*

2. *"You're hurting now, but it will go away." (The hurt will certainly go away, but now it needs to be acknowledged.)*

3. *"Well, you probably wouldn't have had a good time anyway." (Maybe not, but this remark misses the point of what Julie has said.)*

The procedure for phrasing helpful, appropriate supportive statements is as follows:

1. *Listen closely to what the person is saying.*

2. *Try to empathize with the person's feelings. At least try to identify what you regard as the dominant emotion: disappointment? fear? anger? joy? elation? resentment?*

3. *Phrase a reply that is in harmony with the feeling you have identified. Later in the conversation you may be able to say something that will help the person overcome the particular problem involved.*

4. *If appropriate, indicate your willingness to be of service or to help if possible.*

Here are four more examples of supportive statements. Notice that each identifies the prevailing emotion, each statement is in harmony with the person's feelings, and, although you cannot tell from the printed page, each is sincerely meant.

At the end of class, Jan, hoping to get a B or A grade on her paper, is shocked to discover a D grade. As she leaves class fuming, she runs into a friend and says, "He gave me a D on that paper. I worked my tail off, did everything he asked, and he gave me a D." Her friend Lois replies, "A D! As hard as you worked I can see why you're so upset. That's a real blow! Is there anything I can do for you?"

Martha rushes into the house and says, "Dad, I had an accident with the car! No one is hurt, but I really bashed hell out of the fender. I just feel sick about it." Her father replies, "You say no one was hurt! That's good. I can see you're upset, but a car can always be fixed. Can I help you in any way?"

Alex hits his forehead with his hand and says, "I forgot all about the two o'clock meeting! Tony's going to kill me." Hank looks at him and says, "Oh boy—I can see why you feel bad. It can be really upsetting when something important slips your mind. Anything I can do to help you work it out with Tony?"

Art says, "I've really racked my brain over this, and I've decided to go to Peters College rather than State U." Dan replies, "That's an agonizing kind of decision. It sounds as if you really took the time to think it through."

Questioning

When you do not understand what has just been said to you or when you need more information about a specific subject, you will probably ask questions. As you know, **a question is a way of getting additional information.** Although you have no doubt been asking questions ever since you learned to talk, you may occasionally find that the questions you ask arouse defensiveness. Both appropriate wording and a pleasant tone of voice are necessary to a good interpersonal questioner. The questions should be empathic. Let's consider both the goals of questioning and the kind of wording that will be helpful and appropriate.

1. *Questions that encourage a person to give more details:*

Ann: There I was in the middle of dressing when Tom came to the door.

Nell: What happened next?

Fred: They turned down my proposal again.

Sam: Did they give you any reasons?

2. *Questions that seek to clarify the meaning or the use of a particular word:*

Martha: I don't mind Paul being late, but recently he's been late so frequently!

Adelle: How frequently do you mean?

Phil: Norm has been acting obnoxious lately.

Bob: What has he been doing that's obnoxious?

3. *Questions that encourage the sender to share his or her feelings:*

Cal: What a day—to top it off Marge broke our date.

Pete: Did that really make you feel bad?

Norm: Billy didn't win, but he did come in second.

Kay: Were you disappointed that he didn't win?

For questioning to succeed as an appropriate response, it must be perceived by the receiver as an honest effort to discover information that will aid the questioner in helping with the particular problem. If the receiver perceives the questions as actual or veiled attacks, the questioning will be construed in a negative way.

Here are some guidelines for asking helpful, positive questions.

1. *What is the motivation for your question? If the answer is that you need information to be helpful in reply, then continue. If you have some other reason, maybe a paraphrase or some other response is more appropriate. If you are just curious (nosy?), perhaps you need to curb your urge to question.*

2. *What is it you need to know? Is it more details? how a word is used or defined? how the person feels?*

3. *Phrase the question in a way that achieves the goal of the question without creating defensiveness in the receiver.*

4. *Speak with a tone of voice that is sincere—not a tone that could be interpreted as sarcastic, cutting, superior, dogmatic, or evaluative.*

Let's look at some examples of what we'll call *empathic* questions contrasted with examples of less than helpful or inappropriately phrased questions:

Fred comes out of the committee room and says, "They turned down my proposal again!" Art asks:

Empathic: *"Did they tell you whether it was a matter of form or a matter of content? (A sincere request for additional information.)*

Inappropriate: *"Well, did you explain it the way you should have?" (A veiled attack on Fred in question form.)*

In a conversation with Mary about her communication style, Tracy says, "Mary, when you get emotional you tend to make disfunctional statements." Mary says:

Empathic: *"From the context I take it that 'disfunctional' means negative. Am I interpreting the word correctly?" (This question will help clarify the meaning.)*

Inappropriate: *"What the hell does 'disfunctional' mean?" (This question is a very defensive response that is likely to hurt the positive communication climate.)*

Art, talking with Dan about the football game he played in last Saturday, says, "And to top it off, Coach Waldorf was yelling at everyone." Dan says:

Empathic: *"Did his behavior upset you and the rest of the team?" (This question tries to get Art to reveal his feelings.)*

Inappropriate: *"You were probably making a lot of stupid mistakes. Did he say what they were?" (This negative interpretation is very evaluative. It is not likely to encourage Art to talk about the game in a friendly way.)*

Notice that the empathic questions get the necessary information without creating a defensive climate. The inappropriate questions, on the other hand, seem deliberately designed to undermine or attack the person being questioned. To be effective, questions must have a supportive base.

Questioning might be a necessary response, but the information sought should be relevant to the prevailing issue, and it should come out of a spirit of inquiry and support and not from a real or an apparent need to make the person look bad.

Interpreting

 An important but infrequently used skill is interpreting. **Interpreting is an attempt to point out an alternative to or a hidden meaning in an event.** People often interpret ambiguous events negatively, even though they have no reason to. Yet an event may carry a far different meaning from the one that a person assigns to it. For example, consider George's plight. He has just had his first date with Natalie, a woman he thinks he might become very fond of. They had what George regarded as an excellent time, yet the end of the evening was disappointing to George. When he gets back to his room, he says to his roommate: "I take her to dinner and a great show, and when I get to her door she gives me a quick little kiss, says, 'Thanks a lot,' and rushes into the house!"

George is interpreting Natalie's behavior negatively. He sees her action as a rejection of him as a person. Martin, his roommate, replies, "I wonder whether she might not have been afraid that if she said any more you'd get the wrong idea about what kind of a girl she is."

Whose interpretation is correct? We don't know. What we do know is that behavior can frequently be interpreted in more than one way. Too often, especially when we feel slighted, or angry, or hurt, we interpret events in the most negative way. A supportive response that uses interpretation offers a person an alternative to negativism. It is designed to make a person feel better.

Like questioning, a good interpretive response uses language that is supportive of the sender. We are often confused or perplexed by someone else's words or actions. Regardless of the strength of our self-concept, we may be inclined to view the words or actions negatively. The interpretation gives us choices, stimulates thinking, and helps the sender to reason out what has taken place.

When you have a need to interpret, you should examine your motive for the interpretation. In the first place, you are not a mind reader—you cannot know for sure why something was done or said. Your goal should be to help the sender make some sense out of the action—to be a help, not a hindrance to the thinking process. Interpretation works best as a response when it comes with words that are perceived as supportive. Here are three guidelines for interpreting:

1. *Consider your motivation for the interpretation. As with questions, when you desire to interpret you should assure yourself that your goal is to help someone.*

2. *Phrase an alternative to the sender's own interpretation—one that is intended to help the sender see that other interpretations are available.*

3. *When appropriate, preface the interpretive statement with a supportive one.*

Let's look at two examples of appropriate interpreting responses. Notice that both preface the interpretation with a supportive statement.

Polly: "I just don't understand Bill—I say we've got to start saving money and he just gets angry with me."

Angie: "I can understand why his behavior would concern you. Perhaps he feels guilty about not saving money or feels that you are putting him down."

Glen: "I just don't seem to understand Professor Aldrich. He says my writing is really creative, but he never gives me an A."

Sid: "I can see why you'd be frustrated, but perhaps he is trying to motivate you to do even better."

Communication Session

Practice

1. Let's summarize this section by examining a situation. Your goal is to identify the type of response.

   Situation: Joyce is leaving a class in which she has just received her test score and grade. Although she knew she hadn't received an A, Joyce is very disappointed with the D grade that appears on her paper: she feels she should have had at least a C if not the B she was expecting. Jerry, her boyfriend, is waiting for her as she comes from class. When she sees him, a look of anger comes into her eye, and in a trembling voice she says, "He gave me a D—that stinkin' Morten gave me a D!"

   Jerry might make any of several responses. Five possible statements are given in the list. Label each response as A, paraphrase; B, supportive; C, questioning; D, evaluating; or E, interpreting.

   ___ 1. Come on, Joyce, you knew you hadn't studied enough when you went in to take the test.
   ___ 2. A D! I can see why you're angry after all the time you spent studying.
   ___ 3. I get the feeling that you're really shocked by a grade you never expected.
   ___ 4. Did he give you the reasons why he gave the D? Did he write any comments?
   ___ 5. A D is a low grade, but he may well have given it to you to motivate you to do better next time.

2. Supply an S (supportive), a Q (questioning), and an I (interpreting) response to each of the following statements. We have completed the first one for you.

   George: (in a dejected voice) I didn't get the scholarship.
   S: George—I'm sorry to hear that—I know how much you wanted it.
   Q: Are there any other financial aid sources you might tap?
   I: Your grades are certainly high enough—maybe it was given solely on need.

May: Mother says I am not to see Herman anymore!

S:

Q:

 I:

Jerry: They just fired my favorite teacher.

S:

Q:

 I:

Greg: I lost my car keys!

S:

Q:

 I:

Angel: The police just arrested my brother.

S:

Q:

 I:

3. Working in groups of six, have two people role-play a conversation using one of the statements above. The other group members should tally the number of S, Q, and I responses made by each role player. After five minutes, another pair should role-play another set. After all group members have participated, each member should receive the tally of how he did.

Discussion

Discuss how the number of responses per category influenced the outcome of the role-playing.

Answers: 1. D; 2. B; 3. A; 4. C; 5. E.

Paraphrasing

When you don't understand, you ask a question. Should you do anything when you *think* you understand? Yes, because serious communication problems can occur even though you think—or are certain—you understand what has just been said to you. In far more cases than we realize, or care to admit, what we think a person means may be far different from what the person really means. You will be a much more effective listener if you follow this guideline: Before you respond to what a person has said, even if you think you understand, *state your understanding by paraphrasing.*

What is paraphrasing? Simply defined, **paraphrasing means restating a message in your own words.** First, we'll look at how paraphrasing is done, then we'll look at when paraphrasing is appropriate. Although you will probably listen to someone speak several sentences before feeling a need to paraphrase what is being said, for purposes of illustration the following examples are restricted to paraphrases of single-sentence statements.

Right at the start we want to emphasize that paraphrase is not merely repetition:

Charley: "I'm really going to study this time."

George: "This time you're really going to study."

George's repetition shows that he heard the words, but it does not show that he has necessarily understood them. An effective paraphrase puts the message into the paraphraser's own words. George should have tried to make a statement that was *more specific* than the original message.

Charley: "I'm really going to study this time."

George: "From what you say I get the impression that this time you're going to read every chapter carefully and do all the exercises."

Charley: "I'm going to outline the chapters—I don't know that I'll do all the exercises."

George's statement is an acceptable paraphrase of Charley's message because it is more specific than the original statement.

Perhaps you're thinking, "If I were in this situation I'd ask Charley the question, 'What do you mean by *study*?'" As we saw in the last section, a sincere, well-worded question is appropriate when you seek additional information, the definition of a word used, or the feeling of the person making the statement. But in this case, most people think they know what *study* means. So George isn't really seeking new information, he's checking to make sure that what he (George) thinks of when he says *study* is the same as what Charley meant.

When you put a statement into your own words, you may concentrate either on the content of the message or on the speaker's feelings about the message. Either or both are appropriate, depending on the situation. Let's examine the words *content* and *feelings* for a moment. Content means the substance, the denotative meaning, of the message. A message's meaning, however, will go deeper than simple denotation. A person's feelings about the content contribute significantly to its total meaning. Paraphrasing may concentrate on either content or feelings or both. Let's go back to Charley's statement, "I'm really going to study this time," and paraphrase both the content and the feelings behind the message.

Content: *"I take it that when you say 'really study' you mean you're going to outline every chapter and do all the exercises."*

Feelings: *"From what you say, I get the idea that you were pretty upset with your grade on the last test."*

Do you see the difference? Let's try a few more. In each case the content paraphrase will be in the left-hand column and the paraphrase of feelings in the right-hand column.

"Five weeks ago I sent the revised manuscript of my novel to the publisher. I was excited because I felt the changes I had made were excellent. You can imagine how I felt when I got the thing back yesterday, and one reviewer said he couldn't see that this draft was much different from the first."

"You mean the person who reviewed the manuscript said he could see no difference, yet you think your draft was both different and better."

"You seem disappointed that the reviewer didn't recognize the changes you had made."

"Listen, the fact is that it's the student who gets the short end. Education is supposed to be the reason why the school exists, but if you look at what's happened the last few years, I don't think you can find much that has really been beneficial to the student."

"So you're saying that any changes in policy that have occurred have perhaps benefited the faculty or the administration, but not the students."

"You seem to resent the time and energy that have been spent in making changes that you do not perceive as benefiting students."

These examples show that paraphrasing can make you a better listener because it helps you sharpen your understanding of the messages. Try this next one yourself:

Professor Johnson: "Summer really flew by for me. And I didn't get as much done as I'd planned, but I never do. Still, I'm really excited about the new term—it's like a fresh start!"

You: [How would you paraphrase this statement?]

On the surface, Johnson's remark appears to be perfectly straightforward. As with most statements, however, there may be more to what the professor is saying than a few words can convey. For instance, the professor may greatly enjoy teaching, or he may like meeting new students, or he may be getting a chance to teach a new course. To make sure you understand what the professor meant, you will need to paraphrase. Of the many possibilities for paraphrase, you might choose one of the following:

You: "It sounds like autumn is your favorite part of the academic year."

"I get the feeling you've really been looking forward to coming back to school."

"From what you're saying I get the idea that starting the new year is even more important to you than some of your other projects."

Occasionally it will take more than one paraphrase to pin down the message. Consider the following conversation:

Gayle: Wow, that guy Ralph is really weird.

Pat: You think he acts a lot different from most guys in his circumstances.

Gayle: It's not just what he does, it's what he says.

Pat: And what he says bothers you in some way?

Gayle: Well, yes. I kind of like him, but I just never know what he's going to say next, and I feel uncomfortable.

You may think that if a person stated her meaning accurately in the first place you would not have to paraphrase, and you are probably right. However, not everyone is able to state her meaning clearly every time she speaks, and even clear language may be misunderstood.

Paraphrasing is appropriate under the following four circumstances:

1. *Paraphrase when you think you know what a person means or feels but are not absolutely sure.*

2. *Paraphrase when better understanding of a message is necessary before you can continue the interpersonal encounter effectively.*

3. *Paraphrase when you perceive that what the person has said is controversial or was said under some emotional strain.*

4. *Paraphrase when you are inclined to have some strong reaction to what the person has said or how he has said it—and your strong reaction might cause you to misinterpret his message.*

In summary, the procedure for effective paraphrasing is as follows:

1. *Listen carefully to the message.*

2. *Determine what the message means to you.*

3. *Restate the message using your own words to indicate the meaning you have received from the message.*

Communication Session

Reflection

Think of the last time you had a "misunderstanding." Would paraphrasing have helped avoid that misunderstanding?

Practice

1. Try to paraphrase the following statements. To get you started, we've done the first conversation for you.

    Art: It's Sally's birthday, and I've planned a big evening. Sometimes I think Sally wonders whether I take her for granted—well, I think after tonight she'll know I think she's something special!

    You: (content) I get the idea you've planned a night that's totally different from what Sally expects on her birthday.

    You: (feelings) From the way you're talking, I get the feeling you're really looking forward to tonight.

    Angie: Brother! Another nothing class. I keep thinking one of these days he'll get excited about something. Professor Jones is a real bore!

    You: (content)

    You: (feelings)

    Guy: Everyone seems to be talking about that movie on Channel 5 last night, but I didn't see it. You know, I don't watch much TV.

    You: (content)

    You: (feelings)

    Sarah: I don't know if it's something to do with me or with Mom, but lately Mom and I just aren't getting along.

You: (content)

You: (feelings)

Aileen: I've got a test in math and a paper due in English lit. On top of that, it's my sister's birthday and so far I haven't even had time to get her anything. Tomorrow's going to be a bad day.

You: (content)

You: (feelings)

2. Work in groups of three. A and B will hold a conversation on a topic such as "Why I'm majoring in _____," or "The advantages or disadvantages of living in dorms," or "Dealing with drug abuse on campus." C will observe the conversation. For this exercise, neither speaker is allowed to state his ideas until he paraphrases what the other person has just said, to that person's satisfaction. At the end of three to four minutes, the observer (C) discusses the paraphrasing of the two participants. Then, for 3 to 4 minutes B and C converse and A observes; for the final 3 to 4 minutes, C and A converse and B observes.

Discussion

After the exercise is completed, the participants discuss how they felt about paraphrasing and how the paraphrasing affected the conversations.

Describing Behavior

The skills we have discussed so far are supportive responses prompted by verbal messages. How do you respond supportively when the messages are nonverbal? The next two skills—describing behavior and perception checking—relate directly to nonverbal messages.

 Describing behavior means accurately recounting specific observable behavior without labeling the behavior good or bad, right or wrong. The impulse is strong in all of us to draw conclusions about what we have observed. We often use and hear used such evaluative words as *stupid, rude, funny, peculiar, silly,* or other equally vague, judgmental terms. Some people do not seem to mind having their thoughts and actions evaluated—whether the evaluation is positive or negative—but evaluation often interferes with sharing meanings. Consider the following two situations:

1. *Steve and Mark are discussing the future of the Republican party. After Mark has interrupted him for the second time, Steve can say either:*
   a. *"Mark, your behavior is rude!" (evaluative)*

   b. *"Mark, do you realize that you interrupted me before I had a chance to finish either of my last two sentences?" (descriptive)*

2. *Jack picks up Paul before picking up the women with whom they are double-dating. Jack looks at what Paul is wearing. He can say either:*

   a. *"Paul, you've got about as much taste in clothes as a baboon." (evaluative)*

   b. *"Paul, you've got a tartan plaid coat on, a plaid shirt in a different pattern, and a tie with flowers on it." (descriptive)*

Each of these examples illustrates a contrast between describing the behavior and evaluating it. Steve's statement, "Your behavior is rude," supplies no information and may be answered by another evaluative statement ("Steve, you're a jerk!") that will further hinder communication. However, the statement, "Do you realize you interrupted me before I had a chance to finish either of my last two sentences?" recounts Mark's behavior without labeling it right or wrong, good or bad. Steve may still become defensive and misunderstanding may still occur, but the description has been given. As a result, meaning is shared and the communication is more likely to continue satisfactorily.

In the second example, if Jack tells Paul that he has about as much taste as a baboon, Paul may feel hurt, even if Jack and Paul are good friends and even if they enjoy kidding each other. Jack's remark provides no information. On the other hand, the statement, "You've got a tartan plaid coat on, a plaid shirt in a different pattern, and a tie with flowers on it," gives the data. It describes but doesn't evaluate what Jack has observed.

Here are some guidelines for describing behavior:

1. *Become aware of what you are seeing or hearing.*

2. *Report only what you saw or heard.*

3. *Do not judge the merit of what you saw or heard.*

Making judgments may seem easier and more fun than describing behavior. If your goal is to irritate someone, your expressed judgments may accomplish that goal. You may have a kind of unwritten contract with a friend that on certain subjects the fun of arguing and competing is more important than communication. However, if you are interested in contributing to understanding, you will want to rely on description rather than judgment.

Are you a compulsively evaluative person? Are you afraid that you won't be able to break the evaluation habit? If so, we can suggest a two-step approach to evaluation. Our contention is that to contribute to understanding and to avoid defensive reaction, descriptive statements are a necessity. The two-step process that we suggest includes the descriptive statement(s) to be made first, followed by any evaluative, judgmental statement you feel compelled to include. Examine each of the following sets of sentences, which consist of a preferred descriptive statement, an evaluative statement—the kind you should be trying to avoid—and a two-step evaluative statement that begins with a descriptive base:

Descriptive: "Your hair looks curlier than usual."

Evaluative: "I don't like your hair fixed that way."

Two-step statement: "Your hair looks curlier than usual; I prefer it the way you usually wear it."

Descriptive: "You have a flower pattern on the walls of your living room and a different flower pattern on the curtains."

Evaluative: "Those two flower patterns look terrible together."

Two-step statement: "You have a flower pattern on the walls of your living room and a different flower pattern on your curtains—the two different patterns clash!"

You will notice that the evaluative part of the two-step statement is worded a little differently from the evaluative statement. By beginning your analysis with a descriptive statement, you may find that the evaluative part is a little less abrasive than if you used the evaluative statement alone. Whether the evaluative part of your statements is softened or not, at least you will have supplied the data on which the evaluation is based; this alone will reduce the probability of a defensive reaction.

Describing behavior is not an easy skill to use consistently. Do not be discouraged if you occasionally slip into evaluative patterns. We believe that as you gain skill in being descriptive, you will be rewarded by marked improvement in your communication.

Communication Session

Practice

Change each evaluative statement to a descriptive statement:

This report is a mess.

Pat is a good student.

Greg is a sloppy painter.

The movie was boring.

This exercise is stupid.

Television is a waste of time.

Pam is a freak about neatness.

He's a poor communicator.

Professor Green is a great teacher.

Caroline is so disorganized.

Discussion

1. How can you distinguish between descriptiveness and evaluation?
2. Is evaluation ever appropriate? If so, when?

Perception Checking

A perception check is to nonverbal communication as a paraphrase is to verbal communication. You have learned to use paraphrasing to clarify the meaning of verbal messages; the perception check is the skill used to clarify the meaning of nonverbal messages. **Perception checking is a verbal statement that tests your understanding of how another person feels.**

If all of us always said what we are thinking or feeling, perception checking would not be needed. Because some people do not verbalize what they are thinking or feeling and because what they do say sometimes seems at odds with other cues they are sending, you as a receiver must interpret the words and actions. There is no way of judging the accuracy of your perceptions without putting them to the test. Examine the following situations and the efforts at checking out perceptions:

> *George, through various visual and auditory cues that connote displeasure (speaking in short, precise sentences with a sharp tone of voice, and the like), gives Bill his day's assignment. Bill says, "I get the impression that you're upset with me, George. Are you?"*

> *Ted delivers a note to Mary from her friend Gary. As she reads the note, her eyes brighten and she breaks into a smile. Ted says, "You seem particularly pleased with Gary's note, Mary. Is that so?"*

> *Al offers Suzy directions for revising the advertisement she has written for a new product—an advertisement that took her many hours to prepare. As Al talks, Suzy's face reddens, her eyes seem to water, and she sets her lips. Al says, "Am I right that you're angry with the suggestions I'm making?"*

> *Martin listens to what Greg says with virtually no expression other than a slight smile. As Greg speaks, Martin occasionally nods and he looks*

Greg straight in the eye. Greg says, "I'm not sure whether your expression means that you're satisfied or dissatisfied with my proposal."

In each of the above examples, the final sentence is a perception check that is intended to test the receiver's perceptions of the nonverbal communication of the sender.

How do you phrase a perception check?

1. *Watch the behavior of another.*

2. *Describe the behavior to yourself or aloud.*

3. *Ask yourself, "What does that behavior mean to me?"*

4. *Put your interpretation of the nonverbal behavior into words.*

5. *Check to see whether your perception is accurate.*

After the perception check is made, the sender has a chance to speak to the accuracy of that perception.

When should you use perception checking? We recommend that you check your perceptions whenever someone's nonverbal cues suggest that he or she has experienced a mood change. The perception check will enable you to make sure you understand that mood change so that your response to it will be appropriate.

What happens when you respond without checking your perceptions? Let's examine a rather typical conversation based upon the situation described in the first example above.

If, in place of the descriptive perception check ("I get the impression that you're upset with me. Are you?"), Bill were to say, "Why are you so upset with me?" Bill would not be describing his perception—he would be making a judgmental statement related to that perception. Replying as if your perception is obviously accurate requires reliance on mind reading, and few of us can read minds. When mind reading is substituted for perception checking, the result is all too often trouble. Perhaps you are thinking, "Well, I know when another person is upset with me." Perhaps you are correct in your certainty that you can properly identify such feelings accurately much of the time. If you do not respond at all, you are guessing that you know how the other person is feeling. If you choose the judgmental reply, any person so spoken to would be inclined to be defensive about the feelings that you appear to be challenging. In response he might say, "Who said I'm upset?" or more harshly, "What the hell are you talking about?" Such responses might soon lead to further emotional outbursts, and very little communication takes place when communicators lose their tempers.

Because a perception check is descriptive rather than judgmental, the original sender will be less likely to become defensive. The purpose of checking out any perception of behavior is to give a person the opportunity to deal with that perception—to verify it or to correct it. Let's carry through with George and Bill's conversation. When Bill says, "I get the impression that you're upset with me, George. Are you?" George may say either (1) "No, whatever gave you that impression?" in which case Bill can further describe the cues that he received; or George may say (2) "Yes, I am," in which case Bill can get George to specify what has been the cause of the upset. If George is not upset, then Bill can deal with what caused him to misinterpret George's feelings; if George is upset, then he is given the opportunity to explain why in more detail, and Bill has the opportunity of changing the behavior that caused George to be upset.

A perception check will not eliminate defensive behavior. There are times when the emotional stress is so great that calm, logical communication is nearly impossible. Through the use of perception checking, however, you can reduce the probability of defensiveness.

Of all the possible barriers to communication, defensiveness is the easiest to elicit and perhaps one of the most difficult to deal with. We are all sensitive human beings; without giving it conscious thought, we become attached to our own ideas and feelings because they are ours. Then, when we believe that one of our ideas or one of our feelings is being questioned, challenged, or in some way attacked, our immediate reaction is to strike out at the attacker. If, however, we feel that a person is not attacking us, we may develop an empathic bond, and we are less likely to get defensive. In the following exercise, try checking perceptions in a way that is least likely to elicit a defensive reaction.

Communication Session

Practice

1. Respond to the following situations with well-phrased perception checks:

    Vera comes rushing into the room, throws her books on the floor, and sits at her desk with her head in her hands. You say:

    Bob comes out of the instructor's office with pale face and slumped shoulders. Glancing at you with a forlorn look, he shrugs his shoulders. You say:

    As you return Jim's tennis racket, you smile and say, "Here's your racket." Jim stiffens, grabs the racket, and marches away. You say:

In the past, your adviser has told you that almost any time would be all right for working out your next term's schedule. When you tell him Wednesday afternoon at 4 P.M., he pauses, frowns, sighs, and purses his lips. You say:

2. Work in groups of three. A talks with B and C observes. A role-plays a situation, giving off various cues of feelings through words and actions. B uses perception checking to test perception of A's feelings. C discusses the conversation. The exercise continues until everyone in the group has a chance at being sender, receiver, and observer.

Inappropriate Responses

Our discussions of responses have contrasted helpful or appropriate ones with less helpful or inappropriate ones. Let's take a look at some specific types of inappropriate responses that you will want to avoid in your communication.

A response is inappropriate when it increases chances for defensive behavior, when it disconfirms a person, or when it is unlikely to achieve an intended objective. Because we have already discussed defensiveness in some detail, let's turn our attention to the two other consequences of making an inappropriate response.

To *disconfirm* means to cause a person to question his self-worth; it undermines a person's self-concept. Praise is likely to heighten self-worth, but criticism is likely to lower it. Perhaps the most disconfirming statements are those that ignore a person's existence. Children sometimes purposely misbehave to get attention—even though they know the attention will be in the form of punishment. Praise when you can, criticize when you must, but try *never* to ignore a person.

Behavior that does not or cannot achieve its goal is called *disfunctional behavior.* For instance, when your mother asks you "What are you doing?" in an accusatory tone of voice, she may seem to be asking for information, but you will probably perceive the accusing tone as judgmental. Because her question implies a judgment (whatever you are doing is wrong), it is disfunctional.

Here is a summary of the kinds of responses that are likely to cause defensive reaction, to disconfirm, and to fail to achieve their goal:

1. *Irrelevant response:*   An irrelevant response is one that bears no relation to what has been said—in effect it ignores the sender entirely.

Bob: I'm concerned with the way Paul is handling arrangements for the benefit.

Tom: Hey, the Russian gymnasts are coming to town—I've got to get tickets for that.

When the sender is totally ignored, it not only causes him to question whether he was heard, but it may well cause him to wonder about the worth of what he was thinking or saying—for anything important will not be ignored.

2. *Interrupting response:*   When the receiver breaks in before the sender has finished, the response is interrupting.

Bob: I'm concerned with the way Paul . . .

Tom: I know—that Paul is something else, but I don't think there's any real problem.

People are inclined to interrupt when they believe what they have to say is much superior to what the sender is saying, when they believe they know what the sender is going to say and they want the other person to know that they already know, or when they are not paying careful attention. Any of these three common reasons connotes a lack of sensitivity or a dogmatic or superior attitude. As human beings we need to be able to verbalize our ideas and feelings regardless of whether they are already known or not. Constant interruptions are bound either to damage the sender's self-concept or to make him or her hostile—and possibly both. Whatever you have to say is seldom so important that it requires you to interrupt the sender. When you do interrupt, you should realize that you are building a barrier. The more frequent the interruptions, the greater the barrier will become.

3. *Tangential response:*   Tangential responses are really irrelevant responses in tactful language. They are better in that at least the receiver acknowledges hearing the sender's statement. But the net result, changing the subject, is essentially the same:

Bob: I'm concerned with the way Paul is handling arrangements for the benefit.

Tom: Well, you know Paul—Hey, the Russian gymnasts are coming to town—I've got to get tickets for that.

Even though Bob's statement has been acknowledged, Tom appears to be saying that the issue is not important enough to deal with. Again, such responses chip away at the sender's feelings of self-worth. Bob thought that he was raising an issue of great importance. Either Tom has problems because he fails to see the gravity of the situation, or Bob has problems with placing too much emphasis on Paul's methods. The real problem is that the conversation deals with neither of the possibilities. The issue is unresolved. The apparent withdrawal from discussing an issue is in itself a barrier.

4. *Incongruous response:*   In Chapter 4 we indicated that communication problems occur when nonverbal messages appear to conflict with the verbal messages. An incongruous response is an example of this problem.

> **Bob:** Well, we got some things done today.
>
> **Tom:** Yeah, that was a great meeting [stated in sarcastic tones].

On the surface Tom seems to be acknowledging and verifying Bob's statement, but his sarcastic tone causes Bob to wonder whether he is confirming Bob's ideas or whether he is making fun of them. Since nonverbal reactions are likely to override verbal meaning with most people, it is most likely that Bob will take Tom's words as sarcasm. If they are in fact sarcastic, a barrier begins to be built through Tom's insensitivity to Bob's honest statement of feelings. If Tom's words are sincere, a barrier begins to be built as a result of Bob's confusion about Tom's meaning.

5. *Evaluative response:*   Although we have already discussed evaluation in some detail, we list it here because it is often an inappropriate response that results in a barrier to communication. When something intervenes to stop the interaction on a content point, that something is a barrier—and few responses produce more barriers than evaluation:

> **Bob:** I'm concerned with the way Paul is handling arrangements for the benefit.
>
> **Tom:** Questioning Paul's methods is idiotic—he's done this kind of thing more than all the rest of us put together.

Tom's response is inappropriate because it changes the subject from whether Paul's handling of arrangements is appropriate to whether Bob makes idiotic statements. The barrier results initially because the statement has an air of irrelevancy to it, but, more important, it is an attack on Bob—an attack that probably will result in defensive behavior.

Although these are not the only five inappropriate responses, they are the most common ones in building or strengthening communication barriers. How can inappropriate responses be avoided? First, you should really listen to the other person. If you spend your time thinking of what you have to say, your response is likely to be inappropriate—you are more likely to come up with an irrelevant or an interruptive response. If, on the other hand, you really listen to what is being said, you are more likely to acknowledge and to come to grips with the idea or feeling the sender is describing or expressing. Second, you should be sensitive to the needs of the other person. Start with the assumption that what a person says is important to that person—*even if it is not or does not seem to be important to you.* Then deal with the idea or feeling at face value. If what the person has said is not, in your opinion, very important (or worth talking about), then the honest, interpersonal response is one that verbalizes your ideas or describes your feelings.

It is our belief that inappropriate response barriers are common because people do not take the time to be sensitive to the needs of others. You need not compromise your ideas or feelings in any way. Just let the other person know why you are behaving as you are.

Giving Personal Feedback: Praise and Criticism

Giving personal feedback means providing a person with new information or new impressions about himself. Personal feedback takes three forms: (1) description of behavior, (2) praise, and (3) criticism. The skill of describing behavior has already been discussed in some detail. You'll recall that describing behavior means recounting specific observable behavior without labeling that behavior good or bad, right or wrong. Here are four examples of behavior description in the form of personal feedback.

"Bill, you smile when your other behaviors seem to be saying that you are angry."

"Anne, were you aware that you did not let me finish my point?"

"Jed, when you criticize, your voice gets a very sharp tone."

"Jack, whenever Alice joins the group you get a strained look on your face."

Praise is a positive reaction to what a person has done. "Sally, you've got a good backhand," or "Gail, I like the way you sing that song," or

Praise is a positive reaction to what a person has done.

"Guy, you are a warmhearted person," or "Dennis, you have a nice way with words" are all statements of praise. This form of feedback pays a person a compliment.

Criticism is a negative reaction to what a person has done. Constructive criticism is an attempt to phrase the negative reaction in a way that will help the person and not hurt him. The best and most helpful kind of criticism is constructive, but don't forget that it is still criticism. Statements such as "Bill, you're awfully tough on the new recruits," or "Jack, you have a hard time accepting compliments," or "Sue, you're just not helping the team," or "Paul, your paper is not very well written" are all examples of criticism.

Because both praise and criticism require you to make evaluative statements, you should remind yourself that an evaluative statement has two major limitations: (1) it is usually noninformative, and (2) it may cause a defensive reaction. Whenever you are giving feedback, and especially if the feedback takes the form of criticism, the following guidelines will prove helpful.[3]

1. *Make sure that giving feedback is appropriate in the given interpersonal context.* It is safest to withhold feedback until it is asked for. Feedback becomes disfunctional if a person is not interested in hearing it. Even the most open person is not *always* receptive to whatever you might want to say to him.

If a person has not asked for feedback, but you nevertheless feel that some feedback would benefit him, you should be careful about your timing. Look for signs of receptiveness; watch verbal or nonverbal cues indicating that some feedback would be welcomed.

If you are not sure about giving feedback, you can always ask a person if she is receptive. You might say, for example, "Would you like to hear my comments about the way you handled the meeting?" Remember, however, that even if she says "yes," you must proceed carefully. She may have said "yes" out of curiosity or fear that she would hurt your feelings by saying "no." Begin sensitively. Proceed as the guidelines suggest.

2. *Preface a negative statement with a positive one whenever possible.* Feedback is not necessarily negative, although for some reason most of us think that it almost always is—as if the only things that we hear about are things that are wrong. When you are planning to give negative feedback, it is a good idea to start with a positive statement. But use a little common sense. Do not start with a superficial comment and then follow it with a crushing negative statement. "Betty, that's a pretty blouse you have

---

[3]Several of these suggestions were first articulated in the *1968 Summer Reading Book* of the National Training Laboratories Institute for Applied Behavioral Sciences.

on—now, about the perfectly miserable job you did running the meeting,'' is not an example of effective feedback. A good example is ''Betty, you did a good job of drawing Sam into the discussion—he usually sits through an entire meeting without saying a word. But you seem hesitant to use the same power to keep the meeting on track—you seem content to let anybody talk about anything, even if it is unrelated to the agenda.'' The praise should be significant and specific. If you cannot make a positive comment with some substance to it, then don't say anything. Empty comments made just to be ''nice,'' are worthless.

3. *Whether the feedback is praise or criticism, it should include a description of behavior or a discussion of the data on which the evaluation is based.* Betty says, ''What did you think of the way I handled the meeting?'' Instead of saying, ''You did a poor job,'' you might say, ''Many of the people talked about subjects that weren't relevant to the business at hand, and you did a poor job of using the power you have to keep the meeting on track.''

4. *Focus on one behavior at a time.* You might have a list of thirteen mistakes that Betty made running the meeting, but you shouldn't try to tell her all the mistakes at once. What was the major mistake? If you felt that her inability to control the meeting was her biggest mistake, talk about that first and discuss it completely. You may want to mention one or two more, but you want to restrict the discussion to a very few. In the first place, a person is not going to be able to correct every mistake right away. Second, and even more important, you don't want to devastate the person. Any criticism is hard on the ego, and although most of us can handle a little well-stated criticism, few of us can take a barrage of criticism, no matter how accurate it may be.

5. *Be as specific as possible.* It is not helpful to say, ''You had some leadership problems.'' If the person wasn't in control, say so; if the person failed to get agreement on one item before moving on to another, say so. The more specific the feedback, the more effectively the person being criticized will be able to deal with the problem.

6. *Feedback should concern recent behavior.* No one is helped very much by hearing about something he did last week or last month. Problems should be dealt with when they are fresh. If you have to spend time recreating a situation and refreshing someone's memory, the feedback is likely to be disfunctional.

7. *Direct feedback at behavior the person can do something about.* It is pointless to remind someone of a shortcoming over which he has no control. It may be true that Jack would be a better leader if he were taller, but telling him so will not improve his leadership skill. Telling him he needs to work on stating summaries or getting agreement on issues is helpful because he can change these behaviors.

8. *Tell the person you are criticizing what he can do to improve.* Don't limit your feedback to what was done wrong. Tell him how it could be done better. If the chairperson of a committee cannot get its members to agree to anything, you might suggest that he try phrasing his remarks to the committee differently: "Jack, when you think discussion is ended, say something like 'it sounds as if we agree that our donation should be made to a single agency. Is that correct?'"

9. *Even when criticism has been asked for, proceed with caution.* Remember all that you have learned about ways of developing and maintaining positive communication climates. A friendly, empathic approach, accompanied by a warm, sincere voice, will put you on the right track.

Communication Session

Reflection

Think of the most recent times you have given someone feedback.

1. What mistakes, if any, did you make in giving the feedback?
2. If you were to do it again, how would you proceed differently?

Practice

Consider the following two situations. Work out an appropriate phrasing of feedback for each:

1. You have been driving to school with a fellow student whose name you got from the Transportation Office at school. You have known him for only three weeks. Everything about the situation is great except that he drives too fast for you.
2. A good friend says "you know" more than once every sentence. You like her very much, but you see that others are beginning to avoid her. She is a very sensitive girl who does not usually take criticism well.

Discussion

In groups of three to six, share your ideas on how you would phrase the feedback. Which methods seem particularly effective?

Summary

As a listener you have as much responsibility for the effectiveness of communication as the person who forms the original message. The tools of effective listening are helpful responses.

Any effective response begins with good listening. Your heredity and environment influence how well you listen. Your hearing acuity, vocabulary, and ear for language will determine some of your effectiveness. Nevertheless, there are many behaviors you can put into practice to become a better listener. Some of the more important are (1) get ready to listen, (2) make the shift from speaker to listener a complete one, (3) listen actively, and (4) withhold evaluation.

Helpful responses are those that make communication easier: They confirm the person's right to his thoughts or feelings, and they help sharpen understanding of meaning. Supporting, questioning, paraphrasing, perception checking, interpreting, and describing behavior are basic listening and response skills. Inappropriate responses hinder communication—they plant the seeds of discontent within a person about himself or about what he is thinking or feeling, and they ignore or scuttle efforts at understanding meaning. Interrupting, irrelevant comments, tangential statements, incongruous replies, and unsolicited evaluation are some of the most common types of responses that should be avoided.

Personal feedback provides a person with new information or new impressions about himself. Personal feedback takes the forms of description of behavior, praise, and criticism. Making sure the context allows for evaluation, preceding negative statements with positive ones, preceding evaluation with descriptions of behavior, focusing on one behavior at a time, being specific, looking at only recent behavior, and showing what a person can do to correct a problem are some of the most important guidelines for giving effective feedback.

Suggested Readings

Larry L. Barker. *Listening Behavior.* Englewood Cliffs, New Jersey: Prentice-Hall, 1971. You should find several chapters of this book particularly helpful.

Ralph G. Nichols. "Do We Know How to Listen? Practical Helps in a Modern Age." *Speech Teacher,* Vol. 10 (1961), pp. 118–124. This article contains several helpful hints for good listening.

R. Wayne Pace, Brent D. Peterson, and **Terrence R. Radcliffe** (eds.) *Communicating Interpersonally—A Reader.* Columbus, Ohio: Charles E. Merrill Publishing Co., 1973. See particularly John L. Wallen's article, "Developing Effective Interpersonal Communication," pp. 218–233. An excellent discussion of response skills.

Carl R. Rogers. *Client-centered Therapy.* Boston: Houghton Mifflin Co., 1951. This book is especially good for its detailed analysis of evaluative responses. Rogers is a pioneer in the study of empathic communication.

Chapter 8
Interpersonal Influence Skills

PAYOFFS *After you have read this chapter, you should be able to:*

1. *Define power and discuss its sources.*
2. *Discuss power in dependency relationships.*
3. *Explain four strategies that will help develop a balanced relationship.*
4. *Discuss the three levels of positive acceptance of an influence attempt.*
5. *Define influence through persuasion.*
6. *Discuss three means of persuasion.*
7. *Explain the relationship among data, warrant, and conclusion.*
8. *Discuss five categories of reasoning and give an example of each.*
9. *Test the validity of each of the categories of reasoning.*
10. *Explain the function of motivation in the persuasion process.*
11. *Add motivational language to an argument.*
12. *Explain the sources of credibility.*
13. *Outline and defend your own ethical standards.*

Influence is the ability to bring about changes in the attitudes and actions of another person or persons. Knowing that something you said, felt, or stood for has influenced (or seemed to influence) someone to change his attitude or behavior satisfies an important interpersonal need. Influence itself is not a solitary skill. It is a combination of power and persuasion.

Power

A person who is powerless is unable to bring about change. Nothing is more frustrating than to be in a position of knowing that change must occur and lacking the power to bring it about. What is this "power" that is so necessary in the execution of change within interpersonal settings and relationships? *Power* is most often defined as a *potential*; it is the potential for changing attitudes, beliefs, and behaviors of others. The presence of power does not ensure change—but the absence of power makes it nearly impossible for a person to exert any influence.

Everyone has some power at some times and under some circumstances. To determine whether you have power and under what circumstances, we want to examine the sources of social power. Several social psychologists have offered analyses of social power. First we'll examine the sources of power enumerated by French and Raven;[1] then we'll examine Emerson's theory of power in dependency relationships.

French and Raven discuss five bases of power: coercive power, reward power, legitimate power, expert power, and referent power.

Coercive Power

Coercive power derives from the potential to punish. Coercive power can be either physical or psychological; it can be actual or threatened force. The elements of coercion are size, strength, and possession of weapons. If we remember the definition of power as the *potential* for change, we can see that coercive power can be present without a person ever attempting to exercise it. The old vaudeville routine, with the question "Where does a gorilla sit when he comes into a room?" and the answer, "Anywhere he wants to," illustrates the effect of this potential.

How do people use their coercive power? Most often coercive power is used as a threat. You may attempt to coerce your little brother into acting in a specified way by threatening to hit him if he does not. A mugger attempts to coerce his victim to hand over money by threatening

POWER

COERCIVE REWARD LEGITIMATE EXPERT REFERENT

French and Raven discuss five categories of power: coercive power, reward power, legitimate power, expert power, and referent power.

[1]John R. P. French, Jr., and Bertram Raven, "The Bases of Social Power," reprinted in Dorwin Cartwright and Alvin Zander (Eds.), *Group Dynamics,* 3rd ed. (New York: Harper & Row, 1968), pp. 259–270.

to harm with a gun, a knife, or a club. A súpervisor may attempt to coerce an employee by threatening an undesirable assignment or even involuntary termination. Each of these represents the exercising of coercion by threatened punishment. Coercion works when the person being coerced perceives the demanded action as less harmful to him than the threatened punishment; coercion fails as a means of exerting influence if the person perceives the demanded action as more painful than the threatened punishment. Jack Benny, who built his comic image on miserliness, brought about one of the longest sustaining laughs in entertainment history when he responded to the threat, "Your money or your life," with a long pause, then "Just a minute, I'm thinking." If your little brother decides that getting hit is less painful to him than taking a bath, he just may take the punishment, if he cannot run faster than you can.

How effective is coercion as a means of exerting influence in an interpersonal setting? If by "effective" we mean getting the desired result, coercion can be very effective. If, however, we mean getting the desired result in a way that is likely to improve the interpersonal relationship, coercion is likely to be quite ineffective. It is human nature, for those of us who are not masochists, to resent the threat of punishment. Some individuals become so resentful at the threat of even mild punishment that they will subject themselves to brutal hardships rather than submit to even an implied threat of force. Others who comply because of their distaste for the threatened punishment are likely to resort to revenge behavior; a person may look for any way possible to strike back. Coercion often

Coercive power derives from the potential to punish.

has overtones of brute force—and most of us believe that if a person's only way of exerting influence is through force, then he is unworthy of our compliance in change in belief, attitude, or action.

Coercive power is not a part of effective, ethical interpersonal influence. Any of the following four bases of power are far more compatible with ethical interpersonal influence.

Reward Power

Reward power derives from the ability or potential ability of one person to bestow monetary, physical, or psychological benefits on another person.

How do people use their reward power? Most often reward power is used as a motivator for change in attitude, belief, or action. You may offer to reward your little brother if he will take a bath. Your instructor can reward you for good work in this course by a good grade. Your girl friend or boy friend may attempt to motivate you to do something by promising you a special gift for your birthday, Christmas, or Valentine's Day.

Reward power works as a means of exerting influence (1) if the person sees the reward as large enough or important enough to compensate for the pain of the action called for, and (2) if he or she believes the one who promises has the power to give that reward. Let's illustrate both parts of this statement. If you offer to reward your little brother with ice cream for taking a bath, he may well decide that the treat is too small a reward for enduring the pain of such an extensive cleanup. If you offered him all the ice cream he could eat, he may well doubt your financial resources to do what you say you will do. Your instructor offers to reward good work with an A grade in the course. If you believe that the time and effort involved are more than you care to expend, the A grade might not arouse enough motivation in you; or, if you regard grades as unimportant, you are unlikely to make the effort to do the work.

How effective is reward as a means of exerting influence in the interpersonal setting? In comparison with coercion, reward is a much superior motivator. Most of us are more likely to be motivated to work by promise of reward than by threat of punishment. In this context, the reward is seen as a positive element. Ballplayers work hard to have a good season in hopes of a reward of higher pay; students work hard in classes in hopes of a reward of high grades. Just remember that, to be effective, the reward must be perceived as large enough or important enough.

Under some circumstances, reward power is regarded negatively. If for some reason you do not believe a person has a legitimate motive for offering a reward or if the person is offering a reward for actions that are objectionable to you or if you do not respect the person offering the reward, you may reject the offer, reject the reward, or seek to bring down the person or agency misusing the reward power. Reward power is least effective when it is seen as bribery by one who chooses not be be bribed. Bribery by definition is a reward offered for questionable motives to do questionable deeds. For most of us, if we believe the offer to reward is made as bribery, we are likely to resent it.

Legitimate Power

Legitimate power derives from the potential for influence gained as a result of election, selection, or position. The rationale for bestowing legitimate power is the belief that a person in certain positions has the *responsibility* of attempting to exert influence. The president, senators, and members of Congress gain legitimate power through the ballot; your teachers, cabinet members, and committee chairmen gain legitimate power through appointment; and in families the father and mother, the oldest child, or the oldest male child may have legitimate power because of tradition or cultural norms.

If a person is perceived to hold power legitimately, we are likely to cooperate with attempts to exercise that power. It is OK for the chairman of a meeting to ask you to stop talking in order to aid the group effort; it may not be OK for one of the other members to ask you. It is OK for the coach of the team to pressure a player to change his style of play; it may not be OK for another player to do so. It may be OK for the oldest child to give the other children chore assignments; it may not be OK for the second oldest to do so.

The extent to which a person will be influenced by the exercise of legitimate power is likely to depend upon factors other than the legitimate power itself. For instance, if the leader is perceived as powerless to en-

Legitimate power derives from the potential for influence gained as a result of election, selection, or position.

force demands, a member of the rank and file may ignore the call to act. In this instance, the rank and file member may doubt the reward or coercive power potential accompanying the leader's legitimate power. Or a citizen may not do what the president or a member of Congress asks because the citizen has no respect for them.

Probably the most important benefit coming to one who has legitimate power is the right to exercise other means of influence that are not perceived as OK when exercised by a person who does not hold legitimate power. You are likely to "take" more from your instructor because he has the legitimate power to conduct procedures in your particular class. As a result of this legitimate right, then, you give to your instructor more leeway in, for example, criticizing your term paper than you would permit to a person without the legitimate right.

Expert Power

Expert power derives from the potential to influence based on superior knowledge in a certain field. Expert power is present when you admit that another person holds information in a particular field that you need. Your instructor has the potential for expert power in your class because she has knowledge and expertise that you need; a coach has potential for expert power because he has knowledge and expertise that players seek. You, likewise, have the potential for expert power in several areas such as cooking, playing tennis, or repairing automobiles.

How do people use expert power? They attempt to influence others through the promise of revealing information. A coach influences his players when he reveals information about a sport that the players perceive as useful in their efforts to master that sport. A professor influences her students by revealing information about a subject that the students perceive as useful in their education. Expert power fails to influence when a person does not believe that the information is useful to him, when he does not believe that the alleged expert does in fact have the relevant information, when he does not believe that the expert is able to disseminate that information in a usable manner, or when he believes that he has gained parity of information with the expert. An important element of expert power is that its potential exists only within the limited area of expertise. The tennis coach may hold expert power over his players on the subject of tennis but not on the subject of calculus.

How effective is expert power? It seems to be quite effective within its limited scope. However, because information can be exchanged, once a person believes that he has received all the information there is to give, the expert loses the effect of his power. Moreover, expert power must be real to be effective. For example, if one of your friends works as an auto mechanic in a dealer's garage, he has the potential to influence your choice of sparkplugs. If on the basis of the mechanic's opinion that XYZ sparkplugs are superior, you purchase them for your car only to discover two months later that they have burned out, you are not likely to accept your mechanic friend's advice again. He has lost his expert power, as far as you are concerned.

Sometimes people use their expert power as a weapon. A person may purposely withhold information in order to maintain control over others. If a person believes that another is manipulating him with use of expert power, that may be grounds for loss of that power.

Referent Power

Referent power derives from the potential to influence others simply because they identify with the one who influences them. Many persons have power simply because of qualities that cause others to love and trust them. *Charisma* is a word used to label this power. Whatever you wish to call it, people do acknowledge and yield to power residing in certain persons for no apparent reason beyond belief in the individual.

How effective is referent power? Not only does referent power stand on its own as a potential for influence; referent power also underlies the value of the other bases of power we have considered. Expert power, legitimate power, reward power, even coercive power have greater potential for influence if the powerful person is also perceived as having referent power; moreover, if a person doubts the referent power, she is less likely to be influenced by any of the other types of power.

Because of the great importance of the elements of referent power, we will consider them in considerable detail later in this chapter in the discussion of personal credibility.

Although we have considered each of these bases of power separately, in most cases the power we hold is a result of some combination of them.

Power within a Relationship

Our discussion of power implies that power exists within an interpersonal relationship. That is, Irene cannot have power unrelated to other individuals. Irene's power must be over somebody—Ted, for instance. Moreover, Irene has power over Ted only if he grants that power.

Richard Emerson has done some interesting research on dependency relationships. He argues that the power in a relationship is based on the dependency within that relationship.[2] Person A is dependent on person B if (1) person B has something that person A needs or wants and (2) per-

---

[2]Richard M. Emerson, "Power–Dependence Relations," in Carl W. Backman and Paul F. Secord (Eds.), *Problems in Social Psychology* (New York: McGraw-Hill Book Co., 1966), pp. 193–202.

son A is not likely to get it anywhere else. The argument is that person B has power over person A to the extent that person A is dependent on person B to satisfy this want or need. The power of B over A is equal to the dependency of A on B.

Let's look at an example to see how this theory works in practice. George and Mary have been married for eighteen years. During this time, Mary (person A) has never worked outside the home. We could say that Mary is dependent on George (person B) for money, food, shelter, and clothing. Because Mary has never held a job, it would be difficult for her to get the money she needs and has become accustomed to. Our example meets both conditions (1) and (2) cited above.

However, Mary is an excellent cook. George cannot even prepare canned soup. George, then, is to some extent dependent on Mary for food, and we can say that while George's power over Mary is greater than hers over him, Mary nevertheless has some power over George. Perhaps an ideal relationship is one in which power and dependency are equally distributed. In such a relationship both people can feel good because each has power.

In some relationships, however, one person dominates. Dominance exists when one person's dependency is greater than the other person's. Let's say that George hires a cook. George has the upper hand: Mary is still dependent upon him for income, but his dependency on her for food has decreased.

If you find that you are in the lower position of power in a relationship—that is, you are dependent on another person for many things while the other person is not dependent on you for much of anything—you may become uncomfortable. Although some people like to be dominated, most of us need some power. What can you do to balance the power relationship? There are four strategies you can try:

1. *Develop alternative ways to satisfy your needs.* If you have a need that only one person can satisfy, then you are bound to be dependent on that person. You must try to find a way to satisfy that need that will reduce or eliminate your dependency. For instance, Mary might go back to school and learn skills that would enable her to get a well-paid job. If she can earn her own money, she can reduce both her dependence on George and his power over her.

2. *Reduce your desire to have what the other person provides for you.* If you cease to want or need what the other person provides, you are no longer dependent. Although reducing your desires is easier said than done, at times it may be your only choice. George gives Mary money to meet her needs. If Mary can reduce her material needs, then she will no longer be as dependent on George's money. She may have to make sacrifices, but doing so may be better in the long run than being dependent on George.

3. *Reduce the alternatives available to the other person.*   Both parties in a relationship have needs. If you can somehow reduce the other person's ability to satisfy needs outside the relationship, you may be able to bring about a power balance. If George can be shown that the cook he has hired cannot cook all the dishes that Mary can or cook them as well, George may become convinced that the cook is not meeting his needs. Because the cook can't meet his needs, he will have to be dependent upon Mary.

4. *Increase the other person's desire to have what it is that you can provide.*   If you can somehow convince the other person that you are better at meeting a need than anyone else, his desire for you to satisfy that need will increase. Mary might attend a gourmet cooking class. On the cook's days off, Mary prepares such delicious meals that George decides to fire the cook.

Power does not exist in a vacuum; it exists between and among people in a multitude of relationships. In a successful and satisfying relationship, people hope for a certain balance in the dependencies that yield power. But if a relationship is not in balance, if you see yourself becoming powerless, you have opportunities to try to bring the relationship back into a more desirable balance.

Communication Session

Reflection

1. Consider a relationship (with a parent, a brother or sister, a roommate, a boy friend or girl friend) in which you are dominant. What is the principal source of your power?

2. Consider a relationship in which you are in a position of dependency. What is the dominant person's primary source of power? What, if anything, are you doing to try to balance the power relationship?

Practice

1. For each of the statements below decide whether it is an attempt to influence based on reward power (R), coercive power (C), legitimate power (L), referent power (Rf), or expert power (E).

_____ 1. You will wear your hair the way I tell you to wear your hair because I'm your mother.

_____ 2. After studying the effects of radiation for eight years I have concluded that. . .

_____ 3. As long as you do what I say, no one will get hurt.

_____ 4. Sara, I'd be so proud of you if you made the Dean's list.

_____ 5. If you'll drop my books at the library, I'll clean the room.

_____ 6. Trust me—I can do it.

2. Work in groups of six. Your instructor will give you goal cards. One member of each group will pick a goal. He or she must then try to influence another member of the group toward that goal. The other group members will observe from what power bases the people work.

Discussion

What power bases do you most resent? Why?

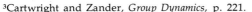

Answers: 1. L; 2. E; 3. C; 4. R; 5. R; 6. Rf.

Persuasion

We said that power is the *potential* for influence; now we want to see how this potential can be enacted through persuasion. **Persuasion is the conscious, usually verbal act of influencing another person's attitude or behavior.** We think persuasion is an especially appropriate means of interpersonal influence. It is appropriate because it allows freedom of choice. The persuader has no hidden motives, nor does he attempt to control the other person's actions. Cartwright and Zander point out that because of the belief in the importance of freedom of choice in a democratic society, persuasion is a positive means of exerting influence.[3] We see a knowledge of means of persuasion as vital in maintaining what Keller and Brown described as the interpersonal ethic, requiring that you meet the need to influence by allowing others freedom of choice.[4]

Whereas an individual's power exists regardless of his or her attempt to use it or exploit it, persuasion is a conscious, usually verbal attempt by one individual to affect the attitudes or behaviors of others. The "means of persuasion," combine reasoning, motivation through emotional appeal, and credibility. These means may be used individually or in concert to achieve the desired result.

---

[3]Cartwright and Zander, *Group Dynamics*, p. 221.
[4]Paul W. Keller and Charles T. Brown, "An Interpersonal Ethic for Communication," *Journal of Communication*, Vol. 18 (1968), p. 79.

Logical Reasoning

Most of you want some justification for changing your attitudes or modifying your behavior. You want to know why you should respond in a particular way. One means of persuasion is a presentation of reasons to adopt the desired attitude or behavior. The persuader need not give complete proof—in fact, complete proof may be impossible to give. The persuader must provide only enough good reasons to satisfy the receiver's need to know.

What are reasons? A reason is any statement that answers *why* a statement should be believed or acted upon. If your friend wants you to go to a particular movie with him (a statement to get you to act), he may be able to persuade you by saying that the movie (1) has an exciting plot, (2) has several excellent actors and actresses playing major roles, and (3) has been nominated for an Academy Award. These three reasons do not necessarily prove the worth of the movie, but they may be enough to get you to act. If the dinner club is unsure where they want to go for this month's gourmet meal, you may be able to persuade them by offering reasons for considering the Chateau Bleu. If from your experience and your reading you have discovered that (1) the chef has won numerous awards for cooking, (2) the atmosphere is elegant, and (3) the prices are comparable with several other less renowned restaurants in town, these reasons alone may be enough to persuade.

Of course, reasons will need to be supported by evidence. It is unlikely that the statement of reasons alone will be persuasive, but when you couple the statement of reasons with examples, documented facts, and opinions of experts, the reasons become more influential.

We could conclude our discussion of logical reasoning here with a summary statement that ethical interpersonal influence is achieved by the persuader presenting reasons and support for the proposition he or she advocates. But the discussion would fall short on one important ground— it would not show how either the sender or the receiver can determine the strength or validity of the reasons presented. To make this determination, a person must have some system of analysis that goes beyond intuitive judgment. In the next several pages we'll describe the rudiments of a system of analyzing logical argument. Knowledge of these rudiments will enable you to make reasonably accurate judgments of the soundness of reasoning. You may wish to go more deeply into the subject. To that end, we have listed sources at the end of this chapter that you should find particularly valuable.

Reasoning is the process of drawing inferences. If you know that the temperature is thirty-eight degrees, the wind is blowing, and rain is falling, you may infer (reason or conclude) that "It's a miserable day." To explain the reasoning process we need to examine the three basic requirements of the process. These requirements are called the data, the conclusion, and the warrant.[5] Your understanding of these words will enable you to construct and analyze both simple and complex forms of reasoning.

Data are the evidence, assumptions, or assertions that provide the basis for a conclusion—in our example, the data are the temperature, the blowing wind, and the falling rain. The *conclusion* is the product of the reasoning, the inference—in our example, the conclusion is "It's a miserable day." The *warrant* is a statement denoting the substantive relationship between data and conclusion—it is the key that provides the essential test of the reasoning, and the only one of the essentials that is usually not included in the statement of the reasoning. Since in our example no warrant is provided, we must frame one. One way of stating a warrant for the example is "low temperature, wind, and rain are three major criteria or characteristics of a 'miserable day.'" Using (D) for data, stated or observed; (C) for conclusion; (W) for warrant; and an arrow to show the direction of the reasoning, our example could be laid out schematically as follows:

(D) Temperature 38°. Wind   ⟶   **(C)** It's a miserable day.
blowing. Rain falling.

 (W) (Low temperature, wind, and
 rain are three major characteristics
 of a miserable day.)

The warrant is written in parentheses because it is implied rather than stated. The warrant, then, indicates how we drew the conclusion, the inference, from the data supplied.

So far you have seen how you can lay out a unit of reasoning. Now we need to show how you can test the components of the unit in order to judge the validity of the reasoning.

There are two tests applied to reasoning: test of data and test of warrant. For a logical conclusion to follow, the data must be sufficient in quantity and quality. If the data are insufficient, you must supply more; if the data are inaccurate, biased, or from a questionable source, the conclusion will be suspect. If you are satisfied that "temperature 38 degrees," "wind blowing," and "rain falling" are accurate, you can examine the logic of the warrant. The warrant is tested by casting it as a question: "Is it true that low temperature, wind, and rain are the major characteristics

---

[5]This analysis is based upon the ideas set forth by Stephen Toulmin, *The Uses of Argument* (Cambridge, England: Cambridge University Press, 1958).

of a miserable day?" If prior experience, observation, or other information lead you to answer "yes," the reasoning is sound; if the answer is "no," the reasoning process is fallacious.

Schematic analysis of reasoning in the framework of data, conclusion, and warrant does not ensure the infallibility of the logic. However, if you take the time to write the process out in this manner and ask whether the warrant is supported by research, the chances of discovering illogical reasoning are increased considerably.

Although warrants could be phrased in many ways for any given unit of reasoning—and literally hundreds of variations are possible in the kinds of reasoning—most methods of reasoning will fall into one of five categories: *generalization, causation, sign, analogy,* and *definition.* Since these categories supply so many warrants, you should familiarize yourself with them. In the following discussion of five kinds of reasoning, the tests after the warrants indicate under what circumstances the warrants are reasonable.

Our goal is not to explain, exemplify, and provide tests for every kind of reasoning link that can be established. What we want to consider are the major forms that will work for you in the great majority of circumstances.

1. *Reasoning by generalization:* You are reasoning by generalization when your conclusion states that what is true in some instances is true in all instances. Generalization links are the basis for polls and predictions. Take, for example, the *data* "Tom, Jack, and Bill studied and got A's" and the *conclusion* based on it: "Anyone who studies will get an A." The reasoning link *(warrant)* can be stated: "What is true in these representative instances will be true in all instances." To test this kind of argument you should ask, "Were enough instances cited? Were the instances typical? Were the instances representative?" (If the answer to any of these questions is "no," the reasoning is not sound.)

2. *Reasoning by causation:*   You are reasoning by causation when your conclusion is based on a single circumstance or set of circumstances. Causation links are one of the most prevalent types of arguments you will discover. *Data:* "We've had a very dry spring"; *conclusion:* "The wheat crop will be lower than usual." The reasoning link *(warrant)* can be stated: "The lack of sufficient rain *causes* a poor crop." To test this kind of argument you should ask: "Are the data (is the evidence) alone important enough to bring about the particular conclusion? If we eliminate the data, will we eliminate the effect?" (If not, the reasoning is unsound.) "Do some other data that accompany the cited data cause the effect?" (If so, the reasoning is not sound.) In real life, one set of circumstances rarely *causes* another, so be careful when using or hearing this type of argument.

3. *Reasoning by sign:*   You are reasoning by sign when your conclusion is based upon the presence of observable data that usually or always accompany other, unobservable data. If, for example, Martha breaks out in hives, the presence of those data (breaking out) might lead Emily to the conclusion that Martha is having an allergy reaction. The reasoning link (the warrant) can be stated, "When one variable [in this case breaking out in hives] is usually or always associated with another variable [an allergy reaction], we can predict the existence of the other, unobserved variable." Signs are often confused with causes, but signs are indications, not causes. Hives is a sign of an allergy reaction. Hives occurs when a person is having such a reaction, but the hives does not *cause* the reaction. To test this kind of argument you would ask: "Do the data cited always or usually indicate the conclusion drawn? Are sufficient signs present?"(If not, the reasoning is not sound.) "Are contradictory signs in evidence?" (If so, the reasoning is not sound.)

4. *Reasoning by analogy:*   You are reasoning by analogy when your conclusion is the result of a comparison with a similar set of circumstances. Although reasoning by analogy is popular, it is the weakest form of reasoning. The analogy link is often stated: "What is true or will work in one set of circumstances is true or will work in another, comparable set of circumstances." *Data:* "A state lottery has proved very effective in New Jersey"; *conclusion:* "A state lottery will prove effective in Ohio." The reasoning link *(warrant)* can be stated, "If something works in New Jersey, it will work in Ohio, because Ohio and New Jersey are so similar." To test this kind of argument you should ask: "Are the subjects really capable of being compared? Are the subjects being compared really similar in all important ways?" (If the answer to these questions is "no," the reasoning is not sound.) "Are any of the ways that the subjects are dissimilar important to the conclusion?" (If so, then the reasoning is not sound.)

5. *Reasoning by definition:*   You are reasoning by definition when your conclusion is a definition or a descriptive generalization that follows from agreed upon criteria. Again, this is a popular form of reasoning. *Data:* "She takes charge; she uses good judgment; her goals are in the best interests of the group"; *conclusion:* "She is a good leader." The reasoning link *(warrant)* could be stated, "Taking charge, showing good judgment, and considering the best interests of the group are the characteristics most often associated with good leadership." To test this kind of argument you should ask: "Are the characteristics mentioned the most important ones in determining the definition? Are those characteristics best labeled with the stated term?" (If the answer to any of these is "no," the reasoning is not sound.) "Is an important aspect of the definition omitted in the statement of the characteristics?" (If so, then the reasoning is not sound.)

Communication Session

Reflection

Do you really listen to the logic of someone's argument? What do you consider good reasons?

Practice

1. Below are some typical arguments you are likely to encounter. Indicate which ones are based on reasoning from (C) causation, (G) generalization, (A) analogy, (D) definition, or (S) sign.

_____ 1. The chess club held a raffle, and they made a lot of money. I think we should too.

_____ 2. Tom is aggressive, personable, and highly motivated—he ought to make a good salesman.

_____ 3. Three of my students last year got A's on this test, five the year before, and three the year before that. There certainly will be some A's this year.

_____ 4. I saw Sally in a maternity outfit—she must be pregnant.

_____ 5. Listen, I like the way Mike thinks, Paul is an excellent mathematician, Craig and Phil are two of my best students, and all four are Alpha Alphas. As far as I'm concerned, the Alphas are the group on campus with academic strength.

_____ 6. If George hadn't come barging in, I never would have spilled my iced tea.

_____ 7. Maybe that's the way you see it, but to me when high city officials are caught with their hands in the till and when police close their eyes to the actions of people with money, that's corruption.

_____ 8. Barb wears her hair that way and guys fall all over her—I'm getting myself a hairdo like that.

2. For each of the eight above, draw a schematic and fill it in. You will have to write appropriate warrants. As an aid, we have done one for you:

We're going to have a bad wheat crop this year—we've had near drought conditions this spring.

(D) Near drought conditions this   ⟶   **(C)** We'll have a bad wheat crop.
spring

(W) (Insufficient spring rain results
in—causes—a poor wheat crop.)

3. Working in groups of six, each group should generate four examples of arguments—one in each category. Record these on paper provided by your instructor. When all groups have completed their work, post the papers at the front of the class.

Discussion

1. Working in groups of four to six, discuss the relative strengths of each argument in no. 2 above.

2. Discuss the nature of the arguments on the paper in no. 3 above. Are they properly identified? Are they valid?

Answers: 1. A; 2. D; 3. G; 4. S; 5. G; 6. C; 7. D; 8. A.

Motivation

Reasoning helps a person decide on the soundness of a particular proposition; motivation provides the trigger for action. Motivation is what arouses a person to *act* on his convictions. Motivation is often brought about by statements that reach the emotions or feelings of the individual. Most of us surround ourselves with a defensive shell that protects us from acting foolishly, in haste, without thinking. For some of us, the shell is thick and difficult to penetrate—for others, the shell is thin and easily penetrated. Motivational means are intended to penetrate the shell and touch the feelings of the individual. Consider an example: The slogan "Give to the March of Dimes, it is a worthy charity" provides one good reason for giving, but it has little if any emotional impact. In contrast, the statements "No one knows when birth defects will mar the life of a newborn child; your son or daughter could be affected. Don't wait to see before caring—that's too late. Give now to help us find the causes for birth defects. In the name of your prospective son or daughter—won't you please give?" make the same plea, but in this case the words touch the feelings. Whether or not you are actually affected by this wording, it stands a much greater chance of motivating you to act than the mere statement of the reason why you should give.

As you think back over causes for your actions, you may hear yourself saying that something impelled you to act. It is as if something inside you took control and directed your actions. That something is often your emotional response to various stimuli. What is an emotion? Simply defined, emotions are "labels we give to bodily feelings."[6] You recognize the presence of such emotions as love, sadness, happiness, joy, anxiety,

---

[6]Robert E. Lana and Ralph L. Rosnow, *Contemporary Psychology* (New York: Holt, Rinehart and Winston, 1972), p. 301.

anger, fear, hate, pity, and guilt. You hear yourself and others say such things as "I'm feeling anxious about the test," "I feel anger toward him for slighting me," or "I feel sad that he's no longer able to work." Many of these emotions are triggered by physical happenings: a dog jumps from behind a tree and frightens you; a friend falls and sprains his ankle and you feel sad; that person puts her arm around you and you feel joy. Emotions are also triggered by words. Someone says, "You idiot, what did you do a dumb thing like that for?" and you feel angry. Someone says, "I'd love to go with you," and you feel happiness. A friend says, "Go ahead with the gang—I'll be all right alone," and you feel guilty. Use of emotion is the conscious effort to phrase ideas in ways that affect the receiver's feelings. In order to do this you must first discover what emotion is most likely to motivate your receiver to do what you want. Then you must phrase your message in a manner that will activate that emotion because the more your receiver feels your words, the more likely it is that he will act.

Interpersonally, motivation is not unethical so long as it is coordinated with or is an outgrowth of logical reasons. Empty emotional appeal for the purpose of arousing—of giving heat without light—is interpersonally unethical.

Communication Session

Reflection

Think of the last time you were persuaded to do something that you normally would not do. Was it a logical argument that swayed you? Was it an emotional appeal? Or was it a logical argument presented emotionally? If the base was emotional, what emotions were involved?

Practice

Try to frame an emotional appeal for each of the following: (1) the Equal Rights Amendment, (2) alleviating hunger in America, (3) registering to vote, (4) welfare reform, (5) not smoking in the classroom.

Discussion

In groups of six, brainstorm a list of the advantages and disadvantages of using emotional appeal. Record on paper. At the end of the discussion post papers at the front of the classroom and compare the lists.

Credibility

All available evidence indicates that persuasion is more likely to be achieved when people like, trust, and have confidence in the persuader. The Greeks called this ability to inspire trust *ethos*. You may call it image, charismatic effect, or the word we prefer—credibility. As a result of our earlier discussion, you may see a relationship between credibility as a means of persuasion and expert and referent power.

Why are we willing to take the word of someone else on various issues? Since it is impossible for us to know all there is to know about everything, we seek shortcuts in our decision making—we rely on the judgment of others. Our thinking often goes something like this: "Why take the time to learn about the new highway when someone we trust tells us it is in our best interest?" "Why take the time to try every restaurant or read the many books telling about restaurants when someone we are willing to rely on tells us that Barney's is the best?" "Why take the time to study the candidates when our best friend tells us to vote for Smith?" Each of us places such trust in some people in order to take shortcuts in our decision making.

How do you determine on whom you will rely? Is it blind faith? Probably not. The presence (or our perception of the presence) of certain qualities will make the possessor a high credibility source. Although the specific number of aspects of credibility differs somewhat in various analyses of that quality, most analyses include competence, intention, character, and personality.

Competence is the knowledge and ability to perform. Perhaps you see your roommate as a competent mathematician. If you perceive her as understanding the mathematical principles and being able to apply them, you may be willing to rely on her to do your income tax, to help you with math, or to be in charge of the budget.

A second important aspect of credibility is *intention*. A person's intentions or motives are particularly important in determining whether people will like him, trust him, have respect for him, and/or believe him. For instance, you know a clothing salesman is trying to sell you the suit he helps you try on, so when he says to you, "That suit is perfect for you," you may well question his intentions. On the other hand, if a bystander looks over at you and exclaims, "Wow, you really look good in that suit!"you are likely to accept that statement at face value because the person has no reason to say anything—his intentions are likely to be good. The more positively you see the intentions of the person, the more credible his words will seem to you.

A third important aspect of credibility is *character*. Character has been defined as what a person is made of. You tend to believe in a person who has a past record of honesty, industry, and trustworthiness.

The fourth important aspect of credibility is *personality*. Sometimes people have a strong "gut reaction" to others based solely on a first impression. Some people may strike you as being friendly, warm, nice to be around. Personality or likability may be the most important aspect of credibility.

Although credibility takes time to build, how people perceive you can be changed. Personality and character are projections of what you are, but competence and intention can be affected by what you say and what you do. A competent person shows that he knows what he is doing and why he is doing it. Some perceived incompetence results from a person's apparent bumbling attempts to do a job. Often incompetence is nothing more than carelessness, trying to do too many tasks at the same time, or not double checking procedures. Similarly, even when your intentions are good, people may perceive them as bad if you are not open in stating why you behave as you do. Remember, people are not mind readers. When you don't explain your behavior, others may assume they know your intentions or may read into your behavior intentions that are incorrect. If people do not see you as a credible person, you may be able to change your image by working on improving your competence and sharing your intentions.

Ethics

We cannot leave the subject of persuasion without some discussion of ethics. What are ethics? Ethics are the standards of moral conduct that determine behavior. Ethics include both how you act and how you expect others to act. When you believe strongly in the righteousness of your cause, you may well be faced with the temptation of bowing to the belief that the end justifies the means—or to put in into blunt English, that you can say or do anything to achieve your goals. As we observe the world around us, we are all too well aware of the many people who have ridden roughshod over any moral or ethical principles operating within our society.

Whether or not you punish those who fail to meet your standards says a great deal about the importance you ascribe to your ethics. Although ethical codes are personal, society has a code of ethics that operates on at least the verbal level in that society.

What is your code of ethics? The following two statements reflect the standards of hundreds of students that we have seen in classes during the last few years. These are but a starting point for a code of interpersonal ethics. These are not rules someone made up—they are statements of attitudes held by large numbers of your peers in our society.

1. *Lying is unethical.* Of all the attitudes about ethics, this is the one most universally held. When people know they are being lied to, they

will usually reject the ideas of the person lying to them. If they find out later, they often look for ways to get back at that person.

2. *Grossly exaggerating or distorting facts is unethical.* Although some people seem willing to accept "a little exaggeration" as human nature and may even use gross exaggeration for dramatic effect, most people regard the use of exaggeration in attempts to influence as the same as lying. Because the line between "some" exaggeration and "gross" exaggeration or "distortion" is often difficult to distinguish, many people see any exaggeration as unethical.

In interpersonal interaction where only two persons are involved, some are not inclined to look at sender responsibility in quite the same way as they do in a public speech, but we believe that any message source has the same ethical responsibility regardless of the setting in which statements are made. Any attempts to influence others should follow some ethical guidelines. Justifying unethical behavior on the ground of "informal setting" is itself unethical and reprehensible.

Communication Session

Reflection

What are your ethical standards? How do you see them operating in the interpersonal setting?

Practice

Try to define your ethical code. You might start by making a series of statements that begin, "It is wrong to _____ ; if someone does this, I am likely to react by _____ ." When you are finished, divide into groups of six and share as much as you feel comfortable in sharing. Notice the similarities in and differences between your code and others' codes.

Discussion

1. How do you develop an ethical code? Has your code changed much?
2. Why were the Watergate and CIA scandals so disturbing to the American public?
3. Who should be responsible for teaching ethics?

Summary

Influence is the ability to affect a person's attitude and/or behavior. Influence can occur without a person knowing that he or she has had any direct influence and without any conscious intent to exert it. For example, if you are a member of your school's debate team, your membership might be enough to influence a friend or relative to try out for the team. When a person engages in a conscious verbal effort to influence another or others, we say the person is trying to persuade. Neither influence nor persuasion is possible without the presence of power.

Power is the potential ability to influence another person's attitude or behavior. Power takes the forms of coercive power, the threat of punishment; reward power, the ability to bestow gifts; legitimate power, the holding of an accepted position of power; expert power, holding needed information; or referent power, having a charismatic effect. Power exists within dependency relationships. Person A has power over person B to the extent that person B is dependent on person A.

The verbal effort to influence is persuasion. Persuasion is the product of several elements that may be used alone or in concert. Persuasion can be a product of logical reasoning, it can be a product of motivation through emotional language, and/or it can be a product of speaker credibility. Effective interpersonal persuasion is always ethical persuasion—it does not depend upon lying, distortion of fact, or acting in the interests of the persuader at the expense of the persuadee.

Suggested Readings

Winston L. Brembeck and **William S. Howell.** *Persuasion: A Means of Social Influence,* 2d ed. Englewood Cliffs, New Jersey: Prentice-Hall, 1976. A standard textbook offering an excellent coverage of persuasion.

Dorwin Cartwright and **Alvin Zander.** *Group Dynamics: Research and Theory,* 3d ed. New York: Harper & Row, 1968. Contains the French and Raven article on power, plus several other articles developing different theories of power. Also has a good explanation of the relationship between power and persuasion.

Howard Kahane. *Logic and Contemporary Rhetoric,* 2d ed. Belmont, California: Wadsworth Publishing Co., 1976. An excellent analysis of forms of reasoning with emphasis on detection of fallacies.

Rudolph F. Verderber. *The Challenge of Effective Speaking*, 4th ed. Belmont, California: Wadsworth Publishing Co., 1979. Chapter 14 provides a more detailed analysis of the reasoning process than is given in the present book.

Chapter 9
Conflict Management Skills

PAYOFFS *After you have read this chapter, you should be able to:*

1. *Define conflict.*
2. *Discuss why ego conflict is so difficult to resolve.*
3. *Contrast a cooperative attitude with a competitive attitude.*
4. *Identify and understand the inappropriateness of withdrawal, surrender, and aggression.*
5. *Discuss the discussion method.*
6. *Apply the problem-solving method to a conflict situation.*
7. *Explain how persuasion can resolve conflict.*
8. *Explain how you might bring someone who views conflict competitively into a cooperative state.*
9. *Explain how negotiation can resolve conflict.*
10. *Discuss the role of arbitration in conflict resolution.*
11. *Devise a plan for dealing with conflicts in your relationship with a close friend.*

Your success as an interpersonal communicator may ultimately depend on the development of conflict management skills. Conflict management uses many, if not all, of the skills we have considered thus far. Conflict management also requires the special application of some of those skills as well as the use of new skills. In this chapter we'll discuss the nature of conflict and look at the skills that have proved most effective in interpersonal conflict management.

Conflict is the clash of opposing attitudes, ideas, behaviors, goals, and needs. It is a rare person who can get through even one day without experiencing conflict. Some of this conflict is *intrapersonal* or psychological conflict, the conflict that occurs within us. Intrapersonal conflict takes four major forms: (1) approach-approach conflict, which results from having to make a choice between two equally desirable goals; (2) approach-avoidance conflict, which is the desire to achieve a goal but at the same time avoid it (for example, you may want to befriend a person of another race but are afraid to); (3) avoidance-avoidance conflict, which results from having to make a choice between two undesirable goals; and (4) double approach-avoidance conflict (for example, you have agreed to care for a neighbor's cat, although you don't want to; you would rather go on a weekend fishing trip with a friend, but if you did you would feel guilty about not keeping your promise to feed the cat).

Intrapersonal conflicts are important, but they are not the primary kinds of conflict we'll be discussing in this chapter. You may find, however, that some of the suggestions for coping with interpersonal conflict may help you to manage intrapersonal conflicts.

How do you react to interpersonal conflict—the conflict that arises between you and others? Does it make you anxious? Do you try to avoid it at all costs? Do you thrive on it? Interpersonal conflict *will* occur—make no mistake about it. How you manage these conflicts may determine the success of your interpersonal relationships and determine the degree of satisfaction you have with the outcome of the conflict.

Conflict inevitably occurs because each of us has unique ideas, feelings, motives, and ways of behaving. However, conflict can be constructive. Conflict forces choice, and choosing helps you to test the relative merits of the attitudes, behaviors, needs, and goals in conflict.

Because conflict will inevitably occur between friends as well as enemies, you need to be aware of various methods of dealing with conflict. You will see that sometimes you can resolve conflict in a manner agreeable to all persons involved; sometimes you can cope with or manage conflict; and sometimes the best you can hope for is to keep the conflict from escalating to interpersonal warfare. In this chapter we'll consider methods for resolving or managing your conflicts.

Kinds of Conflicts

You will be better able to cope with a conflict if you know whether it is pseudoconflict, content conflict, value conflict, or ego conflict.

Pseudoconflict

Pseudoconflict is false conflict that appears to be real. It exists when a person believes that two goals cannot be simultaneously achieved, although in fact they can be. If you are studying for tomorrow's exam in geology and a friend stops by to ask you to go out for a pizza, you may perceive these two actions as being in conflict. The tendency in a pseudo-conflict is to put the choice between actions in an either-or framework, in this case *either* you study *or* you go out. This would be a real conflict if it were impossible to do both within the prescribed time period. More often than not, however, you are likely to set up a false set of choices. It may be possible to do both. Perhaps, in this example, you can find out where your friend is going and then say you will meet him later; or you can go with him for a couple of hours and then come back and study. If either of these schedules for your evening is possible, then you can dispel the pseudoconflict.

In addition to false either-or choices, pseudoconflict can also result from misunderstanding. Suppose a husband and wife have agreed to clean up the apartment before going to play tennis. Yet before the job is finished, the husband puts on his tennis shoes and starts for the door.

When the wife, thinking he is breaking the agreement, asks, "Where are you going?" the husband calls back to her as he reaches the door, "I'll be back in a minute, don't worry." If she is untrusting, his leaving without clearly stating the nature of his action may bring on a pseudoconflict. This pseudoconflict may be dispelled as soon as he returns, realizes her distress, and explains that he had no intention of running out before finishing the cleaning but just had to get a pack of cigarettes. If the explanation is accepted, the conflict disappears.

The plots of many television comedies are built on pseudoconflict played for all it is worth until at the end of the show a simple explanation eliminates the conflict. However, pseudoconflict becomes real conflict when the explanation (1) is not forthcoming or (2) is not satisfactory or (3) is not accepted. If the wife sees the husband's action as symptomatic of his lack of concern for her feelings, a real conflict based on the pseudoconflict may ensue. The conflict may then escalate into either a content conflict or an ego conflict.

Potential conflicts are often resolved by showing that no real conflict exists. Perhaps the very first thing to do when you perceive conflict is to determine whether that conflict is real.

Content Conflict

A conflict concerning message accuracy is known as content conflict. It usually occurs in any of four sets of circumstances.

1. *The conflict may be over a fact.* Two or more persons may come into conflict over whether George Foster drove in more than a hundred runs last year or whether Barbra Streisand won an Academy Award for her performance in the movie *Funny Girl.* Conflicts over facts are easily resolved by looking up the facts. Still, those in conflict may continue to battle if no source is readily at hand. If you find yourself in a conflict over a fact, try to avoid escalating the conflict. Try to disengage until a source for checking the fact can be found.

2. *The conflict may be over an interpretation of a fact or an inference drawn from a fact or series of facts.* Two or more persons may disagree over whether the rise in steel prices will trigger another round of inflation. The rise in steel prices is a fact; what will result from that rise is a matter of opinion based on interpretation of the fact or on inference drawn from the fact. Because there is no way of *proving* that a given interpretation or inference about the future is correct, the participants may determine which choice is more likely to occur.

3. *The conflict may be over a definition.* Two or more persons may come into conflict over whether the use of communication strategies to motivate

people to buy a product is *unethical behavior* or *good salesmanship*. In this type of conflict, the antagonists agree on what is being done; the problems lies in how each person defines the behavior. Again, there is no way to prove the superiority of a given definition. The conflict may be resolved by determining which definition can best be supported.

4. *The conflict may be over a choice among goals, actions, or means of arriving at goals.* Two or more persons may come into conflict over whether building a multilevel garage or using available space more efficiently is the better solution to the campus parking problem. In this type of conflict, the opponents agree on the problem but disagree on the solution. Since you cannot prove that one proposed solution is better, the conflict will be resolved only when the parties involved agree that one solution can be better supported than the other.

Some authorities refer to content conflict as "simple" conflict. Because facts can be looked up, inferences can be tested, definitions can be verified, and competing goals can be weighed and evaluated, the conflict can be resolved rationally. Issues can be clearly stated, and the potential for cooperative effort in resolving the conflict is present. The best procedure for coping with most content conflict is to follow the guidelines for conflict resolution stated in the last section of this chapter and discussed in greater detail in Chapter 12.

Although content conflicts cannot always be resolved, they are still much easier to cope with than either value conflicts or ego conflicts. If you can keep personal emotions out of the conflict situation, you have the *chance* of a friendly resolution.

Value Conflict

Value conflicts arise when people differ in their views of life in general (or an aspect of life), and these differences are brought into focus on a particular issue. A person who believes that the government should be responsible for each individual views life differently from a person who believes that each individual has the right and responsibility to take care of himself. On such issues as welfare, Medicare, and unemployment compensation, these two persons could have value conflicts. Although people whose basic value systems differ can learn to get along in many ways, they will find it difficult if not impossible to resolve most conflicts resulting from their differences in values. For such people to get along, they must seek areas for discussion that do not bring their values into basic conflict. In areas where the basic conflicts occur, they are probably best counseled to agree to disagree.

Can value conflicts be resolved? Perhaps over a period of time. Our values change to some degree from one period of life to another—but these changes are not likely to occur very quickly. Is it bad for people with differences in values to debate those differences? No, provided each person recognizes that he is not likely to change the other person's values. Good friends can often argue over differences for the pleasure of good verbal combat. Persons who are anticipating a long-term intimate relationship should by all means discuss their value systems to determine whether basic differences in values will affect their ability to maintain a relationship.

Ego Conflict

Ego conflicts are probably the most damaging to interpersonal relationships. Ego conflict exists when the persons in conflict view "winning" or "losing" the conflict as a measure of their expertise, personal worth, or image. Ego conflicts develop when in the dialogue over content elements one or both parties introduce personal or judgmental statements. In a discussion of whether Barbra Streisand did or did not win an Oscar for her performance in *Funny Girl*, the simple content conflict may be escalated to an ego conflict when one or both parties see the issue as stupidity versus supreme knowledge—that the eventual winner is the master of supreme knowledge and the loser is relegated to the role of poor, stupid individual.

Who you are, what you are, what competence you have, over whom you should or do have power, and how much you know are some of the factors in the make-up of your self-concept. When a conflict is somehow tied in with your personal worth, the conflict becomes an ego conflict. If you see yourself as a baseball expert, you may perceive conflict over a statement you made about baseball as an attack on your self-esteem; if you see your role as a protector of your brother, you may perceive conflict over whether your brother should be allowed some special privilege as an attack on your ability to handle the responsibility. Once your ego becomes involved in the conflict, your ability to cope rationally is often lost. Before either party realizes it, emotions are involved, words are said that cannot be taken back, and the conflict gets blown all out of proportion.

Since conflict is hard enough to resolve without bringing in personalities and emotions, you must be careful to separate the content of a conflict from your potential ego involvement. This is, of course, easier said than done. In the next section, we'll consider effects of cooperation and competition in conflict resolution—it is through the maintenance of cooperative attitudes that ego conflicts are avoided or resolved.

In this section we have tried to identify four common types of conflict. Before you move on to suggestions for resolving conflict, complete the following exercises.

Communication Session

Reflection

Identify the last three conflicts you had. Were they pseudoconflict? content conflict? ego conflict? or value conflict? What was the outcome of each?

Practice

Decide whether the following are C (content conflict), P (pseudoconflict), V (value conflict), or E (ego conflict).

_____ 1. Joe wants to live together, but Mary wants the two of them to get married.

_____ 2. Stan believes that since he is an insurance salesman Jerry should not dispute his position on annuities.

_____ 3. George defends his failure to present an anniversary gift to Agnes by asserting that their anniversary is not today (May 8) but May 18.

_____ 4. Martin calls to announce that he is bringing the boss home for dinner. His wife replies, "That will be impossible. The house is a mess and I need to go shopping."

_____ 5. Jane says, "Harry, pick up your clothes—I'm not your maid!" Harry replies, "I thought we agreed that it's your job to take care of the house, I take care of the yard."

Discussion

Which of the above examples would be the most difficult to resolve? Why?

Answers: 1. V; 2. E; 3. C; 4. P; 5. C.

Cooperation versus Competition

When a conflict arises, one of the first variables to affect the outcome of the conflict is whether the participants' attitudes are competitive or cooperative. If the attitudes of both individuals are competitive, then each is likely to be ego-involved. If Fred wants to live in an apartment off campus and his father wants him to live in the dorm, Fred and his father have a content conflict. If Fred and his father look at the conflict competitively, then for Fred getting an apartment represents winning and living in the dorm represents losing; from his father's viewpoint, if Fred lives in the dorm Dad wins and if Fred gets an apartment Dad loses.

The problems created by the win-lose conflict are many. First, one member of the conflict must lose. Losing is not pleasant, and the reaction to losing, especially in a high-stakes conflict, may be one in which the loser looks for a way to get revenge against the winner. Second, if the two people engage in several encounters and the same person always wins, the loser may become dejected or hostile. If the loser becomes convinced that he or she will always lose, this may well cause a stumbling block to even the most intimate relationship. Third, and perhaps most important, winning or losing seems to become a measure of personal worth. Battle lines are drawn, and neither party can give in without viewing it as a personal loss.

The alternative to the competitive attitude is the cooperative attitude. If the attitudes of those in conflict are cooperative, then each person looks for mutually beneficial ways of resolving the conflict. You may ask, "How can an outcome be mutually satisfying to Fred and to his father when Fred wants to live in an apartment and his father wants him to live in a dorm?" A mutually satisfying solution is one that meets the needs, wants, and desires of both persons. Why does Fred want an apartment? Why does his father want him to live in a dorm? Through cooperation, the reasons can be discovered. If Dad wants Fred to have good grades and stay out of trouble, and if Fred wants to have privacy and a place of his own, then the two can see whether both sets of needs can be met. Assuming that no third choice exists that may be satisfying to both, through cooperative discussion they may achieve a compromise: If Fred lives in the dorm one term and keeps his grades up, he may move into an apartment the next term; or Fred may get an apartment now and, if he keeps his grades up and stays out of trouble, keep the apartment. A solution then can be mutually satisfying because it meets the needs behind the expressed preferences.

Cooperation means willingness to follow the steps of the problem-solving method: For now we'll simply list these steps—(1) identify the problem, (2) analyze the nature of the problem, (3) suggest possible solutions, and (4) select the solution that best meets the needs determined in problem analysis—later we'll show how to put them into practice. Does cooperation always result in conflict resolution? No, not always; but once the win-lose division is rejected, those in conflict have the potential for working out their conflicts.

In some conflicts one person may initially look at the outcome competitively while the other has a cooperative outlook. In this situation, the nature of the conflict will depend on whether the person looking at the conflict competitively draws the other person into the competition or whether the person looking at the outcome cooperatively influences the other person to cooperate.

A factor that influences whether a person will view a conflict cooperatively or competitively is the importance of the outcome. Suppose Fred and Suzy are discussing plans for the evening. Fred suggests going to a movie. Suzy says she would just as soon stay home and watch television. Fred and Suzy have a content conflict over a choice of actions. If neither sees the decision as important, they are more likely to approach the conflict resolution cooperatively.

Suppose, however, that Fred and Suzy are discussing next summer's vacation plans. If Fred has been thinking for weeks about using the new fly rod he got for his birthday, and he is excited about going off in the wilds for a week of camping, boating, and fishing, where they go will be important to him. If, on the other hand, Suzy has been thinking about going to a plush resort for a week of swimming and sunbathing and eating at exotic restaurants, the conflict that results may be fraught with potential hazards. Because neither will consider vacationing alone, each has significant stake in the resolution of the conflict. If they have time and money for only one week of vacation during the year, the chances that they will maintain a cooperative attitude are not very good. If competitive attitudes develop, then either Fred or Suzy will lose; and, on this issue, losing will hurt. On the other hand, even if both do their best to maintain a cooperative attitude, negotiating an amicable resolution to the conflict will not be easy.

For people who have been resolving conflicts between themselves for years, discovering an issue that is not easily resolved can be a real shock. Often the degree of difficulty is primarily determined by the importance of the outcome. The more important the outcome to you, the more careful you have to be to avoid becoming competitive.

If one person has a strong interest in the outcome and the other person does not, the conflict will usually be resolved in the direction of the stronger interest. The person with little interest is unlikely to offer much resistance to the other person even if a competitive attitude is present.

Let us now consider how you can proceed to keep competition from occurring or how you can deal with it in a way that results in a more cooperative and objective approach. Above all, you need to be aware of competitive statements. If you are alert, you can soon draw perceptive conclusions about another person's attitude toward a subject. When you ask whether the person is a Reds fan, and she replies, "Baseball is a ridiculous game befitting the intelligence of children," you will have no problem drawing a conclusion about her attitude toward baseball. Sometimes, however, we are wrong in our judgments. Since a wrong judgment might well initiate a conflict or heighten one that has begun, we should paraphrase the person's ideas or check out our perception of what the person is feeling. If in response to your comment about some candidate for public office, a person were to say, "Those Democrats are all alike," you might ask, "Are you saying that you believe all Democrats have the same views on all issues?" Such a question will not resolve a conflict, but it might clarify the situation if a conflict does exist, and it might help to determine the exact attitude of the other person.

If a person approaches the potential conflict competitively, how do you go about bringing the person into a cooperative state so the conflict can be considered rationally? First, do not get into the elements of the issue at hand until you demonstrate to the other person that you wish to resolve the conflict in a mutually satisfactory way; second, avoid any statements that would escalate the potential conflict or result in defensive behavior.

Now, let's put these two suggestions into practice. In an apparent conflict over whether your roommate has the obligation to carry out the trash, you would not want to say, "Well, I'm approaching this problem in the spirit of inquiry, so why don't you get off that competitive kick you are on?" Such a statement will only result in the other saying, "What do you mean, 'competitive kick'?" and now you have a new conflict. Remember, your goal is to get the conflict on a cooperative level, without adding to any ego involvement and without compounding the issue. Some of the following wordings may be useful in demonstrating your resolve to be cooperative and in preventing the conflict from escalating:

> *"I know you feel very strongly about what you want to do. Before we consider whether your plan is the answer, perhaps we could consider what we want to accomplish."*
>
> *"I know I sometimes get a little hotheaded in conflict situations, and I'm going to try to look at this problem as objectively as I can, but I may need your help."*
>
> *"You have good reasons for your belief, and I believe I have too. Perhaps if we share our reasons and then consider the consequences of each of them, we can make a mutually satisfactory decision."*

These examples illustrate ways of putting the conflict in an objective cooperative context.

Remember, your language, both verbal and nonverbal, indicates your feelings not only about the conflict, but also about the person with whom you are in conflict. If you approach a person with respect, openly, you should at least get a hearing, but if you demean a person's idea or the person himself by your words or actions, you are likely to create defensiveness, cause hard feelings, and perhaps destroy the entire relationship.

Positive versus Negative Communication

Some kinds of communication are most closely associated with a cooperative attitude, some with a competitive one; some are fundamental to good interpersonal communication and some are destructive. The positive kinds are discussion and persuasion; the negative are withdrawal, surrender, and aggression or combat. Because the negative kinds occur when people react to conflict rather than analyzing it, we will consider them first.

Withdrawal

A common negative way of dealing with conflict is withdrawal, removing oneself physically or psychologically from the situation. We should remember, however, that withdrawal is not always a negative reaction. When withdrawal is a person's major way of managing conflict, then it is harmful, but in at least two types of situations withdrawal may have positive outcomes. (1) When a conflict seems likely between people who communicate infrequently. Jack and Mark live on different floors of an apartment building. They know each other's first names, but don't socialize. For the last two Saturdays Jack and Mark have tried to use the washing machines in the basement at the same time. A potential for conflict exists. In this situation avoidance of the conflict might be a good idea. Jack gets up an hour earlier the next Saturday, and the problem is resolved. (2) When withdrawal can be defined as disengagement. Perhaps we could label this momentary withdrawal—giving a few minutes for temperatures to cool. Bill and Margaret begin to argue over whose responsibility it is to get the car washed. Margaret says, "Hold it a minute—let me calm down before we discuss this." Margaret goes into the kitchen and makes coffee for the two of them. A few minutes later she returns, temper intact and ready to approach the conflict more objectively. Margaret's action is not true withdrawal; it is not meant as a strategy to avoid confronting the issue. It is a cooling-off period that will probably benefit both of them. Withdrawal is a negative response, then, when it is a person's major way of managing conflict.

A common negative way of dealing with conflict is withdrawal, removing oneself physically or psychologically from the situation.

Sometimes when a person senses conflict he will try physical withdrawal:

> Tom says to Doris, "Get your coat and let's get going—we'll be late for the movie." Doris replies, "Oh, I thought it might be nice to sit home, make popcorn, and watch a little TV." When Tom then says, "We already talked about going to the movie," Doris runs to the bedroom and slams the door. Doris offers an alternative to the movie. When Tom emphasizes the conflict, Doris withdraws physically.

Withdrawal behavior does not eliminate the conflict—it is still there. Doris chooses not to deal with it by removing herself from the scene. If Tom follows Doris to the bedroom, the conflict will be resumed there; if not, the conflict will later resurface—probably in an intensified manner and very likely on the ego level.

Withdrawal need not be physical; it can also by psychological. Say, for example, that Marv and Otto begin to discuss a topic on which their values conflict. One way Otto might cope with this situation is not to "hear" what Marv is saying. Otto can think about the movie he saw last night or the date he is having this evening. He can do any sort of day-dreaming. By not hearing Marv, Otto can escape the conflict, and when Marv finishes his statements, Otto might change the subject to something less threatening.

Psychological withdrawal may be less painful than coming to grips with the issue being considered, but it is no answer to conflict.

Surrender

Another negative kind of conflict management is surrender. When the surrenderer senses conflict, he may choose to give in immediately to avoid the conflict. The prevailing attitude of the surrenderer is that actions, goals, and choices are never worth arguing about.

> When Jeff says, "I think we ought to take the money and put it in savings bonds," Marion replies, "I was really hoping we could get the color TV we've been talking about." Then when Jeff says, "OK, we'll talk about it—we have mentioned a TV, but with the economy the way it is . . ." Marion, seeing that conflict is developing, then says, "Oh, no need to discuss it—go ahead and put the money into bonds."

Banking the money may not meet Marion's needs, but rather than express those needs or even consider the comparative advantages of the proposed courses of action, Marion immediately gives in. Sometimes people who feel persecuted develop their reaction into a martyr role with statements that seem to say, "Do it your way—it's just not worth arguing about. I can bear the suffering." Even though the other person gets his way, surrender can be infuriating. It can often result in making the first person angry because the other person will not disclose what he is really thinking.

Aggression

One of the most common reactions to conflict is to become aggressive. Through aggression a person attempts to force another to accept his ideas. When conflict or the suggestion of conflict is perceived, one person strikes out at the other. Aggression threatens or delivers punishment should the aggressor not win the conflict. Aggression is sometimes physical:

> *Bart says to his son, "It's time for you to go to bed, David." When David replies, "I don't want to go to bed now," Bart says, "Get to bed before I beat the living daylights out of you." At the hint of conflict with his six-year-old son, Bart loses his patience and threatens to strike out aggressively at him.*

Aggression can also be verbal. Consider the following exchange:

> *Quinn says, "The game is going to start soon; let's get dressed." Dolly replies, "I don't know if I feel up to going to a game today." Quinn then says, "Right. Any time we talk about going to a game, you're not up to it. Well, maybe I can find someone who is."*

Through aggression a person attempts to force another to accept his ideas.

Verbal aggression is every bit as threatening as physical aggression.

Aggression is an emotional reaction to conflict. Thought is short-circuited, and the person lashes out physically or verbally.

In each of the above reactions, either the conflict is escalated or it is obscured. In none is it resolved or discussed. With these negative reactions, simple conflict becomes ego conflict and may grow into a power struggle. The greater the degree of escalation or withdrawal, the more complicated the conflict and the more difficult resolution of that conflict becomes. Now let's examine the two most positive ways of dealing with conflict.

Discussion

Discussion is a verbal weighing and considering of the pros and cons of the issues in conflict. It depends upon mutual desire of the participants to talk through the various aspects of the conflict. It is a product of a cooperative rather than a competitive attitude toward the conflict. It requires an objectivity in the presentation of the issues, an openness in stating feelings and beliefs, and an openness to acceptance of the solution that proves to be most logical and in the best interests of the needs of both parties. Discussion works best in a climate of mutual respect where neither party is so ego-involved that objectivity is impossible.

Discussion follows the problem-solving method; this method is **an organized procedure for solving problems** that includes the following steps: defining the problem, analyzing the problem, suggesting possible solutions, selecting the solution that best fits the analysis, and working to implement that decision. In everyday give-and-take use of the discussion method, all five steps are not always considered completely nor are they necessarily considered in the order given. Its use requires that, when two people perceive a conflict emerging, they step back from that conflict and proceed systematically in its resolution. Sound ideal? or impracticable? Well, it is difficult. But when two people have agreed to commit themselves to *trying*, beneficial results can be achieved.

Consider the dialogue and its analysis on pages 214–216, which illustrate the discussion method. Both persons have set aside personal needs. Each considers the other's opinion. They weigh and consider together. Is the conflict over? Perhaps not; they have not bought the car yet, but they seem to be on their way to making a cooperative decision. Ego involvement seems to have given way to cooperative analysis. In Chapter 12 we will make a more detailed analysis of the problem-solving method.

What happens if both parties try, but still discussion breaks down? When two people cannot arrive at the same decision through objective weighing and analyzing, then one person may seek to influence the other through persuasion.

Persuasion

As a means of learning to manage conflict, you will want to learn to use the various means of persuasion. Although we discussed persuasion in detail in the last chapter, let's review the key ideas and apply them to conflict management.

Persuasion is the attempt to change either the attitude or the behavior of another person. Suppose that at the point in their discussion of buying a car where Doris said, "Don't we need room?" Jack had replied, "Enough to get us into the car together, but I don't see why we need more than that." If he made such a statement, they would be approaching a new conflict position. Doris might then have said, "Jack, remember the other day when you were cussing out our present car because it doesn't have much back-seat room? We carry a lot of stuff. I do food shopping, you're always carrying equipment for the men at the lodge, and there are a lot of times when we invite another couple to go somewhere with us." Statements like these are attempts to persuade.

Persuasion takes a variety of forms and relies primarily on reasoning, development of an emotional climate (motivation), and credibility of the persuader. *Reasoning* requires the presentation of logical arguments in support of the point of view. In our example, Doris offered reasons why Jack would profit from a roomier car. If you voted for Jones because he has the best qualifications and a good public office record, your action is a result of reasoning. *Development of an emotional climate* means the presentation of the information in language that excites or stimulates the emotions of the listener. When, in our example, Doris spoke of "carrying equipment for the men at the lodge," the language had an emotional thrust—it played upon Jack's responsibilities as a member of his men's club. If you voted for Jones because his position on crime in the streets meshed with your anxieties about personal safety, you were persuaded to vote as you did by motivational factors that played upon your emotions. *Credibility* is a personal means of persuasion that grows from your belief that the sender of the message is knowledgeable on that subject, likable, and trustworthy. If you voted for Jones because your best friend urged you to, you have been persuaded by your personal belief in your friend—by your friend's credibility.

When two people in conflict take adversary positions—that is, each attempts to prove his point to the other—debate occurs. Debate is a type of dual persuasion in which competition is more common than cooperation. Many so-called discussions that people have are really informal debates, wherein neither party accepts the merits of the other's position but instead attempts to demonstrate the strength of his own position. As a result, debates rarely do much to solve the conflict between participants. Still, people sometimes find it useful to debate anyway—it gives each

person a chance to be heard even if there is not much impact on the other.

Debate is an important communication form, but it does not work too well in interpersonal communication. Debate belongs in the legislative assembly and the law court where as a result of the debate other legislators, a judge, or a jury will make decisions on particular issues.

Discussion and Analysis

Doris: Apparently we need to get a new car.

Jack: Yes, the time has come.

Doris: Well, we've talked about getting a station wagon—let's go ahead and do it.

Jack: What do you mean, a station wagon—you know I've been looking forward to a sports car.

Doris: Oh-oh—I can see we're looking at this differently. Before one of us goes off the deep end, let's see if we can't talk this out. We agree we're ready to get a new car, right?

Jack: Yes.

Doris: OK—If there's a hassle, it's over what kind. Look, let's both of us say what we think we *need* in this new car.

Jack: All right—we need a car that gets good mileage.

Doris: I'll buy that, but maybe we'd better be more specific. What is good mileage?

Jack: At least thirty miles per gallon.

Doris: I think we need good gas mileage, but that's really limiting choices, isn't it? How about at least twenty in the city?

The family car has gone haywire. Both Doris and Jack are in agreement on that, but we can see that making the decision is going to result in conflict. At this particular point either we'll see some negative reaction (withdrawal, surrender, aggression), or we'll see something said to put the conflict in a problem-solving climate.

Doris takes the first step to try to put the conflict in a problem-solving framework.

Jack gives verbal agreement. Let's see if he is really cooperative, or whether he is saying he is cooperating as a strategy.

Jack and Doris seem to be cooperating.

Here they are stating criteria that are important in making a rational choice.

Jack: OK. And it's got to look nice—be a little jazzy.

Doris: That's good, and it has to be roomy enough so that we can get in luggage on trips and have room for Judy.

Jack: I don't know—

Doris: Don't we need room?

Jack: I guess so—I'd like to think we didn't, but I get your point. I'd like air conditioning.

Doris: Definitely—and a nice exterior.

Jack: That's what I meant when I said "look nice." How high can we go?

Doris: What do you think the car we have is worth?

Notice how Doris seeks help from Jack in determining various limits.

Jack: Let's say we get around $2,500 in trade. I think that's possible. Maybe $3,500 more?

Doris: So about $6,000 top?

Jack: Give or take a bit.

Doris: OK, let's consider some of the kinds of cars. Can we get a sports car with room?

Now they begin testing specific types of cars against the criteria they have agreed upon.

Jack: Not a real sports car—but we can get a sporty car. Can we get a station wagon that gets twenty miles per gallon in the city?

Doris: A compact wagon would, wouldn't it?

Jack: Maybe, but would it really have the kind of room you're talking about in the back seat?

Doris: Maybe we need a medium sized car that looks kind of sporty.

Both seem to agree that their original choices will not fill the bill. Compromise seems likely.

Jack: So we can forget about a station wagon?

Doris: And a sport car?

Jack: OK.

Communication Session

Reflection

1. Indicate which, if any, of the above means is typical of your communication in a conflict setting.
2. Analyze a conflict that you were involved in recently.

   a. What was the attitude of the participants: cooperative or competitive?
   b. How important was the outcome to each participant?
   c. How complicated was the conflict?
   d. What kinds of communication were used in dealing with the conflict?

Practice

Break into groups of six. One person in each group should be named as an observer. Your instructor will give each of the five participants an envelope. In this envelope are pieces of a puzzle. The task of the group is for each person to construct a square. You may not be able to do this with the pieces in your envelope, so some sharing may have to take place. However, the following rules must be strictly obeyed:

1. Absolutely no talking.
2. You may not take a puzzle piece from someone else.
3. You may not indicate in any way that you would like a puzzle piece that anyone else has.
4. You may give away puzzle pieces to anyone, but you may not indicate where the piece might fit.
5. Your observer will enforce these rules. Observers will also get instructions from the instructor.

Discussion

What does this exercise demonstrate?

Prearrangement of Procedures

Much of the difficulty of conflict resolution in ongoing relationships arises because the parties do not have any procedure in mind. Just as people who have made plans for what they will do in case of a fire, a flood, or a tornado often weather the particular disaster in much better shape than those who have not, so parties to an ongoing relationship weather conflict better if they have a plan for conflict resolution.

At least one of the two parties will know when a conflict is about to occur. It is for him to remind the other of the prearranged procedure. For instance, if two people have agreed to write out advantages and disadvantages of the conflicting actions or plans or ideas before the conflict heats up, then when a conflict occurs the prearranged procedure will take precedence over any actions. Sometimes the time involved in going through the prearranged steps is enough to get people past that explosive moment when each party is likely to say or do something he would like to take back later but never can.

Many of the guidelines offered in this section can be put together into a package that will serve as a conflict resolution procedure. Following a plan encourages rational analysis to take precedence over emotional outburst or evaluative behavior. The plan you draw up might contain provision for negotiation and, if necessary, arbitration.

Cooperation through Negotiation

Although we tend to see conflict in a win-lose context, sometimes we can find a way of resolving the conflict so that neither party wins all or loses all. This may be brought about by negotiation. **Negotiation means resolving conflicts through trade-offs.**

Conflict often results when two actions are proposed but only one can be accomplished. You cannot go to a movie and to a concert at the same time; you cannot eat at a Chinese and at an Italian restaurant at the same time; or, if you can afford only one house payment, you can't *buy* a house and *rent* a house at the same time. Even after you have considered every aspect of the conflict rationally, each person may still truly believe that his way is the best; then perhaps you should negotiate.

With some simple problems, negotiation is easily accomplished. For instance, "I'll tell you what, Joan, I'll go to the concert with you tonight if you'll go to the movie with me this weekend" will probably achieve the desired results. Since in this case there need not be an either/or approach, both activities can be accomplished at different times.

For negotiation to work, the activities, goals, or ideas must be of fairly equal importance. For instance, "Joe, if you'll let me make the decision on where to eat tonight, I'll go along with you on whatever movie you want to see" has a good chance of working. On the other hand, "Alice, if you will let me decide on the kind of car to buy, I'll let you decide on where to eat" does not stand a chance. Obviously, selecting a car is a far more important decision than picking a restaurant, a movie, or any other one-night activity. A person trying such a negotiation is not acting in good faith. Finding situations that are indeed parallel may be difficult, but when they can be found, they make an excellent base for negotiation.

If an issue is truly not negotiable, such as conflict about whether to rent a house or buy one, and you and the other person cannot work out a decision cooperatively, you are not necessarily defeated.

When Negotiation Fails, Seek Arbitration

Arbitration requires the presence of an impartial person who, after hearing both sides, will weigh and evaluate the alternatives and make a decision for you. Labor unions and management sometimes use arbitration. It may work for you.

For interpersonal conflicts, arbitration will work if you can agree on an arbitrator who in turn will agree to make the decision for you. It is important that the arbitrator be a person whose judgment you both trust. The arbitrator also should in some way be competent to make a decision on the issue. Your lawyer may act as arbitrator for you over whether to sue or not to sue about a car accident. Your financial counselor may arbitrate a conflict over whether to invest in a high-risk stock or a high-dividend stock.

Too often we seek to pull in a close friend or a relative to arbitrate. Not only does this person often not have the expertise needed for the particular issue, but more important, a friend or relative is not an independent, impartial agent. He may well be close to both parties, or may have a vested interest in the outcome. Calling on such a person puts him in a no-win situation (somebody may well be upset by his or her decision) or at best makes the person feel very uncomfortable in the role.

If you do agree to arbitration, the verbal contract between you and the other person should include a clause saying that whatever decision is made, you will both willingly and happily comply. Remember you will have gone to a third person because the two of you were unable to come to a conclusion; if you are unwilling to abide by the decision, whichever way it goes, then you should not agree to arbitration in the first place.

In some circumstances the impartial third person will act as a facilitator rather than as an arbitrator. The difference is that instead of the person making the decision for you, the person will *help* the two of you (or you alone in the case of an intrapersonal decision) use the problem-solving method to make your own decision. Psychologists, psychiatrists, marriage counselors, and other clinicians are skilled in facilitating decision making. A good facilitator not only sees to it that you are following the steps of problem solving, but also helps you weigh and evaluate the variables. Even with a good plan there are at least three additional important considerations.

1. *Don't be stubborn.*   Interpersonal communication is not the place for "non-negotiable" demands. If you go into a situation with a defensive attitude or a "this is the way we're going to do it or else" posture, you are more than likely going to heighten the conflict. If, after calm appraisal, it appears that your way is not the best or at least not the only good way, you should try to avoid becoming so ego-involved that any modification of position would cause you to "lose face." Of course, willingness to back off from a position is easier said than done. However, by altering your stance on any issue you pave the way for the other person to make some concessions. If you are in a long-term relationship, it is better to think of the betterment of the relationship than of "winning" on a particular issue.

2. *"Win" and "lose" graciously.*   This guideline is a logical follow-up to not being stubborn. Regardless of any advice we can give, there will be times that you feel very strongly about your position, and having to abandon it or even to modify it will be a tremendous blow to you. Yet, the very worst thing you can do is to punish the other person for "making" you give in. For instance, if your attitude (if not your actual behavior) goes like this: "OK, Laura, I'll go to your party, but, you'll see, I'll be just miserable the whole evening," you are not going to have much fun—and neither will Laura. Moreover, Laura will probably resent your attitude. When a decision is made through objective discussion, both parties should feel an obligation to support the decision. Although our own defenses may not let us concede that the other person's plan is the better one for these circumstances, the continuation of the "war" during the implementation stages will only bring on new conflicts or heighten or regenerate older ones.

3. *Discuss conflict-resolution failures.*   The ideal is to resolve every conflict as it comes up. ("Never let the sun set on your anger.") However, there will be times when no matter how hard both persons try, they will not be able to resolve the conflict. If the person is a friend or a relative, and intimate—so that the relationship is especially important to you—after the heat of the conflict dies down, you should take steps to analyze the failure of the conflict resolution. You should consider such questions as, "Where did things go wrong?" "Did one or more become competitive? or defensive?" "Did we fail to implement the problem-solving method adequately?" "Were the vested interests in the outcome too great?" By seeing why conflict resolution failed, you put yourself in a better position to manage the next conflict more successfully.

Of course, conflicts will arise again and again. Yet, we should have no need to fear conflict. The presence of conflict as such does not mar any relationship; it is the way conflicts are dealt with that is the true measure of a relationship. Some careful analysis after a particular conflict may well save you additional strife in the future.

Communication Session

Reflection

What behaviors do you indulge in during conflict that make resolution difficult? What suggestions from this chapter will help you work on them?

Practice

Working with a person with whom you have a close relationship, design a plan for dealing with conflict before it arises.

Summary

We must all accept the fact that interpersonal conflicts can and do occur. The goal of this chapter was not to teach you how to avoid conflict or even how to prevent it but to describe the skills that will help you to manage it.

Interpersonal conflicts can be pseudoconflicts (conflicts that appear to be real but are not); content conflicts (conflicts over a fact, the reasoning from or interpretation of a fact, choice among means of dealing with facts, or definitions); value conflicts (conflicts that arise from different ways of looking at life); and ego conflicts (conflicts that become battles between personalities and develop a win-lose perspective).

The presence of conflict as such does not mar any relationship.

Interpersonal conflict management depends on the ability of those involved to deal with conflict in a cooperative rather than a competitive way. This ability may in turn depend on how important the outcome of a conflict is to the participants.

People have developed their own styles of dealing with conflict. Styles that use withdrawal, surrender, and aggression are basically negative; styles that use discussion, persuasion, and in some cases debate are basically positive. If your style is basically negative, you should attempt to develop the more positive conflict management skills.

Conflict management between intimates is best accomplished by following a prearranged plan based on discussion. If discussion does not resolve the conflict, people should have a plan for negotiating the conflict; if negotiation fails, people should have a plan for using arbitration.

The various skills of discussion, persuasion, negotiation, and arbitration can help you develop a positive style of interpersonal conflict management.

Suggested Readings

George R. Bach and **Peter Wyden.** *The Intimate Enemy*. New York: Avon Books, 1970. A readable and useful discussion of conflict in marriage.

Fred E. Jandt. *Conflict Resolution through Communication*. New York: Harper & Row, 1973. Of particular value are the two articles on conflict theory and the 18-page bibliography.

Journal of Conflict Resolution. Nearly every issue of the journal has at least one article related to interpersonal conflict.

Gerald R. Miller and **Herbert W. Simons.** *Perspectives on Communication in Social Conflict*. Englewood Cliffs, New Jersey: Prentice-Hall, 1974. Several of the eight articles are relevant to interpersonal conflict. This book also has an excellent bibliography.

Chapter 10
A Synthesis of Skills: Interpersonal Competence and Behavioral Flexibility

1. *Define interpersonal competence.*
2. *Define behavioral flexibility.*
3. *Determine the effectiveness of interpersonal encounters in which you were involved, or have witnessed or read about or both.*

Interpersonal communication is the transactional process of people sharing meaning by simultaneously sending and receiving messages. In the preceding five chapters of Part 2 we have considered more than twenty-five skills that you can use to increase your effectiveness in interpersonal communication. Perhaps as a result of our method you think of these as skills that are individually practiced, but in fact they make up a total package.

In this chapter we want to synthesize the material we have discussed. We want to get back to the idea of skills as a means of achieving the goal of interpersonal effectiveness. First, we'll examine some criteria for interpersonal effectiveness; second, we'll examine methods for analyzing interpersonal communication; and third, we'll give you an opportunity to put what you have learned so far into practice.

Interpersonal Effectiveness

Interpersonal communication occurs (is effective) when people share meaning. This definition assumes that when people communicate they have a conscious meaning to share—they begin with a purpose for communication. Some communication, especially nonverbal communication, occurs *un*consciously: when we're nervous, we may perspire or giggle; when we're angry, we may get a cutting tone in our voice. However, in the latter part of Chapter 1 when we discussed the social and problem-solving functions of conscious interpersonal communication, we were assuming that people speak to some purpose. The skills discussed in this book are most relevant to your behavior when you see purpose in what you are doing.

A speaker may not always be aware of his purpose. For instance, when Charley passes Al on the street and says, "Al—what's happening?" it is not likely that Charley thought: "I see Al coming. I haven't talked with Al for a while. I hope (1) that Al is aware that I recognize him, (2) that he realizes the lines of communication between us are still open, and (3) that I don't have the time to talk with him right now, but that I may like to later—so I'll say, 'Al—what's happening.'" In this case the social need to recognize Al is met spontaneously with the first acceptable expression that comes to Charley's mind.

At other times, however, a person may give careful thought to exactly what she wants to achieve and how she will go about achieving it. Let's look at two examples. Beth goes to the library to do research for a paper. When she consults the card catalog, she discovers that an important source she needs is on microfilm. She knows neither where the microfilm room is nor how to use the equipment. Therefore, (1) she plans to ask the librarian where the microfilm room is, and (2) when she finds the room, she plans to ask the attendant how to use the equipment. Her communication will be effective if she is directed to the room and if someone there explains the use of the equipment to her. Her goal is seeking information.

Now let's consider communication in a different context. Beth wants to use her parents' new Buick this weekend to drive her friends to the beach. She knows her parents are reluctant to let her drive the Buick, so she will need to offer some good reasons why she should be allowed to. Moreover, she is well aware that she must not lose her temper or in any way endanger the positive communication climate she hopes to establish. She will have achieved her goal if her parents consent to let her use the Buick. Her goal in this case is to persuade.

Can interpersonal communication be conscious and still be spontaneous and nonmanipulative? We think it can. *Spontaneous* means occurring impulsively without planning, but there's nothing that says that preplanning a procedure can't lead to spontaneous interaction. Beth has planned her overall procedure. She may even have thought of a wording for her first statement. Her parents' reply will determine how she will continue. Moreover, Beth can change her goals and her methods of achieving them at any time.

Manipulation implies secret and underhanded approaches to goal achievement. Suppose that Beth's mother found her sitting in the living room crying. When her mother asks her what is wrong, Beth sobs, "All my friends want to see the new Buick, but I told them you'd never let me drive it. They all laughed at me and said that it was pretty funny that a girl's parents wouldn't trust a twenty-year-old to take care of a car for one day." After her mother agrees to let her drive the Buick, Beth goes upstairs, smiling to herself. This behavior would be manipulative and counter to all the interpersonal communication methods we've been discussing.

Achieving any communication goal depends on a number of factors. Here are four of the most important. (1) *Ease of the goal.* Finding out what time it is, is easier than finding out why black holes exist. (2) *Attitudes of the people involved.* Convincing a Republican of the merits of a Republican candidate for governor would be easier than convincing a Republican of the merits of a Socialist candidate. (3) *The setting*. Getting people to understand a complicated piece of information is much easier in a well-ventilated room with a moderate temperature than in a stuffy, oppressively hot room. (4) *The skill of the communicator*. Much of what we have discussed thus far is directed to this fourth point. Your effectiveness depends on your competence and behavioral flexibility.

Interpersonal competence is the ability to use interpersonal communication skills in a relevant context. If you see a need to describe your feelings, and if you can make a statement that does in fact verbalize the feelings you are experiencing at the moment, then you have shown proficiency or competence in that skill. We hope that by now you can show some proficiency or competence in nearly all the skills we have presented.

There are, of course, degrees of competence. For instance, saying, "For some reason the tone of your voice is making me edgy and insecure" and saying, "I'm feeling edgy because of the way your voice sounds" may both show a degree of competence. Both sentences are likely to get your meaning across to a listener. The first sentence, however, is preferable. Studies we have conducted with our students show that they prefer those phrasings that are smooth, specific, and show a command of both verbal and nonverbal nuances.

But competence alone is not enough to ensure interpersonal effectiveness. The second important criterion for effectiveness is behavioral flexibility. By *behavioral flexibility* we mean choosing from the various skills the one or ones that are likely to be most effective under a given set of circumstances. Depending on the situation, a supportive statement, a paraphrase, a question, an interpretation, or some combination of them might each be appropriate. Some people see themselves as so competent in a particular skill that they invariably use it to respond, regardless of whether it is appropriate.

When Max says, "Thomas really has it in for me," you will have the competence to *use* any of the appropriate response styles (question, paraphrase, support, interpretation). You should also have the flexibility to *choose* the response (or combination) that will in your estimation be most appropriate.

Most of your conversations require spur-of-the-moment decisions, and therefore you are not always going to make the best decision. Another measure of your understanding of interpersonal communication skills is your ability to look back on a conversation to see what you did right and what you did wrong—or at least what you might have done differently.

Because achieving both competence and behavioral flexibility is a matter of practice and analysis, we believe your best chance for improvement is both to practice the skills and to analyze communication encounters. Let's examine some methods of interpersonal communication analysis.

Analyzing Interpersonal Communication

Of all the forms of communication, interpersonal communication is the most difficult to analyze and evaluate. Why? Because the greatest amount of our interpersonal communication is in informal settings with no "audience." Moreover, the flow is quick, speaker and receiver switch roles rapidly, a response may be as short as one or two words, and some or much of the meaning is sent and verified by nonverbal means.

Nevertheless, to assume that interpersonal communication is beyond analysis is false. You can improve your communication by analyzing what you are doing and how you are doing it, but you need some objective system of analysis. To provide a working base for evaluation, let's take a look at criteria for communication effectiveness and see how these fit together into a method for interpersonal analysis.

The key to an analysis is determining effectiveness. Because communication involves sharing meaning with another, effectiveness depends on communication of meaning. If each partner in a conversation understands or "hears" what the other is saying, then communication has taken place. Of course, the analysis of effectiveness, or outcome, is complicated by the importance of the communication, the length of time involved, and the complexity of the message. A one-hour encounter with your boy friend or girl friend on an important issue over which you are at odds requires a considerably higher level of communication skill than a three-minute encounter with an old friend about getting together for

You can improve your communication by analyzing what you are doing and how you are doing it, but you need some objective system of analysis.

lunch. Likewise, the analysis of each encounter would require differing degrees of skill.

Let's consider two questions on which the evaluation instrument will be based:

1. *What was the apparent purpose of the encounter?*   Was it for enjoyment? Fulfilling social expectations? Building a relationship? Negotiating with others? Exchanging information? Problem solving? Influencing?

2. *How were the elements of communication handled?*   Did the people contribute to or detract from the effectiveness? Did the verbal or nonverbal messages contribute to or detract from the communication? Were any communication barriers present? Were the barriers reduced or eliminated as the encounter continued? Did the barriers interfere with effectiveness?

Before presenting the evaluation instruments themselves, we need to consider who should analyze your interpersonal communication. Because there is seldom an observer present during your conversations, you may have to make the analysis yourself after the fact. Such an analysis is difficult, but it can be done. After an encounter, you have feelings about whether it was satisfactory or not; and it is useful to take the time to "replay" it. You can determine whether your communication is effective and why. Of course, you should be an even more effective critic of encounters you are able to observe.

The first instrument we will consider is a descriptive-analytical, after-the-fact procedure (see Figure 10-1). With this instrument, you can analyze why communication was or was not successful.

The second instrument we will consider enables you to evaluate the means (see Figure 10-2). This instrument calls for you to replay the confrontation noting the presence or absence of various skills.

Communication Session

Reflection

Are you able to be objective in self-analysis? Under what circumstances?

Practice

Using either analysis form (Figure 10-1 or 10-2) as the instrument, analyze one of your communication encounters. Select one that occurred during the past day or two so that the dialogue is fresh in your mind.

Figure 10-1

Communication Analysis: Descriptive

---

1. Participants:

---

2. Apparent purpose of the encounter:

---

3. Outcome:

---

4. Describe the entire encounter. Use dialogue wherever possible.

---

5. List and discuss the reasons for the success or failure of the communication.

Figure 10-2

Communication Analysis: Skills

---

1. Participants:

---

2. Apparent purpose of the encounter:

---

3. Outcome—what was the result:

---

4. In column one, place a check mark (√) by those skills that were well done.

In column two, place a check mark (√) by those skills that were crucial in determining outcome.

1	2	**Analysis of climate:** Check the skills that you think were used effectively. Briefly indicate how.
		Empathy
		Openness 　Self-disclosure 　In receiving feedback
		Describing
		Provisionalism
		Equality
1	2	**Analysis of message formation skills:**
		Dating
		Indexing
		Accuracy
		Specific-concrete

1	2	**Analysis of message formation skills (continued):**
		Fluency
		Crediting
		Describing feelings
		Assertiveness
1	2	**Analysis of listening and responding skills:**
		Supporting
		Questioning
		Paraphrasing
		Interpreting
		Praising
		Criticizing
		Describing behavior
		Perception checking
1	2	**Analysis of influence and conflict:**
		Power relationships
		Influence
		Persuasion
		Discussion
		Problem solving
		Negotiating
		Arbitrating
1	2	**Analysis of barriers:**
		Noise
		Suspicion
		Inappropriate responses
		Defensiveness
		Hidden agenda
		Aggressiveness
		Passivity or withdrawal

5. List and discuss the reasons for the success or failure of the communication.

Communication Session

Practice

1. Form a team with another member of your class. Together you are to prepare a four- to six-minute role-play, during which you will demonstrate competency and behavioral flexibility. Each person is required to include a paraphrase, a perception check, and a description of feelings. Select a topic on which you are inclined to take opposite sides. Your goal is to explain your positions. You may or may not reach any agreement. Dialogue is to be spontaneous. Although you may want to have practice sessions, do not try to write out scripts or memorize parts.

2. Beginning on this page is a transcript of a role-play. Read this role-play through aloud in its entirety. After you have considered its merits, read it again, noting the analysis in the right-hand column.

3. On page 236 you will find another transcript of a role-play. You are to write an analysis similar to the one written for role-play 1, or, if you prefer, analyze it by using either Figure 10-1 or Figure 10-2.

Role-Play 1

Sheila and Susan talk about the advantages and disadvantages of dating exclusively within one's own religion.[1] Read the role-play aloud in its entirety. After you have considered its merits, read it again, this time noting the analysis in the right-hand column.

---

[1]Conversation presented in Interpersonal Communication class, University of Cincinnati. Reprinted by permission of Sheila Slone and Susan Lautman.

Susan: How are you and Bill getting along these days?

Susan introduces the subject with a question.

Sheila: Not too well. I think you could say our relationship is coming to an end. The feelings just aren't there, and so many problems have been building up.

Sheila's answer is neither as specific nor as concrete as it could have been.

Susan: I get the impression from the expression on your face that you're having problems. Is there one specific problem?

Susan responds with a *perception check* wording when a *feelings paraphrase* wording would be better. She's responding both to Sheila's spoken words and to what she is implying. Better: "From the way you're talking, I get the impression that you're very sad about the outcome of the relationship."

Sheila: Well, there are a lot, but one that I didn't think would make such a difference at the beginning of the relationship that's made a difference now is the fact that we're from different religions. I'm Jewish and he isn't, and at first I never thought it would affect me, but it does make a difference.

Sheila says, "It really does make a difference," but she doesn't go on to say what the difference is. We would expect Susan to ask about the difference.

Susan: I think I was kind of lucky, well, lucky in the long run. When I was in high school, my parents wouldn't allow me to go out with anybody who wasn't Jewish. I really resented that at first, but now I'm kind of glad since I'm thinking about the future now. And as my parents said, you don't know what could come out of a high-school relationship.

Susan assumes she understands. She needs a question or a content paraphrase here. Instead, she changes the emphasis to her own experience. Now apparently the conversation will focus on Susan and an implied contrast in upbringing.

Sheila: It seems like you were a little upset at first, but now you're pretty happy with the whole situation.

Although Sheila's paraphrase is satisfactory, the wording could be even more specific: "It seems like you were a little upset at first, but now that you're older you have a better understanding of your parents' position."

Susan: Yes, now that I look around, I'm not in the predicament that you are of having to get out of a relationship for something that's not what you want.

Susan's response has a slightly superior ring to it. Note the implications of the word *predicament*. Susan needs to empathize with Sheila more directly.

Sheila: I can see what you mean, but I'm also happy that my parents didn't restrict me because I think I would have felt a lot of pressure just to always . . . I wouldn't have had a choice of whom to go out with, and I wouldn't have felt very independent. But I feel I have to make my own choices. As long as I know what I want, I feel it's all right.

Sheila's reaction is to defend her parents' policy. Then she makes a statement about the value of independence. Notice that even though the statements are at odds, Sheila and Susan seem to be maintaining a good climate.

Sheila says "feel," but she's not really describing feelings.

Susan: That was my problem—having to pick and choose. My parents would say, "Oh, is he Jewish?" "I don't know, should I ask him?" They wanted me to say, "Are you Jewish? Oh, you're not? Well, you can't go out with me, then."

Susan begins a response to the subject of the last sentence: choices. But then she returns to her parents' policy.
Good, clear statement of position.

Sheila: I can see how you feel—that's a tough situation, but I see now that I feel pretty frustrated because I want to date people who are Jewish, but I'm not going to go around picking on them saying this one is and this one isn't. It's too hard to do that. You can't turn your feelings on and off. You have to be interested in someone. So I get pretty frustrated a lot of times.

Sheila's acknowledgement of Susan's feelings is in the right direction, but her wording appears a bit half-hearted. She needs a good paraphrase of feelings. In the midst of her response, she switches to a description of her feelings. The rest of the sentence is well-worded. She needs a clearer division between her response to Susan and her description of feelings.

Susan: Are you saying that you are kind of glad that your parents didn't restrict you in that manner,

This is probably one of the best responses in the dialogue. Although it is cast in question form, or are you saying that you're glad they didn't but wish they had?

Sheila: I guess I'm glad they didn't, but maybe it would have been better if they had. I would have been more conscious about it.

Susan: In the long run, I feel it's best to start early to get an idea in your mind of what you really want to do. I never thought a relationship in high school would go anywhere, but the man I'm dating, it's been four years already. That's a long time.

Sheila: You seem happy together. I saw you the other day and that's really nice. I wish I could find somebody that . . .

Susan: I saw you start shrugging Bill off and just ignoring him.

Sheila: Yes, that's a hard situation. I get pretty depressed about it, too. I just never thought religion could make such a big difference. But it means a lot to me, and that's why it makes such a difference.

Susan: What are you planning on telling him?

Sheila: Well, I guess I'll just say that it won't work out. It depresses me to think about that, too.

Susan: You should really try to go easy—don't let it upset you too much. It's what you want, right?

Sheila: I guess so. I'll have to try to do the best I can.

it is still a good attempt at seeking clarification of Sheila's feelings.

Notice the use of the word *feel* when *believe* or *think* would be more appropriate.

A nicely phrased personal feedback statement—a nice compliment.

Sheila again describes her feelings quite well.

Here's one of the few times when Susan focuses her attention on Sheila. Good question.

Sheila states her plans and continues to describe her feelings.

Susan gives advice that is meant to be supportive of Sheila's predicament.

In trying to help Sheila deal with her problem, Susan probably spent too much time talking about her own background and situation. Although some of her remarks show that she heard what Sheila was saying, some of her comments did not deal directly with Sheila's problem. Since the dialogue began as a response to Sheila's problem, Sheila's attempts at directing conversation to her problem are in order.

Both speakers made satisfactory attempts at paraphrasing and describing feelings; however, there were no good examples of perception checking. Still, the conversation was friendly (nonverbal responses were very supportive, but you can't see that on paper), and no major barriers developed.

Role-Play 2

Daryl and Lyn talk about whether a woman should share the costs of a date.[2] Read the conversation and then make comments on skills and barriers in the margin. Then analyze the dialogue, using Figure 10-2 as your instrument.

Daryl: I just don't understand it—sometimes women make me so mad! I don't know what I can do!

Lyn: I can understand how women might make you mad, but Daryl, you have to learn how to dish it out yourself.

Daryl: Well, it seems like you—women—have your hands in my

---

[2]Conversation presented in Interpersonal Communication class, University of Cincinnati. Reprinted by permission of Daryl Rush and Lynnette Braddell Petitt.

pockets. I took this woman out the other night—or I wanted to take her out, but I hadn't gotten paid that week—and I suggested to her that we go out and she pay her way and I pay my way, but she wouldn't buy it. What's wrong with you women? Why don't you want to help out a little bit? You must realize that none of us has money to throw away when you want . . . Why not help us out a little bit?

Lyn: Are you saying that you always want women to pay their way when they go out with you? Or just sometimes pitch in to help things a little?

Daryl: It would be helpful if we could have a little help and support . . . Some people have expensive tastes.

Lyn: Well, I feel that if a man is going to take a woman out, he should be prepared to spend money, no matter what she wants to do.

Daryl: I can understand that in certain situations. But every time a person goes out? I just can't see spending five, ten dollars—you can go out to a movie and spend fifteen dollars very easily—just for a movie. If you're going to take somebody out, it would seem to me that you should be able to expect a little bit of help from that person every now and then.

Lyn: I'm not going to give anybody any help when he takes me out. I mean, it's like saying that if a man is going to take me out, then I'm expecting him to give me some kind of royal treatment, but if I take him out, then I'll give him a treat.

Daryl: You're crossing your arms—I hope I'm not making you upset or anything. I'd rather not get into a fight. Let's keep this down to a discussion. I'm not making you mad, am I?

Lyn: No, you're not making me mad, but you should realize that paying the expenses on a date is one of the things you're supposed to do because you're one of those male chauvinists . . .

Daryl: I can understand what you're trying to say, and I realize a woman expects a man to make her feel good, but when that gets to a point where it's too expensive, then the woman ought to make some concessions.

Lyn: Well, in certain situations, maybe, but I still think that a man should do all the paying.

Daryl: I think you're just being kind of stubborn.

Lyn: I'm *not* being stubborn.

Daryl: Are you sure?

Lyn: Yes.

Daryl: I don't think you're even trying to see my point of view.

Lyn: I can see it, but I don't see why when you ask me to go out for the first time, I don't see why *I* should have to pay.

Daryl: Yes, I can see what you're saying there, but you're not seeing my point. If I had taken you out say three or four times, maybe the fifth time you could pay your own way—and maybe pay my way, too.

Lyn: Well, maybe—because I'm starting to see your point about that fifth date, and if you come up say five or ten dollars short I could lend it to you. But otherwise, I'll stick to my point.

Daryl: It still seems that there's something you're thinking, but you're not really telling me about this issue . . . It seems like you're getting very upset with my point of view.

Lyn: I'm not upset with your point of view, it's just that you're stuck on one side and I'm stuck on the other. I would be willing to lean a bit, but . . .

Daryl: I'm trying to understand why women think that way— that's the reason I'm having this conversation with you. But it's a delicate issue because my money is always disappearing very quickly. I'm trying to get a better idea of how women think about having men take them out.

Lyn: A woman feels that she should be pampered to a certain extent when a man takes her out. If she gets this kind of pampering, she'll give it back—if you take me out for a certain amount of time, and I'm pleased with the way you've behaved, then you'll . . .

Daryl: Oh, so you're saying I'll get it back in ways other than monetary—I can understand that part . . .

Lyn: Maybe—we'll have to see how the relationship evolves.

Daryl: I'm happy that I had this time to talk about this issue with you, and I'm really trying to understand. I'm making an effort —when I get mad next time, I'll think it over two or three times! I'd like to discuss it further with you. Do you want to go to a movie with me Saturday night?

Lyn: Are you paying?

Daryl: We'll discuss that later!

Summary

We have discussed more than twenty-five basic interpersonal communication skills. The goal of this chapter was to synthesize those skills.

Interpersonal communication is effective when it achieves its conscious or unconscious goals. Most goals are related to meeting social needs and solving problems.

The effectiveness of any communication is a product of many factors, including ease of the goal, attitude of the participants, and nature of the setting. In this book the focus has been on the skill of the interpersonal communicator.

Effective interpersonal communication depends on a competent and behaviorally flexible communicator. Competence means showing the ability to accomplish the skills with at least some proficiency; behavioral flexibility means being able to choose the skill or skills that are most appropriate for the particular circumstances.

In addition to practicing your own skills, you can develop your effectiveness through analysis of interpersonal encounters. You can do an after-the-fact analysis of an encounter in which you were involved, or you can analyze encounters that you've witnessed or read.

Suggested Readings

Alton Barbour and **Alvin A. Goldberg.** *Interpersonal Communication: Teaching Strategies and Resources.* ERIC/RCS Speech Communication Module. New York: Speech Communication Association, 1974.

Arthur P. Bochner and **Clifford W. Kelly,** "Interpersonal Competence: Rationale, Philosophy, and Implementation of a Conceptual Framework," *The Speech Teacher,* Vol. 23 (November, 1974).

Part Three
ADAPTING SKILLS TO YOUR ENVIRONMENT

Chapter 11
Bridging Gaps between People

PAYOFFS *After you have read this chapter, you should be able to:*

1. *Discuss the three viewpoints on how sex-role differences develop.*
2. *Explain how socialization results in sex-role differences.*
3. *List and explain what men and women are doing to cope with changes in sex roles.*
4. *List and explain the functions communication serves in the family.*
5. *Discuss communication strategies for overcoming communication problems in the family.*
6. *Define culture.*
7. *List and explain the problems that lead to difficulties in cross-cultural communication.*
8. *Explain what can be done to bridge the gaps between cultures.*

When two people attempt to communicate, they must face the differences between them. Some of these differences—a few inches in height, a few pounds, hair color, perhaps a few years in age—are unlikely to affect communication significantly. Differences in religion, sex, race, income, and place of birth, however, can cause very real difficulties in communication. These important differences between people are called *gaps*.

If two people are able to focus on their similarities, they will probably find that whatever gaps exist between them are not particularly relevant. But if they focus on their differences, they will begin to grow apart. The further apart they get, the more difficulty they will have in finding a communication base. At some point they may have grown so far apart they feel themselves incapable of communicating.

In this chapter we want to look at means of bridging gaps in male-female, family, and cross-cultural communication. We'll begin with an analysis of male-female communication, a subject that has too long been ignored or made light of. Then we'll consider family communication. It may seem that communication in the family should come easily, but it often turns out to be very difficult. And finally, we'll turn to cross-cultural communication, perhaps the most difficult test of your mastery of inter-personal communication skills.

Male-Female Communication

A little girl who was playing in the park suddenly stopped, ran over to a bench, threw herself on it, and began to cry. Her playmate, seeing her crying, came over and gently asked, "Alexia, what's wrong?" The little girl looked up and shook her head sadly. "Never mind," she said, "you wouldn't understand." Her playmate persisted, "Sure I would. Tell me." But Alexia refused, saying, "No, you couldn't understand; you're a boy!"

What may have been bothering the little girl is hard to say. What we want to focus on here is her response to her male playmate: "You couldn't understand; you're a boy!" Like it or not, the biological sex of your communication partner often affects the transaction between you.

In this section we explore how sex and gender affect communication. We'll discuss why male and female behavior differs, we'll look at the role of socialization in male-female behavior, and we'll discuss how men and women are coping with changing sex roles.

Differences between Male and Female Behavior

The behavioral differences between men and women have been attributed to biology, to environment, and to a combination of both. Those who attribute the differences to biology hold that all differences in female and male behavior are genetic. For example, they would say that a woman's maternal behavior stems from an innate biological drive or instinct that men lack. The environmental viewpoint, by contrast, claims that the differences between female and male behavior result solely from differences in the social environments and experiences of the two sexes. In other words, if male and female infants could be reared exactly alike and as adults have the same experiences, they would behave alike. But because the two sexes are treated differently from birth, they behave differently.

The third, or interactionist, viewpoint is a compromise position. Interactionists say that the behavioral differences between women and men can best be explained by biologically determined tendencies reinforced by experience. Because most of the evidence and research supports this third position, we'll use it as the basis of our discussion.

Biological tendencies are the directions an organism tends to take because of the genes it inherits—if these genes can act unhindered. For example, a pine tree tends to grow straight and tall, but if the tree is growing in a crack in a rock, or in an area of strong prevailing winds, or in a bonsai artist's pot, it may end up short and twisted. An organism's tendency toward a certain behavior, then, does not guarantee that the behavior will occur. It is merely more *likely* to occur. What determines whether the behavior will occur is the organism's environment.

To use a human example, research has shown that throughout their lifetime males tend to be more aggressive than females. Does this mean that all males are aggressive? Does it mean that all men are more aggressive than all women? Certainly not. In fact, in some cultures the women are notoriously more aggressive than the men. In our culture, if a little boy acts aggressively and is rewarded (or at least not punished) for the aggressive behavior, then he is likely to develop what initially was just a tendency. If, however, the same little boy is punished for aggressive behavior, then the tendency will probably diminish as he learns what will and will not be accepted in a particular situation. Behavioral tendencies can be—and regularly are—modified by a person's family and society.

Socialization and Behavior

Most of the male-female differences that create communication problems are socialized (that is, environmentally conditioned) differences. In order to appreciate these differences let's briefly discuss how the socialization process teaches people their appropriate sex-role behavior.

If you look into the nursery of any American hospital, you may be able to see first-hand the beginning of the sex-role socialization process. You may be able to spot nurses picking up girls somewhat more gently than boys. At least one study shows that parents do so—and parents let their boy babies cry longer before picking them up and speak to them differently as well. Very young babies are often surrounded by toys that their parents believe are right for a child of that sex. A new father may buy his son a football, even though it will be six years or more before the child can begin to use it. Early on, a child's behavior is guided by what the parents think is appropriate to the child's sex.

As the child grows, the sexual indoctrination becomes more intense. Parents worry if their son plays with dolls or their daughter prefers cars and trucks. If these preferences persist, the children are often labeled deviant and firmly steered in the "proper" direction. Perhaps something like this happened to you.

Eventually a little girl learns that society expects her to be demure, quiet, passive, neat, caring, nurturing, and emotional. Likewise, a little boy comes to realize that society expects him to be strong, dominant, assertive, manually dexterous, persuasive, athletic, and in control of his softer emotions.

Although few people fit the stereotype perfectly, many have low opinions of themselves for deviating from it, even if they are living rich and congenial lives. A successful career woman may inwardly downgrade herself because she's aggressive and doesn't like to cook. A successful male kindergarten teacher or florist may believe himself incompetent because he can't fix a leaky faucet.

In addition to lowering the self-concepts of people who think they don't fit, sex-role stereotyping can keep individuals from developing their abilities to the fullest. The fastest and best-coordinated girl in the school may never become a star soccer player, for example, if she learns her passivity lessons too well.

Neither men nor women can develop their communication skills to the fullest as long as they are prisoners of the stereotypes. As we have seen, one important set of communication skills helps you to nurture other people and deal with emotion. Others help you present your own point of view clearly and firmly. Traditionally, the first set of skills is considered feminine, the second, masculine, and thus no one person is likely to develop them both—or at least not equally well. You see the costs of this rigidity every day.

Because the goal of communication is accurately shared meaning and sharing meaning accurately requires all possible communication skills, the key to communication effectiveness is behavioral flexibility. In other words, both men and women need to be able to step outside the stereotypes, acquire each other's traditional skills, and become well-rounded communicators.

Some of you are probably thinking, "I'm not locked into a rigid sex role, and neither are most of my friends. The old sex roles are changing." It is highly unlikely that you have fully escaped sex-role indoctrination, but you are right—sex roles are changing, for several reasons. First, the nature of our society's work is changing. In the past, many jobs required strenuous manual labor, but many of today's jobs require more brain power and less muscle power. Women can now compete for jobs that a few decades ago would have been physically impossible for them. For instance, with the increased use of power tools and lifts, more women are working as auto mechanics.

The second reason sex roles are changing is the widespread use of contraceptives. American family size has dropped drastically, which means that the average American woman is spending fewer of her years raising children. Moreover, she can choose which years they will be. As a result of both the technological advances and acceptance of contraception, more women are entering or returning to careers. This new reality is changing the nature of the relationships in families. When both adults work outside the home, then homemaking tasks that were traditionally the woman's responsibilities must be shared. Men are performing tasks new to them—and in many instances finding the family-centered work an interesting and stimulating experience.

Coping with Changes in Sex Roles

Now that we've seen how sex roles develop and how socialization affects male-female behavior, let's look at what men and women *can* do and *are* doing to cope with changing sex roles.

Acknowledging effects of conditioning on communication   One of the first things people can do and are doing is to acknowledge the effects of their early conditioning on their interpersonal communication. For example, it is hard for Mark to describe his feelings. Yet describing feelings, as you have learned, is one of the most important communication skills. Unless Mark is willing to probe his upbringing to find out why he is having difficulty developing this skill ("Be brave, Mark—big boys like you don't cry"), he may never integrate this particular skill into his behavior. Similarly, unless Mary understands that the socialization process has encouraged her to be passive ("Nice girls don't talk back, Mary"), she will find it hard if not impossible to learn to be assertive and stand up for herself.

You'll recall that effective communication occurs when meanings are shared. Sharing meaning requires the ability to empathize, and empathy results from common experience. Unfortunately, sex-role differentiation sees to it that women and men have all too few common experiences, which sometimes makes it hard for women and men to empathize with each other. For example, if Marge believes that any form of aggressiveness is unfeminine and therefore undesirable, she will probably have trouble being assertive when returning damaged merchandise to a store. In fact, she may dread this experience. If her husband, Bob, as is traditionally expected of men, has no trouble being assertive, he may not be able to empathize with Marge at all.

Similarly, many women complain that their boy friends, lovers, or husbands don't verbalize their affections. Often a woman feels unloved or unwanted because the man is unwilling to say, "I love you," often enough. Is it because he doesn't love her? More likely, he's simply filling the traditional male sex role that discourages men from expressing their feelings. Since the feminine sex role encourages expressing feelings, women often have trouble empathizing with silent men. These are only two of the many ways in which different sex-role orientations create meaning-sharing problems for women and men.

Examining dependency relationships   A second step people can take and are taking is to examine the dependency relationships that result from sex-role stereotypes. Because society values traditionally masculine behaviors more highly than feminine behaviors, men have a power advantage.[1] Under these circumstances, as you can imagine, a positive climate of equality is hard to establish in communication between women and men. A man who adopts a superior attitude toward a woman undermines the effectiveness of their communication.

The fact that society values masculine over feminine behaviors has ramifications for same-sex relationships as well. In our society, for example, Amy will probably cancel her plans to go shopping with Beth if Joe calls to say he'd like to stop by for lunch. Yet if Joe has plans to go out with his friend Tom, he probably will not cancel them to spend the eve-

[1]A research study of college students showed that both women and men saw more of the typically masculine traits as desirable. See Paul S. Rosenkantz et al., "Sex Role Stereotypes and Self-Concept in College Students," *Journal of Consulting and Clinical Psychology*, Vol. 32 (1968), pp. 287–295.

ning with Amy—even if she really wants to see him. Men's company is more valued than women's. Women sometimes jeopardize their relationships with other women to advance what they believe to be a more socially desirable relationship with a man. Since masculine behavior is more valued, however, men don't often risk same-sex friendships in this way.

Confronting sexist attitudes and behaviors   A third way to cope with changing sex roles is to become aware of and confront sexist attitudes and behaviors. Sexist behavior—or sexism—is any behavior, however insignificant it may seem, that is negative and results solely from differences in sex. Sexism limits both women and men to rigid, stereotypic roles. Sexist attitudes and behaviors are seen not only in men's behavior toward women, although such attitudes and behaviors are under heaviest attack because of the economic and social disadvantages they cause women in a society where men have more power. Sexism is also seen in attitudes men have about how other men should behave, attitudes women have about men, attitudes women have about other women, and the accompanying behavior. For example, many women never think of paying their own way on a date. That is sexist. Similarly, many women believe that *all* women should stay home with small children. That is sexist. Likewise, many men believe women have no place in the executive suites of corporate America unless they have a memo pad or a vacuum cleaner in their hands. That is sexist. Some men feel that a man (but not a woman) who cries is weak. That too is sexist.

Very few people escape all sexist attitudes and behaviors. By becoming aware of yours, you can guard against frustrating communication by automatically assuming that other people feel and act the same way you do. You can also guard against saying or doing things that offend other people and perpetuate outdated sex roles.

The language we use often reflects sexist attitudes. A man who refers to his fifty-year-old female office assistant as "my girl" is using sexist language. Although language reflects reality, you should remember from the discussion of the Sapir-Whorf Hypothesis in Chapter 3 that language also *affects* reality. Those who wish to avoid sexism in language use champion the development of non–sex-based terminology. They want the word *chair* or *chairperson* or *presiding officer* to replace *chairman*. They prefer *mail carrier* or *letter carrier* to *mailman*, *firefighter* to *fireman*, *police officer* to *policeman*. Is all this concern with language important? We believe it is. Since the language that you use affects the way you think, the use of sex-neutral terms will help you realize that roles are changing. Using them will also enable you to discuss ideas and issues with anyone without fear of offense.

Not only individual words but also some of our common expressions can be offensive: "You're acting like a little old lady," or "Well, what can you expect; he's a man, isn't he?" These familiar expressions are based not on information about any one person but rather on generalizations about all women or all men—in other words, stereotypes. As such, they are harmful to accurate and meaningful communication.

Monitoring the tendency toward dominance or passiveness   A final step is to monitor sex-role–based tendencies toward communication dominance or passiveness. If as a normal part of your sex role you tend to assume either an obviously dominant or an obviously passive communication role, then you are likely to create defensiveness in your communication partners. Remember, a good communication climate results in part from equality, which is impossible to achieve if one person is dominant.

A climate of equality makes people more willing to accept nontraditional sex-role behaviors. Even though more and more women hold nontraditional jobs, many people still have trouble acknowledging their right to do so. Men who pursue nontraditional jobs may have even more trouble getting accepted. "Househusband" is all too often a term of ridicule. It does not matter whether you personally wish to lead a nontraditional life. What does matter is this: If you want successful interpersonal communication, you must be willing to accept behavior that is different from your own.

Communication Session

Reflection

1. Try to remember specific incidents in your life when other people taught you what behavior was appropriate for your sex.
2. Which of the communication skills have you had the most trouble learning? Is it a sex-inappropriate one?

Practice

1. Working in pairs, have one person begin, "Girls should be . . ." and the other person finish the sentence. Repeat until the first person cannot think of any more endings, then switch roles. When both persons have had a chance to say what girls should be, start over with "Boys should be . . ." After this is done, two pairs could form a group to discuss individual reactions to the exercise.
2. In mixed-sex groups discuss your personal histories. When did you first notice that boys acted differently from girls? How did this affect your relationship with boys or girls?

Discussion

In groups of four to six brainstorm a list of "famous old sayings" on sex roles (example: "Big boys don't cry"). Take a poll in class to determine which of the sayings seemed to be the most commonly heard. As a class, discuss your reactions to these sayings when you first heard them. Discuss your reactions to them now.

Family Communication

What is the most important group you belong to? If your answer takes into account the effect of that group on your growth and development, the most important group you belong to is your family. What you are, how you behave toward yourself and others, and the plans and hopes you have for the future are very much a product of your interaction with your family. Yet of course you are not a member of your family by choice. Children do not select their parents, and a child has little if anything to say about whether she or he will have brothers or sisters. Humans spend the most important years of their lives with a group of people that they have not chosen to be with.

In this section we'll discuss the nature of communication in the family and the importance of communication for the family members, and finally we'll suggest some strategies for overcoming family communication problems.

The Nature of Families

The family is a basic social unit composed of people with dependency relationships characterized by unequal power distributions. (You will recall our discussion of power and dependency relationships in Chapter 8.) Some of these dependencies are obvious: The infant is dependent on the other family members for food, warmth, and clothing. Other family dependencies are not as obvious: the family members depend on certain individuals (usually one or both parents) to provide income; the family members depend on others for transportation, clean clothes, love, and affection, to name but a few of the dependencies.

Because of these dependencies, the distribution of power within the family is unequal. Society gives parents legitimate power over their children, and since parents usually control the family budget and are physically larger than their children, they have considerable reward and coercive power. Older children often have great amounts of coercive and referent power over their younger brothers and sisters as well as the legitimate power given them by the parents. Within any family with children, then, some of the members will have more power than others. Family communication is often strongly influenced by these dependencies and the power distribution they give rise to.

The Importance of Family Communication

Communication within the family unit is critical to the individual members. This communication serves at least four major purposes: (1) the family is primarily responsible for self-concept formation in children; (2) the family is the primary source for validating an individual member's self-worth; (3) family communication is the source of family cohesiveness, which ensures its survival; (4) the family members in high power positions serve as models of behavior for other family members. As we'll see, these purposes entail certain responsibilities.

In Chapter 2, The Perceptual Base of Communication, we discussed the relationship between self-concept and communication. An individual's self-concept is well-established by the time he is a teenager. It has been formed mostly by feedback from other family members. The years during which the self-concept is formed are crucial to a person, yet, unwittingly at times, family members will say things that are damaging to developing self-concepts.

Statements that *tease, blame,* and *evaluate* are particularly damaging to children. Teasing questions like, "How are you today, clumsy?" or "Still sucking your thumb, eh? Are you going to be doing that when you're twenty-one?" or "Look at George with his doll—you going to grow up to be a mother, George?"; blaming statements like, "You know, if I didn't have to raise you, I could be back at college" or "No, *you* didn't drop the plate, but your constant whining made me so nervous that I dropped it"; and evaluations like, "Terry, why are you trying to make breakfast? You know you can't even boil water" or "Marty, didn't you learn how to add? If what you want to do in life involves numbers, you'd better think of a different profession" are all negative. Statements like these are stored in a child's mind and may be played back over and over until the child believes them. An occasional negative statement like the ones quoted may not have any lasting effect, but if the family's normal communication style is negative teasing, blaming, and evaluating, damaged self-concepts are likely to result.

One of the first communication responsibilities that family members have to one another is to make statements, especially to young children, that contribute to the development of strong self-concepts. Statements of praise like, "Jim, you really did a nice job of cleaning your room" or "Betty, that's one of the best pictures you've painted"; statements of acceptance and support like, "If you have good reasons to drop out of the Glee Club, we accept your decision" or "Andy doesn't see eye to eye with us, but he's welcome in our home because he's your friend, and we respect that," and statements of love like, "Bart, I know it hurts to play poorly in front of your family, but we love you and we'll be here again next game" or simply "We both love you very much, Tom" can do a great deal to enhance a person's self-concept.

A second major communication responsibility in families is to validate (to confirm the worth of) individual members. The importance of this responsibility cannot be overstated. Your family is (usually) made up of the people with whom you feel safest, and you often turn to them when you need to be praised, comforted, and reassured. Yet, in many families this important responsibility is forgotten in the rush of day-to-day living.

Consider this family of four. Arthur, the father, works as a sales representative. Martha, the mother, divides her day between working in the home and a part-time job in a social service agency. The two children, Julia and Jack, are in school all day. Each person thinks that what he or she is doing is important; each person suffers the stresses and strains that affect his or her feelings; and each person needs validation, confirmation, and support.

Picture the following situation. Julia, the daughter, had a great day at school. She won a prize for having the neatest desk and she also got an A on an arithmetic test that she had been worried about. She needs to share her pleasure and have it validated. Jack, her brother, tells her he has better things to do than to listen to his kid sister, so Julia plans to share this important news with her mother. "Mom," she shouts as she bursts through the door, "I won a prize for the neatest desk and I got an A on the arithmetic test!" Mom, who did *not* have such a great day—the federal grant proposal she had worked on for two months was denied, and the meat that was supposed to be tonight's dinner still lies in the freezer—replies, "Fine, Julia—listen, will you go play in your room? I've got to work something out for dinner." Julia waits until her father comes home. As he walks through the door, Julia says, "Dad, I got a prize for . . ." "That's great, Julia," he interrupts, "you'll have to tell me about it later, but right now I have to make a phone call." Slowly Julia walks into her room, picks up her old worn teddy bear, and begins to tell him her news.

Everybody in the family needs support and validation. In this case, perhaps Julia needed it most. When a person can't get this validation within the family, he or she may go outside the family. This brings up a third and closely related function of communication between family members: to develop and maintain the cohesiveness that ensures the family's survival as a unit. Today one in every four marriages ends in divorce. Although some divorces are unavoidable, many of them *might* have been avoided had the family members been able and willing to communicate openly throughout their relationship. Divorce, however, is not the only threat to family cohesiveness. Each year more and more children are running away from the family or psychologically withdrawing from family life. Again, the causes are many, and again some of the problems could be solved by more open communication within the family.

The fourth function of communication within a family is that family members in high power positions serve as models of behavior for other family members. Parents, especially, serve as models, whether they want to or not. The saying, "Do as I tell you, not as I do" just doesn't work—it breeds only hypocrisy. If Julia sees her mother carefully describing how she feels, Julia will be more likely to describe her feelings openly. If Jack sees his father freely disclosing when he has made a mistake, Jack will be more inclined to admit his mistakes. How many times do we hear a family member lament, "I don't understand Tim's or Betty's behavior," when that behavior is much the same as another family member's?

Improving Communication within the Family

As we have looked at the nature of the family and at the importance of communication within the family, we have already made some suggestions for bridging gaps within the family. Now we analyze four specific communication behaviors that can further efforts at bridging those gaps.

1. *Open the lines of communication.*   Whether because of unequal power distribution or concern with personal problems or one of many other possible reasons, lines of communication within a family are often scrambled or broken. Sometimes members of a family can feel the communication isolation. Think of the typical day in your household. Discounting requests and orders from parents ("Clean up your room," or "Don't play the stereo so loudly"), how many minutes each day do you spend interacting with each of the other members of your family?

Perhaps the best time for families to spend together is during the evening meal. But the rush of busy lives and the ever-present television set—which competes for the attention of the family even when they are

A family should set aside some time each day to get together and talk.

physically together—threaten the evening meal conversation. Family members often spend more time in conversation with people outside the home than they do with their husbands, wives, children, brothers or sisters.

Opening lines of communication begins with setting up time for communication. A family should set aside some time each day to get together and talk. Each member of the family needs and should have the opportunity to talk about what happened to him or her that day. Maybe it is difficult to have a family hour every day of the week, but there should be some time set aside at least a few days each week when everyone can share ideas and experiences.

2. *Confront the effects of power imbalances.* If lines of communication within a family are open, then it is possible to identify and confront the family power imbalances and the inequities they may be causing.

Let's look at some typical family power imbalances. In most families older children are given more responsibilities than younger children. For instance, the oldest child may be given the responsibility of caring for the younger children. A power imbalance has been created: the younger child may be placed in the position of having to please three "parents"— mother, father, and an older brother or sister. If the demands of all three are in accord, there is usually little problem. If, however, the older sibling begins to abuse the power relationship, the younger sibling may react by becoming hostile or withdrawn.

Along with the legitimate power that parents give the oldest child, he or she usually has a great deal of referent power for the younger brothers and sisters. Referent power imbalances occur between two children when one of the children will go to almost any length to please the other (usually older) child. For instance, Todd, a younger child, often accepts abusive treatment from his older brother, Mark, since during that time Todd at least has the "privilege" of being with Mark.

In many families children are not treated equally. The parents may realize that one of the children has certain gifts or talents that the others do not have, so the parents give this child privileges that the others do not enjoy. Occasionally a parent simply makes a mistake and treats the children unequally because one child is more demanding or because the parent has forgotten how he treated the other children under similar circumstances.

If lines of communication are open, the power imbalances and their effects can be confronted. First, parents can explain *why* they are behaving as they are. Too often parents rely on their authority: "Why should you be in by 10:30? Because I said so, that's why!" If parents will level with their children and give them reasons for their behavior, then children will get into the habit of leveling with their parents. A child will feel free to ask why an older brother's rules are different from a parent's rules or why George got to drive the family car when he was sixteen but Matthew is denied such permission.

3. *Recognize change in family members.*   Members of a family know each other so well that they can often predict how a particular family member will think, feel, or act under many different circumstances. However, these predictions will not always be accurate. All people change with time—family members included. This change in family members is likely to be gradual. It isn't until Todd goes away to camp for six weeks that another member of the family is likely to recognize the changes that have been taking place in him over the last year.

Even as children grow and change, their brothers and sisters—and especially parents—continue to see them as they once were, not as they are or are becoming. How often is a younger member of the family likely to hear such statements as, "Don't tell me you like asparagus—remember I'm your brother—I know you" or "You're going to be a doctor! Come on, you faint at the sight of blood." The skill of dating is an important one for members of a family to master. It may well be true that Maggie didn't like asparagus or that Ginger used to faint at the sight of blood, but as the years go by, Maggie and Ginger change.

4. *Care more.*   Perhaps the most important recommendation for improving communication within the family is for members of the family to care about each other just a bit more. Chapter 5 discussed the importance of empathy and the fact that people need people. Yet, family communication can often be marked by indifference or apathy.

Too often individual family members are concerned with what is important to them and do not consider the feelings of others. For instance, in our story about Julia coming home with a prize for having the neatest desk, the first reaction of some members of the family might be "Big deal—an award like that is not important." But such an award might have been very important to Julia. Moreover, if other family members recognize what she thinks is important, perhaps she'll return the favor.

Communication Session

Reflection

Think about your family. Analyze the power relationships between you and (a) your mother or father, (b) your siblings, or (c) your children. How do these dependencies affect your communication?

Practice

1. Select an actual problem you are having with a member of your family. With another member of the class, role-play this problem. Try to use confronting, dating, or caring as a means of attempting to resolve this problem.

2. Develop an action plan for increasing the time your family spends communicating. Remember, you needn't try to schedule any one large block of time. Are there times for increasing communication with any member of the family that you have not pursued?

Cross-Cultural Communication

We have been discussing some of the problems that are caused by gaps between males and females and between members of a family. But certainly the largest and most difficult gap to bridge is that between people from different cultures.

Why do most people overreact to cultural differences? Mostly because differences represent unknown quantities. The more different one person is from another, the less either is able to predict the behavior of the other. When a person does not believe he knows how another person will behave, fear is a probable result. Some people respond to fear by withdrawing, some become compliant, and others mask their fear with aggressive behavior.

Many of the problems that arise when people from different cultures meet are communication problems. In this section we want to examine the concept of culture, look at some of the problems that make cross-cultural communication so difficult, and then discuss a plan for bridging gaps between people from different cultures.

The Concept of Culture

A culture is a system of shared beliefs, values, symbols, and behaviors that characterize a group. Each nation of the world contains cultures that differ from our own. Some, like Canada to our north and England across the Atlantic, have a culture much like the dominant white American culture. On the other hand, the cultures of the Middle East, black Africa, the Far East, and even Mexico right across our southern border are so different from our own that communication can be difficult.

You don't have to cross national borders to encounter different cultures. Every dominant culture contains subcultures, groups both large and small that maintain their individual cultural identities. The United States has been called a melting pot of people and cultures, but since "melting pot" implies a total assimilation, our nation is anything but a melting pot. This nation is more accurately described as one with a large, dominant white American culture within which are major subcultures, including black American, Mexican-American, Hispanic-American, Oriental-American, native American, Appalachian, and others.

When we speak of cross-cultural communication, then, we are not speaking just of international communication. We are also speaking of communication between and among groups of Americans.

Major Problems That Lead to Cultural Gaps

In this section we want to consider some of the major problems that make it difficult for people from different cultures to communicate effectively. Communication across cultures can be helped (1) by recognizing when one of the problems exists or is likely to exist and (2) by consciously attempting to overcome the problem.

Stereotyping and prejudice   We link these two problems because one follows from the other. As we noted in Chapter 2, when we characterize another person on the basis of the category or group to which that person belongs, we are stereotyping him. For instance, Tom has certain beliefs about Muslims. He discovers that a man he has just met is a Muslim. Tom would be stereotyping the person if he reacted to him on the basis of his beliefs about Muslims rather than on the basis of how the individual behaved.

Prejudice is an unjustified attitude toward a person or group. Moreover, a prejudiced person is likely to continue to maintain his prejudices even in the light of evidence that disproves them. Roy, a black man, may stereotype all whites as racist. When Roy meets Phil, a white man, Roy will believe that Phil is racist. Later, if Roy is confronted with evidence showing that Phil's behavior is not racist, Roy may refuse to acknowledge the evidence or may reject the source of the evidence. Then we would say that Roy was prejudiced.

Stereotyping is a shortcut in thinking. By developing an attitude or belief about an entire group and then applying that attitude to every member of the group, a person no longer has to consider the potential for individual differences. The stereotypic view applies to all. It provides some people with a certain comfort to believe that blacks are lazy, Italians are naturally hot-headed, Arabs are so emotional they're incapable of reasoning, and white Americans are racist. When the person meets a black, an Italian, an Arab, or a white American, the person already "knows" how to treat the new acquaintance.

One form of stereotyping that causes major problems in cross-cultural communication is racism. Racism is any behavior, however insignificant it may seem, that results solely from racial stereotyping. Do you believe anything or behave in any way that is racist? Remember, the behavior may seem insignificant. For instance, leaving more space between you and another person on a bus, on a plane, in a lounge, or at a counter in a restaurant—a space wider than the space you would leave if the person you were sitting next to were of your race, is racist behavior. Telling jokes, listening to jokes, or encouraging repetition of jokes that demean people of other races is racist behavior. Ignoring the presence of another person when that person is of another race is racist behavior. You may say, "But I didn't *mean* anything by what I did"; if, however, your behavior is perceived as resulting from racial stereotyping, it will be perceived as racist and seriously harm attempts to communicate.

Stereotyping, prejudice, and racism are hard to overcome because (1) a person can always find someone who will conform with his or her preconceived attitudes and (2) the person is likely to ignore any information or discount the source of any information that is counter to the attitude. Still, the only way to fight these attitudes is with accurate information. If a person is confronted with enough information over a long enough period of time, his or her attitude can be changed.

Basic premises   Although we may not think about it very much, nearly everyone has certain beliefs that he thinks are self-evident. In the dominant white American culture, the belief that people have a "right to life, liberty, and the pursuit of happiness" is one of the basic premises on which American values rest. Basic premises tie into or form the bases for our value systems.

What happens when an American encounters a Taoist from Asia who believes that human life is conditioned and unfree and that only when a person recognizes this limitation and makes himself dependent upon the harmonious and beneficent forces of the cosmos does he achieve success? The two are deadlocked from the start. They have a conflict of values resulting from different basic premises.

Such a difference can be resolved (or at least understood) if each person takes the time to explain the basis of his beliefs. Then through describing feelings, perception checking, paraphrasing, and questioning, the people can at least gain an understanding of each other's positions.

Role and role prescription   When a person interacts with a person from another culture, both people might expect that they will view role relationships the same way, but roles differ between and among cultures. If one person is identified as a professor, a minister, or a doctor, the other person may have expectations based on preconceived notions of the roles these positions symbolize in his or her particular culture. *Before* making any assumptions, a person should determine whether the preconceived notions are in fact valid.

In our own society we are having conflict over the roles of the mother and father in raising children. Why should we expect people from another culture to see things as we do when we are having conflicts among ourselves? Before getting too deeply involved with a person on the issue of preschool education, for instance, we should be careful that we have some understanding of what the role of father or mother has to do with education of children within that culture.

Language   Language can obviously be a barrier to communicating across cultures. It is, however, a particularly interesting barrier to examine. When two people speak a different language, they expect to have some problem communicating and seem to take extra care to keep that barrier from becoming insurmountable. Language becomes a greater barrier when two people speak the same language, because they are likely to believe they mean the same things when they use the same words. When one person says that his government wants what is best for the nation, it would seem that people should have no difficulty understanding what is meant. Yet "best for the nation" can and does mean many different things, depending on basic premises, role prescription, and other factors. When someone from another culture uses a word and you perceive that word as particularly important to understanding, you should take the time to get examples so that you can be sure of what the person means.

Nonverbal elements   Time, space, facial expression, gesture, and posture may be used quite differently in one culture than in another. Since nonverbal communication is not coded to the extent that verbal communication is, the meanings we think we get may be very different from the meaning intended, if in fact *any* meaning was intended.

One nonverbal element that can be a problem is time. White Americans see promptness as a sign of interest in work, but often black Americans, Hispanics, Japanese, and people from many other cultures see promptness from a different perspective. For instance, to black Americans a designated time may be considered an approximation rather than a set time.[2] Edward Hall has done extensive research to show the link between views of time and culture.[3]

Space also reflects differences in cultures. People around the world have different attitudes about what is an appropriate personal distance. For instance, we Americans consider the space of up to a foot or eighteen inches from our bodies as intimate space—we do not expect people to violate that space. In the Middle East, however, men will seek to get much closer to other men when they are talking. When an Arab talks with an American, one of the two is likely to be uncomfortable. Either the American will experience a territorial invasion or the Arab will feel himself at an uncomfortable distance for serious conversation.

---

[2] Arthur L. Smith, *Transracial Communication* (Englewood Cliffs, New Jersey: Prentice-Hall, Inc., 1973), pp. 31–32.
[3] Edward Hall, *The Silent Language* (Garden City, N.Y.: Doubleday, 1959).

The cultural differences in the meaning of facial expression, gesture, and movement are too numerous even to begin to discuss here. For instance, cultures differ widely on the amount of emotional expression they will permit in their communication.[4]

Because of these nonverbal differences, description of behavior and perception checking should precede any assignment of meaning to the nonverbal communication of people from different cultures. As we pointed out earlier, these should also become an important part of your communication style with people from your own culture!

A Program of Bridge Building between People from Other Cultures

Building bridges between cultures is desirable both for the society as a whole and for its individual members. As the world continues to shrink, effective cross-cultural communication becomes crucial to the survival of all people. To make headway in bridging cross-cultural differences, you will need to take the following steps:

1. *Be personally committed.*   If you care, if you understand the importance of cross-cultural communication, you will increase your chances for success.

2. *Be willing to work.*   Understanding different cultures is not easy. It takes time and energy. You may find that the attitudes and behaviors that have become a part of your value system over the years are being seriously challenged. You must be open to ideas different from your own, and you must be willing to listen.

3. *Be able to use all available skills.*   Throughout this book we have been trying to help you develop competence and behavioral flexibility. Overcoming cross-cultural differences will test your abilities to use these behaviors.

4. *Be willing to fail.*   Not all your attempts at cross-cultural communication will be successful. Sometimes they will fail because your skills are not yet developed enough. Other times failure will result because someone is trying to sabotage your efforts. The person you are trying to communicate with must try too. In your attempts to communicate, you will gain needed experience and learn to identify others who are willing to try.

Now let's consider specific communication strategies for overcoming cross-cultural differences.

---

[4]J. R. Davitz, *The Communication of Emotional Meaning* (New York: McGraw-Hill, 1964), p. 14.

1. *Work to widen your perspectives.*   You widen perspectives with information. When we spoke of perception in Chapter 2, we noted that people's perceptions of other people may be wrong. Perceptions of cultural characteristics are likely to be wrong as well.

One way to proceed is to learn all you can about the culture of the person with whom you want to or must communicate. A second and perhaps more stimulating way is to list your beliefs about that culture and its people and attempt to test them. By confronting some of your stereotypes and prejudices, you may achieve great success in widening your perspectives.

2. *Practice indexing statements.*   The secret to intercultural communication is to break through the barriers of stereotyping and prejudice. Widening perspectives is one step; using indexing is the second.

Remember that indexing is a verbal device for taking individual cases into account. You are going to find people of other cultures who are despicable, mean, racist, unsavory, untrustworthy, lazy, and every other negative adjective imaginable. But as long as you can deal with them as individuals and not as proof of class behavior, you will be well on your way toward improving your intercultural communication.

Communication Session

Reflection

List all the racial and cultural stereotypes you have heard. Now think of people you know who are in these stereotyped racial or cultural groups. Do they fit the stereotype? How does your communication behavior toward them differ from your communication behavior with people of your own cultural background?

Discussion

If your class does not include members of cultures other than white American, get in touch with an international students group on your campus and invite several members to join your class for a day. In groups of four to six, discuss how cultural differences create communication problems. Be sure to discuss the potential problem areas mentioned in this section of the chapter (and remember to use the appropriate communication skills).

How has your perception of cultural differences changed as a result of the discussion with people from other cultures? Will this changed perception alter your communication strategies when you next communicate with people from different cultures?

Summary

In this chapter we have looked at means of bridging differences in male-female, family, and cross-cultural communication.

Women and men often have trouble communicating because of the sex-role differences between them. These differences occur because of the interaction of biological factors and environmental ones. The sex-role differentiation results in a lack of the behavioral flexibility that is necessary for healthy communication.

Male-female communication can be improved by people acknowledging the effects of conditioning on communication, by examining dependency relationships, by confronting sexist attitudes and behavior, and by monitoring the tendency toward dominance or passiveness.

The family is the most important group that people belong to. What happens during a person's years of living with the family is likely to shape the rest of his or her life. Family communication is important because the family is primarily responsible for self-concept formation in the children, because the family members in high power positions serve as models of behavior for other family members, because the family is the primary source for validating individual members' self-worth, and because family communication is the major source of the family cohesiveness that ensures its survival as a unit.

Family communication is improved by opening lines of communication, by confronting the effects of power imbalances, by recognizing change in family members, and by caring.

Perhaps the most formidable communication gaps to bridge are cross-cultural. Some of the major problems in cross-cultural communication are stereotyping and prejudice, basic premises, role and role prescription, language, and nonverbal elements.

You can learn to improve your communication across cultures if you will be personally committed, willing to work, able to use all available skills, and willing to accept failure. Two of the most important strategies you can practice for improving your communication are to work to widen your perspectives and to practice indexing statements.

Suggested Readings

Kay Deaux. *The Behavior of Women and Men.* Monterey, California: Brooks/Cole Publishing Co., 1976.

Barbara Westbrook Eakins and **R. Gene Eakins.** *Sex Differences in Human Communication.* Boston: Houghton Mifflin Co., 1978.

Bobby R. Patton and **Bonnie Ritter Patton.** *Living Together . . . Female/Male Communication.* Columbus, Ohio: Charles E. Merrill Publishing Co., 1976.

Larry Samovar and **Richard E. Porter.** *Intercultural Communication: A Reader,* 2d ed. Belmont, California: Wadsworth Publishing Co., 1976.

Virginia Satir. *Peoplemaking.* Palo Alto, California: Science and Behavior Books, 1972.

Carol Tavris and **Carole Offir.** *The Longest War: Sex Differences in Perspective.* New York: Harcourt Brace Jovanovich, 1977.

Sven Wahlroos. *Family Communication.* New York: Macmillan Publishing Co., 1974.

Chapter 12
Small Group Communication

PAYOFFS   *After you have read this chapter, you should be able to:*

1. *Distinguish among questions of fact, value, and policy.*
2. *Analyze a problem.*
3. *Brainstorm for solutions.*
4. *Discuss how to choose among possible solutions.*
5. *Solve a problem using the problem-solving method.*
6. *Differentiate among authoritarian, democratic, and laissez-faire leadership.*
7. *Discuss the assets and liabilities of each leadership style.*
8. *Plan an agenda.*
9. *Apply the leadership skills of directing the flow of discussion, questioning, and summarizing.*
10. *Discuss the characteristics of responsible contribution.*
11. *Explain how you can ensure objectivity of approach.*
12. *Identify and explain the task roles.*
13. *Identify and explain the maintenance roles.*
14. *Help someone who is fulfilling negative roles to start fulfilling positive ones.*

Do you belong to a fraternal, governmental, or religious group? Have you ever worked on a committee of such a group? Has a professor ever divided your class into groups for some class project? Your answer to at least one of these questions is likely to be "yes." The fact is that some of our most important communication time occurs in groups.

In this chapter we'll focus on those communication skills that are essential for the smooth functioning of a work group. We are defining a *work group* as a small unit whose members interact face-to-face and who strive toward a common goal. The size recommended for an effective group varies, but many researchers set five to eight members as ideal. The type of goal for which a group strives also varies: a family may gather to plan a vacation; a student committee handles details of a campus concert series; a board of directors sets policy for a major corporation. Yet for each of these groups to succeed, its members must not only use the skills we have discussed so far, they must also be able to understand and use the problem-solving method; there must be effective leadership; and participants must be able to fill necessary role functions.

Preparation for Problem-Solving Group Work

If a group is to be successful, it must be able to use the problem-solving method of stating the problem, analyzing the problem, suggesting solutions, and selecting the best solution.

Stating the Problem

In many groups, much wheel-spinning takes place during the early stages of group discussion. Much of it results from members' questions about the function, purpose, or goal of the group. As soon as possible, the group should decide exactly what it is going to be doing. It is the duty of the person, agency, or parent group that forms a particular work group to give the group specific responsibility for solving a problem. For example, a group may be formed for the purpose of "determining the nature of the spring social" or "preparing a guideline for hiring at a new plant." If the responsibility is not this clear, it is up to the group leader or representative to find out exactly why the group was formed and what its goals are. If stating the problem is up to the group, then the group should move immediately to get it down on paper; until everyone agrees what they have to do, they will never agree on how to do it.

Problems may be stated as questions of fact, questions of value, and questions of policy.

1. *Questions of fact.*   These consider the truth or falsity of an assertion. Implied in the question is the theoretical possibility of verifying the answer. For instance, "Does cigarette smoking cause cancer?" is a question of fact because the relationship between smoking and cancer can be measured. "Is Smith guilty of robbery?" is also a question of fact; either Smith committed the crime or he did not.

2. *Questions of value.*   These consider relative goodness or badness. They are characterized by the inclusion of some evaluative word such as *good, cool, reliable, effective, worthy.* The purpose of the question of value is to compare a subject with one or more members of the same class. "Who is the best lecturer on campus?" is a question of value. Although you can set up criteria for "best" and measure your choice against those criteria, there is no way of verifying your findings. The answer is still a matter of judgment, not a matter of fact. "Is John Denver's music superior to Bob Dylan's?" "Is a small-college education better than a large-college education?" are both questions of value.

3. *Questions of policy.*   These questions call for decisions as to whether future actions should be taken. The question is phrased to arrive at a solution or to test a tentative solution to a problem. "What should we do to lower the crime rate?" seeks a solution that would best solve the prob-

lem of crime. "Should the university give equal amounts of money to men's and women's athletics?" provides a tentative solution to the problem of how we can achieve equity in financial support of athletics. The inclusion of the word *should* in all questions of policy makes them the easiest to recognize and the easiest to phrase of all problems.

Analyzing the Problem

Once the group is in agreement about exactly what the problem is, it should move on to the next step, analyzing the problem. *Analysis* means determining the nature of the problem: its size, its causes, the forces that create or sustain it, and the criteria for evaluating solutions. Sometimes analysis takes only a few minutes; at other times it may take longer. Both in preparation for problem solving and in the discussion itself, analysis is too often ignored because most groups want to move directly to possible solutions. For instance, if your problem is to determine what should be done to solve the campus parking problem, you may be inclined to start by listing possible solutions immediately. Because this procedure sounds logical, the tendency is then to pursue these prematurely offered solutions. However, a solution or a plan can work only if it solves the problem at hand. Before you can shape a plan, you must determine what obstacles the solution must overcome and what obstacles the solution must eliminate, as well as whom your plan has to satisfy. Before you even begin to suggest a solution, you should check to make sure that the following questions about the problem have been answered:

I. *What is its size and scope?*

   A. *What are its symptoms? (What can we identify that shows that something is wrong or needs to be changed?)*

   B. *What are its causes? (What forces created it, sustain it, or otherwise keep it from being solved?)*

II. *What criteria should be used to test the solution? Specifically, what checklist must the solution meet to best solve this problem? Must the plan eliminate the symptoms, be implemented within present resources, and so on?*

Suggesting Possible Solutions

Most problems have many possible solutions. Although you need not identify every one of the possibilities, you should not be content with your work until you have considered a wide variety of solutions. If you are considering a problem that needs only a "yes" or "no" solution, your procedure may be simple. Should financial support for women's sports be increased? This question has only two possible answers.

How do you come up with solutions? One way is to use *brainstorming* as a method of generating ideas. The procedure for brainstorming is to free-associate, that is, to state ideas as they come to your mind in random order until you have compiled a long list. In a good ten- to fifteen-minute brainstorming session, you may think of ten to twenty solutions by yourself. Depending on the nature of the topic, a group may come up with a list of a hundred possibilities in a relatively short time. Other possible solutions will come from your reading, your interviews with authorities, or your observation.

Selecting the Best Solution

If the group has analyzed the problem carefully and suggested enough possible solutions, then the final step involves only matching each proposed solution against the criteria. For instance, if you have determined that hiring more patrols, putting in closed-circuit TV, and locking outside doors after 9 P.M. are three possible solutions to the problem of reducing crime on campus, then you begin to measure each against the criteria. The one meeting the most criteria or that meets several criteria most effectively would then be selected.

Now let's put these all together with a sample (and somewhat abbreviated) outline that would help the group proceed logically. The group is being convened to discuss "meeting the needs of women on campus."

1. *State the problem—suggested wordings*

    What should be done to improve the status of women on campus?

    What should be done to increase opportunities for women on campus?

    What should be done to equalize social, athletic, and political opportunities for women on campus? [1]

2. *Analyze the problem of meeting the needs of women*
    I. *What is the size and scope of the problem?*
        A. *How many women are there on campus?*
        B. *What is the ratio of females to males on campus?*
        C. *What opportunities are currently available to women?*
            1. *What social organizations are there? What is the ratio of women to men who belong?*
            2. *Are women involved in political organizations on campus? To what extent?*

---

[1] Since the outline is made before the actual discussion, there is no guarantee that the remainder of the outline will relate entirely to the agreed-upon wording of the problem. As is illustrated by this example, however, outlining may anticipate group directions or at least serve as a valuable point of departure for the remainder of the discussion.

> 3. *What athletic opportunities are open to women? Intramural? Intercollegiate?*
>
> II. *What are the causes of the problem?*
>   A. *Do women feel discriminated against?*
>   B. *Does the institution discriminate?*
>   C. *Do societal norms inhibit women's participation?*
>   D. *Do certain groups discriminate against women?*
>
> III. *What criteria should be used to test solutions?*
>   A. *Will women favor the solution?*
>   B. *Will it cope with discrimination if discrimination does exist?*
>   C. *Will it be enforceable?*
>   D. *Will it comply with Title IX?*

3. *State possible solutions*
   (The list can only be started at this point—other possible solutions will be revealed as the discussion progresses.)

   A women's center should be initiated?

   A special-interest seat on all major committees should be given to women?

   Women's and men's athletic teams should be combined?

   (Others to be added.)

4. *Determine best solution*
   (To be completed during discussion.)

Communication Session

Reflection

Think of the last group with which you worked. Did the group follow the problem-solving method? If not, what steps were left out? What effect did leaving out steps have on the discussion? on the quality of the solution?

Practice

1. Label the following questions fact (F), value (V), or policy (P).

_____ 1. Is Ohio State the largest single-campus university in the United States?

_____ 2. Should the United States support any government that seeks to remain free of Communism?

_____ 3. Which computer costs the least to own and operate?

_____ 4. Is Sparky Anderson the best manager in the American League?

_____ 5. Should tuition be increased at Miller University next year?

2. Take one of the questions listed above. Outline the problem-solving method you would use to deal with this question.

Discussion

In your group of four to six people, discuss a plan for solving this problem: changing the foreign language requirements for graduation. Be sure to follow all the problem-solving steps.

Answers: 1. F; 2. P; 3. F; 4. V; 5. P.

Leadership in Problem-Solving Groups

A problem-solving group will not work well without effective leadership. Ordinarily, we think of a single appointed or elected individual as leader and all others in the group as contributors of content. A group can be so organized, however, that everyone shares the leadership. A group can have leadership whether or not it has a designated leader. In order to decide whether your group should vest leadership responsibilities in one person, you must understand the advantages and disadvantages of single and shared leadership.

When someone is appointed or elected leader, the group looks to that person for leadership. If he or she is a good leader, the group will benefit. Each participant can concentrate on considering the issues being raised, confident that the leader will guide the group justly. There are pitfalls in this kind of leadership. When the leader is unsure, the group may ramble about aimlessly; when the leader dominates, participants do not feel free to contribute spontaneously, and the discussion follows a path predetermined by the leader; when the leader is unskilled, the group can become frustrated and short-tempered. Good leadership is a necessity. When the appointed leader cannot provide it, the group suffers.

When the group is leaderless, everyone has the right and the obligation to show leadership. Ordinarily, leadership will emerge from one, two, or perhaps three members of the group. Because no one has been given the mantle of leadership, everyone is on equal footing, and the discussion can be more spontaneous. Disadvantages become evident in situations in which either no one assumes leadership or a few compete for leadership. In such situations the discussion becomes "leadershipless." Depending on the qualities of the participants, discussion by a leaderless group can arrive at good group solutions, or it can degenerate into rambling, meaningless chatter.

Because of its importance to group effectiveness, let's consider the question of leadership in greater detail by examining traits necessary for leadership, methods of gaining leadership, and styles of leadership.

Leadership Traits

There have been numerous research efforts to find those particular leadership traits that would enable us to predict leadership ability and account for leadership success. Modern researchers have largely abandoned the search for the simple reason that although some leadership traits have been identified, they are traits that are found in *all* people to varying degrees. Despite the conclusion that the trait approach to predicting leadership is futile, it may still be useful for us to examine those traits that are thought to be indicative of leadership.

Marvin Shaw, a leading authority in group research, found some correlation between individual traits and leadership measures.[2] The three traits cited are ability, sociability, and motivation. In group studies, he found that relative to ability, leaders exceed average group members in intelligence, scholarship, insight, and verbal facility. Relative to sociability, leaders exceed group members in such things as dependability, activity, cooperativeness, and popularity. Relative to motivation, leaders exceed group members in initiative, persistence, and enthusiasm. This does not mean that a person with superior intelligence, or the one who is most liked, or the one with greatest enthusiasm will necessarily be the leader. We believe it does mean that a person is unlikely to be the leader if he does not exhibit at least some of these traits to a greater degree than do those he is attempting to lead.

Do you perceive yourself as having any or many of these traits? If you see these traits in yourself, then you are a potential leader. Since several individuals in almost any grouping of people have the potential for leadership, determination of the one who ends up actually leading others depends on many things other than possession of these traits.

Who Will Attempt to Lead?

In a group or societal setting, a person is usually appointed or elected to act as leader. In an interpersonal setting, however, the struggle for leadership proceeds without benefit of election or appointment. In fact, those involved may not perceive that a struggle takes place. In settings in which one individual has high needs to control and the other has high needs to be controlled, leadership will be established with no struggle at all. In most interpersonal settings, however, leadership is shared,

---

[2]Marvin E. Shaw, *Group Dynamics* (New York: McGraw-Hill Book Company, 1971), p. 269.

switches back and forth, or develops into power struggles in which each party exercises his or her need or desire to lead.

To some extent, whether you will be permitted to lead again may well depend upon how you lead when you have the opportunity. Since leadership requires exerting influence, then how you lead may well depend upon whether this influence is a product of power, persuasion, or some combination. In effect, who will lead may well be a matter of style.

Leadership Styles

The collection of a person's behaviors is called *style*. In a pioneer study, Ralph White and Ronald Lippitt trained leaders to interact in one of three leadership styles: democratic, authoritarian, and laissez-faire.[3] The democratic leader may suggest specific policy, procedure, and tasks and/or roles for members, but this style of leadership allows the group to make the decisions. Group discussion is encouraged and assisted by the leader. Everyone is free to participate in appraisal of group efforts.

The authoritarian style calls for the leader to be the sole determinant of policy, procedure, and tasks and/or roles of members. The leader makes personal praise or criticism of individual contributions.

The leader who adopts the laissez-faire style does nothing but supply information and material when asked. He does not take part in or direct

Authoritarianism seems to create aggression and discontent.

[3]Ralph White and Ronald Lippitt, "Leader Behavior and Member Reactions in Three Social Climates," reprinted in Dorwin Cartwright and Alvin Zander (Eds.), *Group Dynamics*, 3rd ed. (New York: Harper & Row, 1968), pp. 318–335.

decisions of the group. The group has complete freedom in determining policy, procedure, tasks and/or roles of group members, and appraisal. Laissez-faire procedure is essentially nonleadership.

In summary, as you can see, democratic leadership involves participants in decision making, authoritarian leadership is largely dictatorial, and laissez-faire provides no leadership.

After training these leaders, White and Lippitt subjected several groups to the various styles and then analyzed the results. The following synopsis of White and Lippitt's conclusions also includes other research to verify, supplement, and occasionally modify their conclusions.[4]

1. *More work is done under a democratic leader than in a laissez-faire setting.*   For all practical purposes, laissez-faire leadership means no leadership at all. Whether you are seeking to lead another person or a group of people, laissez-faire style is least effective under all circumstances.

2. *More work is done under an authoritarian leader than under a democratic leader.*   Whether this finding is true most of the time or only some of the time is open to question. According to Shaw, either the authoritarian group is more productive or there is no significant difference.[5] This means that if the sole criterion is getting a job done, the democratic group is never more effective and is usually less so.

3. *Work motivation and originality are better under a democratic leader.*   Evidence for this conclusion is quite consistent. In a democratic group, the members have a greater sense of participation, and they feel as if they have been active in the decision-making process. As a result, under democratic leadership individual members are more likely to blossom. Not only is individual growth potential the greatest, but individuals feel better about the group process.

4. *Authoritarianism seems to create aggression and discontent.*   However, the discontent may not appear on the surface. Again, research continues to support this point. Notice that under an authoritarian leader members may not be very vocal with their discontent during the group process—in fact an authoritarian group often gives the impression of complete harmony. However, below-the-surface discontent usually manifests itself in other ways. It may be in grousing after the meeting about what took place in discussions; it may be in foot dragging in implementation stages of the proposal; it may be in abandonment of the decision if the going gets rough during implementation; it may be in just an indifference to or hostility about taking time to work with the group.

---

[4]White and Lippitt, "Leader Behavior," p. 334.
[5]Shaw, *Group Dynamics*, p. 274.

5. *There is more dependence and less individuality in authoritarian groups.* Democratic leadership may help the individual to blossom, but authoritarian leadership seems to stifle the individual. Because the authoritarian leader has power and is quick to exercise it, everyone looks to the leader to see what to do, how to do it. There is very little chance for individuals to take initiative. Moreover, if the leader is absent, the authoritarian group tends to flounder.

6. *There is more group-mindedness and more friendliness under a democratic leader.*   People enjoy the group process more when they work under a democratic leader. They often look forward to meetings, get caught up in the group action and become oblivious to time, and look back on the group activity as a positive experience.

This summary of White and Lippitt's study indicates that the researchers favor democratic leadership. True. However, there are times when the democratic style is inappropriate and may lead to chaos. Participatory democracy has its limits. For instance, during a closely contested basketball game, the coach who calls a time-out has one minute to help his players handle a particular defensive alignment the other team is using. He will not use his minute in democratic processes—asking his players if they have any ideas or suggesting a plan and giving the players the opportunity to evaluate it. He will tell the players how to proceed, make a substitution if he needs to, and give the players encouragement to do what he tells them. When the accomplishment of the task is or appears to be more important than the feelings of members, then authoritarianism may be appropriate. (This is not to say that a basketball coach or any other leader who adopts the authoritarian style for the moment can disregard group feeling.) As studies have shown, a job gets done as fast or faster and often with fewer errors under an authoritarian leader. Authoritarian leadership also seems to work well when the authority is much superior in knowledge and skill to the participants. Again, the basketball example bears this out. The coach is the coach because of what he knows—as long as the players respect his superior knowledge, they will work under the authoritarian style.

There is at least one other advantage of the authoritarian form of leadership—it is easier. Learning to be a good democratic leader sometimes ends in the frustrations of laissez-faire nonleadership. In other words, some people confuse being a democratic leader with not leading at all. Since there is little ambiguity in authoritarian leadership—the leader gives directions and the group follows them—it is far easier to understand and administer.

If authoritarian leadership appeals to you—and many authoritarian leaders do exist, are effective, and even win the approval of their groups—perhaps you should consider one other point. The best authoritarian model seems to be "benevolent dictatorship." If the authority arises out of the need to control—and perhaps even to crush dissent—authority leads to tyranny.

Our advice is that you examine your style very closely. What is your natural inclination? How has it worked in the past? Would it be useful to blend some of the characteristics of another style with what comes naturally to you? Remember, these categories are not necessarily hard and fast. Still, the style you adopt is yours. If you have determined your approach, now you must consider your leadership behavior.

Communication Session

Reflection

1. What is your leadership style? What are the strengths and weaknesses of that style?
2. Under which leadership style do you work best? Why?

Practice

Break into three groups. One person from each group should be elected leader. These three will report to the instructor to get further direction on what the group is to discuss and how it is to proceed.

Discussion

Discuss your group's functioning. How did the leader help or hinder your group's success?

Responsibilities of the Leader

Regardless of whether a leader is appointed or whether several members of the group share leadership, there are certain leadership responsibilities that must be met. In this next section, let's assume that you have or wish to assume the responsibilities of leadership.

Establishment of a Climate

As leader, your first job is to set up a comfortable physical setting that will encourage interaction. The leader is in charge of such physical matters as heat, light, and seating. Make sure the room is at a comfortable temperature. Make sure that there is enough lighting, and, most important, make sure the seating arrangements are conducive to spirited interaction.

Too often, seating is too formal or too informal for the best discussion. By "too formal," we mean board-of-directors style. Imagine the long polished oak table with the chairman at the head, leading lieutenants at right and left, and the rest of the people down the line. Since seating may be an indication of status, how the seating is arranged can facilitate or hamper real interaction. In the board-of-directors style, a boss-and-subordinates pattern emerges. People are unlikely to speak until they are asked to do so. Moreover, no one has a really good view of all the people present. However, an excessively informal seating may also inhibit interaction—especially if people sit together in small groups or behind one another.

The ideal is the circle. Everyone can see everyone else. At least physically, everyone has equal status. If the meeting place does not have a round table, you may be better off with either no table at all or a setting of tables that make a square at which the members can come close to the circle arrangement.

Planning the Agenda

A second responsibility of the leader is to plan the agenda. You should do this alone or in consultation with the group. When possible, the agenda should be in the hands of the group several days before the meeting. How much preparation any individual member will make is based upon many factors, but unless the group has an agenda beforehand, members will not have an opportunity for careful preparation. Too often, when no agenda is planned, the group discussion is a haphazard affair, often frustrating and usually unsatisfying.

What goes into the agenda? Usually a sketch of some of the things that need to be accomplished. In a problem-solving discussion, the agenda should include a suggested procedure for handling the problem. In essence, it is an outline form of the steps of problem solving discussed earlier in this chapter. So if you are leading a group concerned with integrating the campus commuter into the social, political, and extracurricular aspects of student life, the following would be a satisfactory agenda.

1. *How many students commute?*

2. *Why aren't commuters involved in social, political, and extracurricular activities?*

3. *What criteria should be used to test possible solutions to the problem?*

4. *What are some of the possible solutions to the problem?*

5. *What one solution or combination of solutions will work best to solve the problem?*

Directing the Flow of Discussion

The leader is responsible for directing the discussion. It is in this area that leadership skill is most tested. Let's examine carefully four of the most important elements of this responsibility.

Give everyone an equal opportunity to speak   Decisions are valid only when they represent the thinking of the entire group. However, in discussions, some people are more likely or more willing to express themselves than others. For instance, if a typical eight-person group is left to its own devices, two or three people may tend to speak as much as the other five or six together; furthermore, one or two members may contribute little if anything. At the beginning of a discussion you must operate under the assumption that every member of the group has something to contribute. To ensure opportunity for equal participation, those who tend to dominate must be held somewhat in check, and those who are content to observe must be brought into the discussion.

Accomplishing this ideal balance is a real test of leadership. If an ordinarily reluctant talker is embarrassed by another member of the group, he or she may become even more reluctant to participate. Likewise, if a talkative yet valuable member of the group is constantly restrained, he or she may lose value.

Let's first consider the handling of the shy or reluctant speaker. Often, apparently reluctant speakers want to talk but cannot get the floor. As leader you may solve this problem by clearing the road for that speaker. For instance, Mary may give visual and verbal clues of her desire to speak; she may move to the edge of her seat, she may look as if she wants to talk, or she may even start to say something. Because the reluctant speaker may often relinquish the opportunity if another, more aggressive person competes to be heard, you can help considerably with a comment such as "Just a second, Jim, I think Mary has something she wants to say here." Of course, if Mary is sitting back in her chair with a somewhat vacant look, such a statement would be inappropriate. A second method of drawing out the reluctant speaker is to phrase a question that is sure to elicit some answer and then perhaps some discussion. The most appropriate kind of question is one requiring an opinion rather than a fact. For instance, "Mary, what do you think of the validity of this approach to combating crime?" is much better than "Mary, do you have anything to say here?" Not only is it specific, but also it requires more than a "yes" or "no" answer. Furthermore, such an opinion question will not embarrass Mary if she has no factual material to contribute. Tactful handling of the shy or reluctant person can pay big dividends. You may get some information that could not have been brought out in any other way; moreover, when Mary contributes a few times, it builds up her confidence, which in turn makes it easier for her to respond later when she has more to say. Of course, there are times when some members do not have anything worth saying because they just are not prepared. Under such circumstances, it is best for you to leave them alone.

As a leader, you must also use tact with the overzealous speaker. Remember that Jim, the talkative person, may be talkative because he has done his homework—he may have more information than any other member of the group. If you turn him off, the group may suffer immensely. After he has finished talking, try statements such as, "Jim, that's a very valuable bit of material; let's see whether we can get some reactions from the other members of the group on this issue." Notice that a statement of this kind does not stop him; it suggests that he should hold off for a while. A difficult kind of participant to deal with is the one who must be heard regardless of whether he or she has anything to say. If subtle reminders are ineffective with this individual, you may have to say, "Jim, I know you want to talk, but you're just not giving anyone else a chance. Would you wait until we've heard everyone else on this point?" Of course, the person who may be the most difficult of all to control is the leader. Leaders often engage in little dialogues with each member of the group. They sometimes exercise so much control that participants believe that they can talk only in response to the leader.

There are three common patterns of group communication (see Figure 12-1, in which the lines represent the flow of discussion among the eight participants). Discussion *a* represents a leader-dominated group. The lack of interaction often leads to a rigid, formal, and usually poor discussion. Discussion *b* represents a more spontaneous group. Since three people dominate and a few are not heard, however, conclusions will not represent group thinking. Discussion *c* represents something

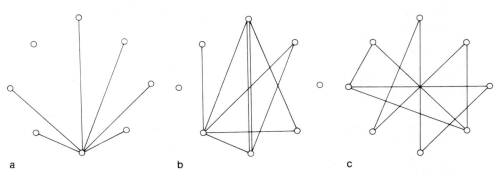

a   b   c

Figure 12-1

close to the ideal pattern. It illustrates a great deal of spontaneity, a total group representation, and—theoretically at least— the greatest possibility for reliable conclusions.

Ask appropriate questions   Although the members of any group bring a variety of skills, information, and degrees of motivation to the group, they do not always operate at peak efficiency without help from the leader. Perhaps one of the most effective tools of leadership is the ability to question appropriately. This skill requires knowing when to ask questions and knowing what kinds of questions to ask.

By and large, the leader should refrain from questions that can be answered "yes" or "no." To ask a group member whether he or she is satisfied with a point that was just made will not lead very far, for after the "yes" or "no" answer you must either ask another question to draw the person out or change the subject. The two most effective types of questions are those that call for supporting information and the completely open-ended question that gives the member complete freedom of response. For instance, rather than asking John whether he has had any professors who were particularly good lecturers, you could say, "John, what are some of the characteristics that made your favorite lecturers particularly effective?"

When to ask questions is particularly important. Although we could list fifteen to twenty circumstances, let's focus on four purposes of questioning.

1. *To focus the discussion.*   Individual statements usually have a point; the statements themselves relate to a larger point being made; and the general discussion relates to an issue or to an agenda item. You can use questions to determine a speaker's point or to determine the relationship of the point to the issue or agenda item; for instance, "Are you saying that the instances of marijuana leading to hard-drug use don't indicate a direct causal relationship?" Or, to what has just been said, "How does that information relate to the point that Mary just made?" Or, to ask about an issue or an agenda item, "In what way does this information relate to whether or not marijuana is a health hazard?"

2. *To probe for information.*   Many statements need to be developed, supported, or in some way dealt with. Yet often members of a group apparently ignore or accept a point without probing it. When the point seems important, the leader should do something with it. For instance, on a question of source, you can say, "Where did you get that information, Jack?" Or, to develop a point, "That seems pretty important; what do we have that corroborates the point?" Or, to test the strength of a point, "Does that statement represent the thinking of the group?" Or, to generate discussion, "That point sounds rather controversial—should we accept the point as stated?"

3. *To initiate discussion.* During a discussion there are times when lines of development are apparently ignored, when the group seems ready to agree before sufficient testing has taken place. At these times, it is up to the leader to suggest a starting point for further discussion. For instance, "OK, we seem to have a pretty good grasp of the nature of the problem, but we haven't looked at any causes yet. What are some of the causes?"

4. *To deal with interpersonal problems that develop.* Sometimes the leader can help a member ventilate very personal feelings. For instance, "Ted, I've heard you make some strong statements on this point. Would you care to share them with us?" At times, a group may attack a person instead of the information that is being presented. Here you can say, "I know Charley presented the point, but let's look at the merits of the information presented. Do we have any information that goes counter to this point?"

Questions by themselves are not going to make a discussion. In fact, some questions can hurt the discussion that is taking place. The effective leader uses questions sparingly but decisively.

Summarize frequently Often a group talks for a considerable period, then takes a vote on how the members feel about the subject. A good problem-solving discussion group should move in an orderly manner toward intermediate conclusions represented by summary statements seeking group consensus. For instance, on the question, "What should be done to lower the crime rate on campus?" the group would have to reach consensus on each of the following questions:

1. *What is the problem?*

2. *What are the symptoms of the problem? (Draw intermediate conclusion; ask whether group agrees.)*

3. *What are the causes? (Draw intermediate conclusion on each cause separately or after all causes have been considered; ask whether group agrees.)*

4. *What criteria should be used to test the solutions?*

5. *What is one criterion? (Draw conclusions about each criterion.)*

6. *What are some of the possible conclusions? (Determine whether all possible solutions have been brought up.)*

7. *What is the best solution?*

8. *How does each of the solutions meet the criteria? (Discuss each and draw conclusions about each; ask whether group agrees.)*

9. *Which solution best meets the criteria? (The conclusion to this final question concludes the discussion; ask whether all agree.)*

During the discussion the group might draw six, eight, ten, or even fifteen conclusions before it is able to arrive at the answer to the topic question. The point is that the group should not arrive at the final conclusion until each of the subordinate questions is answered to the satisfaction of the entire group.

It is up to the leader to point up these conclusions by summarizing what has been said and seeking consensus on a conclusion. Everyone in the group should realize when the group has really arrived at some decision. If left to its own devices, a group will discuss a point for a while, then move on to another before a conclusion is drawn. The leader must sense when enough has been said to reach a consensus. Then he must phrase the conclusion, subject it to testing, and move on to another area. You should become familiar with phrases that can be used during the discussion.

"I think most of us are stating the same points. Are we really in agreement that . . ." (State the conclusion.)

We've been discussing this for a while and I think I sense an agreement. Let me state it, and then we'll see whether it does summarize group feeling." (State the conclusion.)

"Now we're getting into another area. Let's make sure that we are really agreed on the point we've just finished." (State the conclusion.)

"Are we ready to summarize our feelings on this point?" (State the conclusion.)

Maintain necessary control   A leader must maintain control of the discussion. Remember, absence of leadership leads to chaos. Group members need to feel that someone is in charge. If the group has a set of formal rules, be sure that the rules are followed (at times bending is necessary, but total breaking does not help the group). As leader, remember that some members will be playing negative roles in the discussion; do not let them spoil the outcome. You are in charge. You are responsible. You have authority. You will need to exercise it on occasion for the benefit of the group. If John is about to talk for the fortieth time, it is up to you to harness him. If Jack and Mary are constantly sparring with each other, it is up to you to harmonize their differences. If something internal or external threatens the work of the group, it is up to you to deal with it. Also, when the group has solved its problem, end the discussion smoothly. Some discussion groups meet by time instead of by problem. Just because you are scheduled to discuss for an hour does not mean that you cannot stop in forty-five minutes if you have done the job.

Responsibilities of Group Members

Even the most successful leader will fail if the members of the group do not fulfill their responsibilities. Good discussion occurs when group members contribute responsibly, contribute objectively, perform positive task and maintenance roles, and avoid negative roles.

Members Should Contribute Responsibly

One of the greatest differences between a work group and an informal social group is in the quality of the developmental material included. Responsible decision making is characterized by documented factual material, careful analysis of every item of information, and sound conclusions and evaluations about and from the factual material. Let's examine each of these characteristics. Because you need documented factual material, your preparation should be extensive. The more material you have sampled, the better knowledge you will have of the subject and the more valuable your contributions will be. Since, of course, you cannot predict all of the ideas that will be covered in the discussion, you cannot prepare your actual contributions ahead of time. Nevertheless, you should be familiar enough with the material to be able to find any item you need when you need it. Usually, you will bring your sources with you to the meeting.

A second characteristic of responsible contribution—careful analysis of every item of information—is shown by raising questions about and probing into contributions of others. Your obligation does not end with the reading into the record of items of information. Once an item of data has been submitted, it is the obligation of the membership to determine whether the item is accurate, typical, consistent, and otherwise valid. Suppose that in a discussion on reducing crime a person mentioned that, according to *U. S. News & World Report*, crime has risen 33 percent in the past five years. The group should not leave this statement until they have explored it fully. What was the specific source of the data? On what were the data based? What years are being referred to? Is this consistent with other material? Is any contradictory material available? The purpose of these questions is not to debate the data but to test them. If these data are partly true, questionable, or relevant only to certain kinds of crime, conclusions based on them should be tentative.

Reaching sound conclusions about and from the material, a third characteristic of responsible contribution, refers to the real goal of the group. Participants must pool information to provide a basis for conclusions about the question. You can still offer opinions, but unlike social sessions in which opinions substitute for data, in problem-solving groups opinions are based on the previously tested materials.

Members Should Be Objective

Let's focus on two recommendations for ensuring objectivity of approach. First, report data, do not associate yourself with them. If you report that crime has risen 33 percent in the past five years, do not feel that because you presented the data you must defend them. An excellent way of presenting data with a degree of disassociation is illustrated by the following: "According to *U. S. News & World Report,* crime has risen 33 percent in the past five years. That is a startling statistic. I wonder whether anyone else found either any substantiating or any contradictory data?" Presenting data in this way tells the group that you want discussion of the data and that, whether they are substantiated or disproven, you have no personal relationship with them. Contrast that disassociative approach with the following statement: "I think crime is going up at a fantastic rate. Why, I found that crime has gone up 33 percent in the past five years, and we just can't put up with that kind of thing." This member is siding with the data. Since anyone who questions the data or the conclusions is going to have to contend with the speaker, there is a good chance that the discussion that follows will escalate into an ego conflict.

A second recommendation for ensuring objectivity is to solicit all viewpoints on every major issue. Suppose you were discussing the question, "Should financial support for women's sports be raised?" Suppose that after extensive reading you believed that it should. If in the discussion you spoke only to support your position and took issue with every bit of contrary material, you would not be responding objectively. Although there is nothing wrong with formulating tentative opinions based upon your research, in the discussion you should present material objectively whether it supports or opposes your tentative claims. If the group draws a conclusion that corresponds to your tentative conclusion, fine. At least all views have had the opportunity to be presented. If the group draws the opposite conclusion, you are not put in a defensive position. By being objective, you may find that during the discussion your views will change many times. Remember, if the best answer to the question could be found without discussion, the discussion would not really be necessary.

Members Should Fill Positive Roles

Everyone in the group has a responsibility for certain functions of the group. These functions are served as members carry out various roles. A *role* is a style of behavior that you determine for yourself or that is determined for you by expectations of the group. Sometimes a person plays one role and only one role in the group. At other times a given person may play several roles simultaneously or alternately, and, of course, more than one person can play a given role. In a successful group, all the positive roles are usually played sometime during the interaction; an unsuccessful group may be one in which no one plays the positive roles or one in which negative role-playing predominates. Let's examine the most common and most essential positive roles.

Group roles perform both task and maintenance functions. Task functions are those behaviors that are designed to get the work done, while maintenance functions are behaviors whose purpose is to assure harmony and good feeling among group members. In a successful group, both functions are usually satisfied. When we analyze a group interaction, we look first to see how and whether they solved the problem; second, we look to see how well the group worked together, whether members like, respect, and understand other members of the group.

Task roles   In most groups there are at least four major task roles.

1. *The information or opinion giver* provides content for the interaction. Actual information provides about 50 percent of what is done in a group. Without information and well-considered opinions, the group will not have the material upon which to base its decisions. Probably everyone in the group plays this role during the discussion. Nevertheless, usually one or more persons have really done their homework. Either as a result of past experience with this or a related problem, long conversations with persons who have worked with similar problems, or a great deal of study, these group members are relied upon or called upon to provide the facts. In some groups, there is a designated resource person or consultant called in solely to fulfill the information-giving role. In most groups, one or more persons take it upon themselves to be especially well prepared. The information giver identifies himself by such statements as, "Well, when Jones Corporation considered this problem, they found. . . ." Or, "That's a good point you made—just the other day I ran across these figures that substantiate your point." Or, "According to Professor Smith, it doesn't necessarily work that way. He says. . . ."

2. *The information seeker,* the opposite of the information giver, is a role played by the member of the group who sees that at a given point the group will need data in order to function. Again, in most groups more than one person will take this role during the discussion, yet one or more are especially perceptive in seeing where more information is needed. The information seeker identifies himself by such questions as, "What did we say the base numbers were?" Or, "Have we decided how many people this really affects?" Or, "Well, what functions does this person serve?" Or, "Have we got anything to give us some background on this subject?"

3. *The expediter* is the individual who perceives when the group is going astray. Whether the group is meeting once or is an ongoing group, almost

invariably some remarks will tend to sidetrack the group from the central point or issue before them. Sometimes apparent digressions are necessary to get background, to enlarge the scope, or even to give a person an opportunity to get something off his chest. Sometimes these momentary digressions take the group far afield from their assignment. Because these tangents are sometimes more fun than the task itself, a tangent often is not realized for what it is, and the group discusses it as if it were important to the group decision. The expediter is the person who helps the group stick to its agenda; he or she helps the group stay with the problem at hand. When the group has strayed, the expediter helps lead it back to the main stream. This role is revealed by such statements as, "Say, I'm enjoying this, but I can't quite see what it has to do with whether permissiveness is really a cause." Or, "Let's see, aren't we still trying to find out whether these are the only criteria that we should be considering?" Or, "I've got the feeling that this is important to the point we're on now, but I can't quite get hold of the relationship—am I off base?" Or, "Say, time is getting away from us and we've considered only two possible solutions. Aren't there some more?"

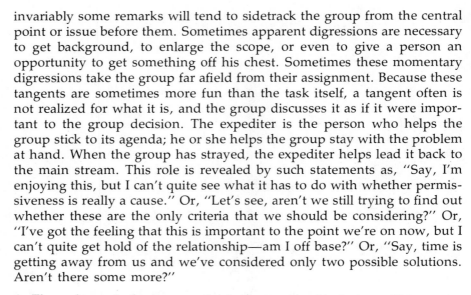

4. *The analyzer* is the person who is the master of technique. This person knows the problem-solving method inside out. The analyzer knows when the group has skipped a point, has passed over a point too lightly, or has not taken a look at matters it needs to. More than just *expediting*, the analyzer helps the group penetrate to the core of the problem it is working on. In addition, the analyzer examines the reasoning of various members. The analyzer may be recognized from such statements as, "Tom, you're generalizing from only one instance. Can you give us some others?" Or, "Wait a minute, after symptoms we have to take a look at causes." Or, "I think we're passing over Jones too lightly. There are still criteria we haven't used to measure him by."

Maintenance roles In most discussion groups there are at least three major maintenance roles that encourage good working relationships.

1. *The active listener* is the person who responds with supportive statements, paraphrases, questions, and praise for good ideas. People participating in groups are likely to feel better about their participation when their thoughts and feelings are recognized—the active listener meets these needs. In any group we expect nearly everyone will exhibit active listening skills at some time, but people tend to get so wrapped up in their own ideas that they may neglect to respond to comments that are made.

The active listener is recognized through such nonverbal cues as a smile, a nod, or a vigorous head shake. Verbally he or she is recognized by such statements as "You've put a lot of thought into that plan, Mel—we'll have to consider it very carefully," "I think I get your point Ann," "You seem a little upset by what Mary said, Tom, am I right?" and "It's obvious you've really done your homework, Marsha."

2. *The harmonizer* is essential. It is a rare group that can expect to accomplish its task without some conflicts. Even when people get along well, they are likely to get angry over some trivial points in heated discussion. Most groups experience interpersonal conflicts caused by different personality types. The harmonizer is responsible for reducing and reconciling misunderstandings, disagreements, and conflicts. Good at pouring oil on troubled waters, he or she encourages objectivity and is especially good as a mediator for hostile, aggressively competing sides. A group cannot avoid some conflict, but if there is no one present to harmonize, participation can become an uncomfortable experience. The harmonizer may be recognized by such statements as, "Bill, I don't think you're giving Mary a chance to make her point." Or, "Tom, Jack, hold it a second. I know you're on opposite sides of this, but let's see where you might have some agreement." Or, "Sue, I get the feeling that something Todd said really bugged you, is that right?" Or, "Hold it, everybody, we're really coming up with some good stuff; let's not lose our momentum by getting into name-calling."

3. *The gatekeeper* is the person who helps to keep communication channels open. If a group has seven people in it, the assumption is that all seven have something to contribute. However, if all are to feel comfortable in contributing, those who tend to dominate need to be held in check and those who tend to be reticent need to be encouraged. The gatekeeper is the one who sees that Jane is on the edge of her chair, ready to talk, but just cannot seem to get in, or that Don is rambling a bit and needs to be directed, or that Tom's need to talk so frequently is making Cesar withdraw from the conversation, or that Betty has just lost the thread of discussion. As we said earlier, a characteristic of good group work is interaction. The gatekeeper assumes the responsibility for facilitating interaction. The gatekeeper may be recognized by such statements as, "Joan, I see you've got something to say here . . ." Or, "You've made a really good point, Todd; I wonder whether we could get some reaction on it . . ." Or, "Bill and Marge, it sounds like you're getting into a dialogue here; let's see what other ideas we have."

Discussants Should Avoid Negative Roles

There are four common negative roles that group discussants should try to avoid.

1. *The aggressor*   is the person who works for his or her own status by criticizing almost everything or blaming others when things get rough. This person's main purpose seems to be to deflate the ego or status of others. One way of dealing with the aggressor is confrontation. Ask this person whether he or she is aware of what he or she is doing and what effect it is having on the group.

2. *The joker's*   behavior is characterized by clowning, mimicking, or generally disrupting by making a joke of everything. Usually trying to call attention to himself, the joker must be the center of attention. A little bit of a joker goes a long way. The group needs to get the joker to consider the problem seriously, or the joker will be a constant irritant to other members. One way to proceed is to encourage this individual when tensions need to be released but to ignore him or her when there is serious work to be done.

3. *The withdrawer*   refuses to be a part of the group. Withdrawers are mental dropouts. Sometimes they are withdrawing from something that was said; sometimes withdrawal is merely indifference. Try to draw this person out with questions. Find out what he or she is especially good at and rely on him or her to do it. Sometimes a compliment will bring out the withdrawer.

4. *The monopolizer*   needs to talk all the time. Usually this person is trying to impress the group that he or she is well read, knowledgable, and of value to the group. Encourage this person when his or her comments are helpful. But when the monopolizer is talking too much or when the comments are not helpful, the leader needs to interrupt the steady flow and draw others into the discussion.

Evaluating Group Communication

Now that we have considered the criteria for group effectiveness, we can consider instruments for analyzing the group decision, individual participation, and the group process.

The Decision

The first instrument (Figure 12-2) to be considered gives you an opportunity to look at the group *decision*. The rationale behind the use of this instrument is that since the group's goal is to arrive at a decision, a decision-based critical instrument will consider the end product of group communication. This instrument calls for you to discuss four major questions:

1. *Did the group arrive at a decision?*   Just because a group meets to discuss does not necessarily mean that it will arrive at a decision. As foolish as it

Figure 12-2

Decision Analysis

---

1. Did the group arrive at a decision?

---

2. What action is taken as a result of the discussion?

---

3. Was the group consensus a good one?

---

4. Is there evidence that the product of the group interaction is something different from what would have resulted from an immediate combination of individual beliefs and reactions?

---

may seem, some groups thrash away for hours only to adjourn without having arrived at a decision. Of course, some groups discuss such serious problems that a decision cannot be reached without several meetings, but we are not talking about a group that plans to meet later to consider the issue further—we mean the group that "finishes" without arriving at some decision. Not arriving at a decision results in frustration and disillusionment.

2. *What action is taken as a result of the discussion?*   Problem-solving discussion implies implementation. If the group has "finished" without considering means for putting the decision into action, then there is reason to question the practicality of the decision.

3. *Was the group consensus a good one?*   This may be the most difficult question to answer. Whether a decision is good or not is of course a value judgment. We suggest applying six criteria for such an evaluation. (1) Was quality information presented to serve as a base or foundation for the decision? (2) Were the data discussed fully? (3) Did interim conclusions relate to information presented or were they stated as opinions that had no relation to content? (4) Did a given conclusion seem to be the product of consensus or was it determined by the persuasive or authoritarian power of the leader? (5) Was the final decision measured against some set of criteria or objectives? (6) Did the group agree to support the decision?

4. *Is there evidence that the product of the group interaction is something different from what would have resulted from an immediate combination of individual beliefs and reactions?*   Discussion is or should be a process. If the end product is indistinguishable from what could have been concluded at the beginning, then discussion was not the factor that brought about the decision.

Individual Members

Although a group will have difficulty without good leadership, it may not be able to function at all without members who are willing and able to meet the task and maintenance functions of the group. The next critical instrument in group analysis (Figure 12-3) incorporates each of the elements considered earlier in the chapter and provides a simple check list that can be kept for each individual.

Leadership

Although some group discussions are leaderless, no discussion should be leadershipless. An important element of the evaluation process is to consider the nature of the leadership. If there is an appointed leader, and most groups have one, you can focus on that individual. If the group is truly leaderless, then you must consider attempts at leadership by the

Figure 12-3

Individual Member Analysis

For each of the following questions, rate the participant on a 1 to 5 basis: 1, high; 2, good; 3, average; 4, fair; 5, poor.

Content:	1	2	3	4	5
Seems to be well prepared?					
Interacts?					
Maintains objectivity?					
Analyzes material as presented?					
Draws conclusions?					
Organization:	1	2	3	4	5
Is aware of the problem?					
Analyzes the problem?					
Suggests possible solutions?					
Tests each solution?					
Carrying Out Roles:	1	2	3	4	5
As information or opinion giver?					
As information or opinion seeker?					
As expediter?					
As analyzer?					
As active listener?					
As harmonizer?					
As gatekeeper?					
Carrying Out Negative Roles: (For this category a 1, high, would show that the person was not playing that negative role.)	1	2	3	4	5
As aggressor?					
As joker?					
As withdrawer?					
As monopolizer?					

Analysis: Write a short profile of this person's contribution to the group based on the above check list. Consider the person's relative effectiveness in helping (or hindering) the group in achieving its goal.

---

various members or focus on the apparent leader who emerges from the group.

The last instrument (Figure 12-4) is a simple check list for evaluating group leadership.

Figure 12-4

Leadership Analysis

For each of the following questions, rate the leadership on a 1 to 5 basis: 1, high; 2, good; 3, average; 4, fair; 5, poor.

Leadership Traits:	1	2	3	4	5
Has sufficient understanding?					
Stimulates group?					
Has the respect of the group?					
Leadership Methods:	1	2	3	4	5
Establishes a good working climate?					
Has an agenda?					
Promotes systematic problem solving?					
Directs the flow of discussion?					
Encourages balanced participation?					
Asks good questions?					
Clarifies and crystallizes ideas?					

Summarizes frequently?					
Maintains necessary control?					
Brings the discussion to a satisfactory close?					

Analysis: Write a short profile of this person's leadership, based on the above check list. Consider the person's relative effectiveness in helping the group achieve its goal.

Communication Session

Reflection

What role do you usually take in groups? Are you effective in that role?

Practice

1. Each classroom group is given or selects a task that requires some research. Each group should be given approximately thirty to forty minutes for discussion. While group A is discussing, members of group B should observe and after the discussion give feedback during the remainder of the class period. For practice in using the various instruments, one observer could be asked to do a decision analysis, one could be asked to do an individual member analysis, and one could be asked to do a leadership analysis. In the next class period, group B would discuss and group A would observe and critique. Sample questions:

   What should be done to improve parking (advising, registration) on campus?

   What should be done to increase the participation of minorities in college or university teaching (governance, administration)?

2. Each classroom group has ten to fifteen minutes to arrive at a solution to the following dilemma: Five people are boating: the father, a 55-year-old heart

specialist reputed to be the best in the state; his 36-year-old wife, a dermatologist; their 8-year-old child; their neighbor, a 43-year-old industrial salesman for a major corporation; and his wife, a 35-year-old former model who appears in television commercials. If the boat started to sink and only one of the five could be saved, who should it be? One observer will be appointed for each group. The observer will use one of the three evaluation instruments discussed.

Discussion

After the exercise, the group should determine (1) what roles were operating in the group during the discussion, (2) who were performing those roles, and (3) what factors helped or hurt the problem-solving process.

Summary

As an effective group participant, you have many responsibilities. The first is to be prepared. Whether you need only to think about the problem or whether you need to carry out some research, you should have some solid material to take into the discussion with you.

Your preparation should consider the possible organization the group will follow. Determine the kind of questions you are discussing. Analyze the size and scope of the problem—determine the criteria you will need to apply to tentative solutions to the problem. Outline some possible solutions to the problem. In the discussion itself you will weigh and evaluate to determine the best solution.

The measure of your value in the group discussion will be in your participation. You may perform one or more of the task roles of giving and seeking information, expediting, analyzing, and coming up with creative ideas; you may perform one or more of the maintenance roles of active listening, harmonizing, gatekeeping, compromising, or reducing tension through humor. You will want to try to avoid the negative roles of aggressor, joker, withdrawer, or monopolizer.

Leadership is exerting influence to accomplish a goal. Although leaders may show greater degrees of ability, sociability, and motivation than others in the group, the presence of such traits does not guarantee that you will lead effectively.

Do you want to lead? If so, you will want to understand the group expectations, study the subject area, be prepared to work hard to get the job done, be willing to be decisive, be committed to the goals of the group, interact freely with members, and develop task and maintenance skills.

Still, how well you lead may depend on your style and how you put it into operation. Some "leaders" adopt the laissez-faire style of no leadership; some leaders try to dictate what will be done, when, and how; but most effective leaders try to adopt the democratic style of giving the group direction, while letting them participate in decision making.

Once you hold a position of leadership you must establish a good working climate, plan an agenda, be able to direct the flow of discussion, summarize when necessary, and maintain the necessary control to keep the discussion from getting out of hand.

Suggested Readings

Ernest G. Bormann. *Discussion and Group Methods: Theory and Practice,* 2d ed. New York: Harper & Row, 1975. This is a comprehensive textbook on the subject of group discussion.

John K. Brilhart. *Effective Group Discussion,* 3d ed. Dubuque, Iowa: Wm. C. Brown Company, 1978. This paperback is a very popular textbook.

Dorwin Cartwright and **Alvin Zander.** *Group Dynamics: Research and Theory,* 3d ed. New York: Harper & Row, 1968. This book is basic to any library of group research. It contains a wealth of information on all facets of group process.

David Potter and **Martin P. Andersen.** *Discussion in Small Groups: A Guide to Effective Practice,* 3d ed. Belmont, California: Wadsworth Publishing Co., 1976. Although this is a much shorter book than Bormann, it is still quite comprehensive. Contains a practical approach to group discussion.

Chapter 13
Interview Communication

1. *Contrast the methods of interviewing.*
2. *Be able to identify and phrase open and closed questions, primary and secondary questions, and neutral and leading questions.*
3. *Know the steps in planning for an information-getting interview.*
4. *Develop a schedule of questions for an information interview.*
5. *Conduct an information interview.*
6. *Explain the procedure used by job interviewers.*
7. *Write a résumé.*
8. *Participate in a job interview.*

Although only a relatively small amount of your future interpersonal interaction will include interviewing, the time you spend interviewing may be very important. *Interviewing* is a form of interpersonal interaction based primarily on the asking and answering of questions. Unlike most of your interpersonal communication, interviewing can be planned ahead and is usually focused on one content area.

An interview may be for appraisal (making value judgments that may lead to hiring, promotion, reward, or firing), for counseling (helping a person to examine and perhaps solve his problems), or even for persuasion (influencing a person to buy a product). We believe that the two most important types of interviewing skills students need to study are those for gaining information and for job interviewing.

In this chapter we'll consider methods of interviews, the phrasing of questions, and procedures for gaining information and job interviews.

Methods of Interviewing

The two major methods of interviewing are directive and nondirective. A *directive interview* is one in which the interviewer is in control. He or she knows what is to be accomplished and has a well-conceived plan for achieving the goals of the interview. The advantages of the directive interview are that its techniques are easy to learn, it takes less time than the nondirective interview, it provides verifiable data, and it can be used to supplement other methods of data collecting. Its disadvantages are that it is inflexible, limited in variety and depth of subject matter, and narrow in scope.

The *nondirective interview* is one in which the interviewee is in control. It provides an opportunity to deal in depth with a wide range of subject matters, allows interviewer flexibility, and provides an opportunity to establish an ongoing relationship between interviewer and interviewee. However, it is time-consuming, requires acute psychological insight and sensitivity, and generates nonverifiable data.

Some interviewers prefer the directive interview, some prefer the nondirective, and some like a blend of the two. Since we believe you must learn to be in control before you can allow the other party to take control and still achieve the purpose of the interview, most of the suggestions in this chapter relate to the directive interview. Moreover, the directive method is more common in information-getting and job interviews. Before moving to the specifics of these two kinds of interviews, we need to discuss the one element common to all interviewing—questioning.

Questions in Interviewing

An interview differs from other forms of interpersonal communication in its reliance on the asking and answering of questions. Although we deal here specifically with questions in the interview situation, a knowledge of good question construction can be applied to any interpersonal encounter. Questions may be phrased as open or closed, primary or secondary, leading or neutral.

Open versus Closed Questions

Open questions are broadly based—often specifying only the topic to be covered. They allow considerable freedom to the interviewee. Closed questions are those that can be answered "yes" or "no" or with only a few words.

Open questions range from those with virtually no restrictions—"Tell me about your life"—to those that give some direction—"Tell me about your experiences with the speech department." Why do interviewers use open questions? Mostly to encourage the person to talk, allowing the interviewer maximum opportunity to listen and observe. As a result of this type of question, the interviewer discovers what the person perceives as important to him or her. By asking open questions the interviewer is likely to elicit information that would not be forthcoming in response to closed questions. For instance, by his answer to an open question, a person may reveal prejudices, peculiarities, and other personal perceptions. Open questions take more time to answer, and the interviewer can lose control of the interview if she does not know how to work with the answers.

Closed questions range from those requiring only "yes" and "no" answers ("Do you like avocados?") to the short-answer variety ("How many years have you worked here?"; "What kinds of beer do you buy most frequently?"). The obvious advantage of the closed question is that the interviewer can maintain necessary control of the interview. Moreover, he can get a great amount of usable information in a short period of time. When you add that a schedule can be well-planned in advance and that the interview itself requires less time and less effort on the part of the interviewee, you begin to see why closed questions are popular with interviewers. The obvious disadvantage is that the interviewer will seldom know why the person responded the way he did. The closed question gives little room for talking about ideas and feelings that fall between the "yes" and "no" extremes. Moreover, since the respondent has little opportunity to talk, he is less likely to volunteer useful information.

Which type of question is superior? A great deal depends upon what kinds of material you are seeking and how much time you have at your disposal. We'll consider the possibility of blending the two types of questions as we talk about specific interviewing procedures.

Communication Session

Reflection

Have you ever interviewed or been interviewed by anyone? If so, what type of interview was it? What method of interviewing was used? Were the questions mostly open or closed? How did the type of questions affect the interview?

Practice

1. Indicate which of the following are (O) open questions and which are (C) closed questions:

    _____ 1. What makes you think Fox's chances are good in the upcoming election?

    _____ 2. Have you ever thought of running for City Council?

    _____ 3. How many persons are involved in the process of developing a new product?

    _____ 4. What is your opinion of the company's vacation policy?

    _____ 5. How do you think the student affairs office should be organized?

    _____ 6. Do you agree with Mr. Sheldon's position on attendance?

2. Reword the questions above to make the open ones closed and vice versa.

3. Select a subject for an interview. Determine what information you would like to know about that subject. Frame five open questions and five closed questions that attempt to yield the same information.

Discussion

In groups of four to six, share your open and closed questions. Discuss the advantages and disadvantages of the list of open questions and the list of closed questions.

Primary versus Secondary Questions

A second useful distinction is between primary and secondary questions. *Primary questions* introduce topics; *secondary questions* follow up on the answers to primary questions. Some people refer to the secondary question as the "probing" question because it asks the interviewee to go more deeply into ideas and feelings behind his answers. A good list of primary questions can be made before the interview; good secondary questions call for you as an interviewer to listen carefully and be sensitive to both the content and the intent of the respondent's statements. Skill at use of secondary questions comes with interviewing experience.

Some secondary questions are just supportive statements designed to encourage the respondent to continue but in greater depth. Such priming questions as, "And then?" "Is there more?" and "What happened next?" give the respondent reason to continue with his comments.

A second-level secondary question is a more specific probe such as, "What did you do after . . .?" "I'm not sure I fully understand what you were thinking at the time—can you tell me?" and "What do you mean by 'frequently'?" Questions of this kind encourage continuation, but along a specific line that you as the interviewer determine.

A third-level question is one that probes the feelings of the respondent. Such questions as, "How did you feel when you were cut from the squad?" "How did you react when you got such a beautiful gift?" and "What words best describe exactly what you were feeling when it happened?" encourage the person to reveal emotions and moods.

One of the major reasons for a secondary or probing question is to motivate the respondent to enlarge on an answer the interviewer believes is inadequate. Such follow-ups are necessary because the respondent may be purposely trying to be evasive, incomplete, or vague, or because the interviewee may not really understand how much detail you are looking for. Your follow-up questions show the person how much leeway you will give him in giving answers.

Keep in mind that the effectiveness of the follow-up questions may well depend on your interpersonal skill in asking them. Since probing questions can alienate the interviewee (especially when the questions are perceived as threatening), such in-depth probes work best after you have gained the confidence of the respondent and when the questions are asked within the atmosphere of a positive interpersonal climate.

Leading versus Neutral Questions

A third essential distinction to make is between the neutral and the leading question. A *neutral question* is one in which the respondent is free to give an answer without direction from the interviewer. In contrast, a *leading question* is one in which the interviewer suggests the answer she expects or desires. Notice the difference in wording in the following pairs of questions:

Neutral: How do you feel about working with Roger?

Leading: Working with Roger makes you feel uncomfortable, doesn't it?

Neutral: How would you compare a Volkswagen with other cars?

Leading: Wouldn't you like to own a Volkswagen?

Neutral: Tell me about the ways you respond to pressure.

Leading: When was the last time you had a drink to cope with the pressures you faced?

Notice that the neutral question leaves it to the respondent to determine how she will answer. The leading question makes the person feel some pressure to answer a particular way.

Leading questions are frequently used by a person who conducts a persuasive interview with the intention of controlling the attitude or behavior of the respondent. Since your interviewing experience is more likely to come through information and selection interviews, you should probably avoid the frequent use of leading questions, which tend to elicit biased responses rather than usable information.

Communication Session

Practice

Change each of the following leading questions to a neutral question:

Doesn't it depress you to see so many patients who will never get well?

After what Angelina did, I bet you are really out to get her, aren't you?

Aren't you excited about your new promotion?

Wouldn't you be upset about going to Philadelphia if you were traded?

Discussion

Under what circumstances if any are leading questions preferable to neutral questions?

Information-Seeking Interviews

Interviewing can be a valuable method of getting information on nearly any topic. Students can use the interview to get information for papers, lawyers interview witnesses to get facts to build their cases, doctors interview patients to get medical history before making diagnoses, and reporters interview sources to get facts for their stories. A good interviewing plan requires selecting the best person to interview, determining a procedure, conducting the interview itself, and interpreting the results.

Selecting the Best Person

Somewhere on campus or in the larger community there are people who are experts in the areas you want to research. Your first step should be to find out who they are so you can arrange to talk with them. Suppose you are interested in published textbooks by faculty members. Whom should you interview? To find out, you would try to locate a list of publications written by faculty members and determine prospective interviewees yourself. Or, you could call the office of the provost or the dean and ask for names of faculty members who have written textbooks. After you had made a list of names, you would make an appointment with one or more persons on the list. Making an appointment is very important— you cannot just walk into an office and expect the prospective interviewee to drop everything on a moment's notice. You are going to get very little valuable information if the person is not willing to cooperate with you. To get an appointment you must know (1) why you need to interview this particular person (why the person should take time to talk with you) and (2) what information you hope to get from the interview.

Before going into the interview, you should do some research on the person you will be interviewing. If you are going to interview a faculty member who has written college textbooks, you should already have reviewed some material about publishing and you should know something about the faculty member. Not only will evidence of your preliminary research encourage the person to talk more openly with you (few people will either respect or talk in detail with a person who obviously knows nothing about the subject or the person), but also this familiarity with material will enable you to frame more penetrating questions.

In addition, you should be forthright in your reasons for seeking the interview. If you are interviewing the person as part of a class project, if you are writing a newspaper article on campus authors, or if you have some other reason, say so.

Determining a Procedure

Good interviewing results from careful planning. The plan includes overall interview method and preparation of specific questions.

You must determine the kind of interview that is most likely to achieve your goals. As we mentioned earlier, interviews may be directive or nondirective, but we recommend the directive method—especially for the information-getting interview. You should write down the subject areas you want information on. Then write down all the questions you can think of, revise them until you have worded them clearly and concisely, and then put them in the order that seems most appropriate. On your written question schedule, you should leave enough space between questions so that you can fill in answers as completely as possible. Moreover, you should leave enough space for answers to secondary questions that are related to the primary questions you have prepared. Some interviewers try to play the entire interview by ear. Even the most skilled interviewer needs to have some preplanned questions to ensure his covering important areas. The order and type of questions depend somewhat on what you are hoping to achieve in the interview. Let's look at the interview opening, the body, and the closing.

Initial stages—the interview opening   You should begin by thanking the person for taking time to talk with you. In this initial stage, you are trying to develop rapport between you and your respondent. Start by asking questions that can be answered easily and that will show your respect for the person you are interviewing. For instance, in an interview with your professor on textbooks he has written, you might start with such questions as, "I know writing is a big project—how long does it take to write a book?" or, "Do you find you work better in the office or at home or some other place?" Such questions will set the interviewee at ease and get him talking freely. Because the most important consideration at this initial stage is to create a positive communication climate, keep the questions easy to answer, nonthreatening, and encouraging.

The body of the interview   The body of the interview consists of the major questions you have prepared. After the initial stages, you can move into the planned schedule. The following example gives you an idea of the method of setting up an interview question schedule. Notice that the questions are grouped, and notice that the hard-hitting questions that require careful thinking are placed late in the schedule. For instance, the question, "Should a school use a book written by a professor teaching at that school?" is the final question on the list.

If you were planning to interview one or more teachers about textbook publishing experiences, you might prepare the following questions schedule:

I. *About textbook publishing in general*

  1. *How do you go about getting a company to publish your work?*

  2. *Is there a difference between getting a textbook published and getting a novel published?*

  3. *Does a textbook author need to have an agent?*

  4. *How does an author apply for a copyright?*

II. *Experience of this author*

  1. *How many books have you written?*

  2. *What company publishes your book(s)?*

  3. *Besides money, what motivated you to write a textbook?*

  4. *How long did it take you to write this book?*

  5. *What are the most difficult aspects of writing a book for you?*

  6. *Do you have to write many drafts?*

  7. *How is a book edited?*

  8. *Do you do the illustrations, pictures, and other visuals? If not, how are they done?*

III. *Opinions of this author*

  1. *How would you react if a teacher at another school photocopied a chapter from your book to hand out to his students?*

  2. *Do most textbooks need to be revised or brought out in new editions as often as some are?*

  3. *Do you think a school should use a book written by a professor at that school? Please explain.*

You may or may not ask all of these questions in the actual interview. Before you begin, however, you must be satisfied that you have enough questions to yield the kind of information you want. As you get into your questions, you must be particularly sensitive to both content and intent of the respondent's answers so that you can frame secondary questions that will yield additional information.

Closing the Interview   As you draw to the end of your planned questions, thank the person for taking time to talk with you. If you are going to publish the substance of the interview, it is courteous to offer to let the person see a draft of your reporting of the interview before it goes into print. Although this practice is not followed by many interviewers, it helps to build and maintain your credibility.

Conducting the Interview

The best plan in the world will not result in a successful interview unless you practice good interpersonal communication skills in conducting the interview. Let's focus on a few of the particularly important elements of good interviewing. Perhaps more than anything else, you should be courteous during the interview. Listen carefully—your job is not to debate or to give your opinion, but to get information from a person who has it. Whether you like the person or not or whether you agree with the person or not, you must respect his opinions—after all, you are the one who asked for the interview.

Put into practice your best receiver skills. If the person has given a rather long answer to a question, you should paraphrase what he has said to make sure your interpretation is correct. Also, keep the interview moving. You do not want to rush the person, but he is probably busy with a full schedule of activities. It is usually a good idea to ask for a given amount of time when you make the appointment. "I'd like to talk with you for about half an hour" is a statement that lets the person know how much time you have in mind. Sometimes the interviewee will want to extend the time. Ordinarily, however, when the time is up, you should call attention to that fact and be prepared to conclude.

Finally, you should be very much aware of the impression you make nonverbally. You should consider your clothes—you want to be dressed appropriately for the occasion. Since you are taking the person's time, you should show an interest in the person and what he has to say. How you look and act may well determine whether or not the person will warm up to you and give you the kind of interview you want.

Interpreting and Evaluating the Results

The interview serves no useful purpose until you do something with the material you have gathered, but you should not do anything with it until you have reviewed the material carefully. Especially if you took notes, it is important to write out complete answers carefully while information is still fresh in your mind. After you have processed the material from the interview, you may want to show the interviewee a copy of the data you are going to use. You do not want to be guilty of misquoting your source.

You may also find it necessary to check out the facts you have been given. If what the person has told you differs from material from other sources, you had better double check the accuracy of the material.

The most difficult part is making interpretations and drawing inferences from the information. Facts by themselves are not nearly so important as the conclusions that may be drawn from the facts. Be careful to see that you check and double check your thinking before you present the substance of the interview in a speech or for publication.

Communication Session

Reflection

Have you ever conducted an interview? Did you use the steps outlined above? What was the result?

Practice

1. Working in groups of four to six, determine a topic on which you might wish to conduct an information-getting interview.

   a. Decide on the best person or persons to interview on this topic.

   b. Devise a list of questions for this information-seeking interview. Remember to frame open as well as closed questions. Make sure that you have appropriate secondary questions to use as follow-ups. Check to make sure that most questions are neutral rather than leading. Group the questions under major headings. Make sure you have some questions that are appropriate for opening the interview. Write the finished product on paper for posting.

   c. The class should compare the various interview plans. Look for poorly worded questions; make sure the organization of questions is logical.

2. Conduct an in-class interview with a classmate in an area of his or her expertise.

3. Conduct an interview outside of class and submit a written report.

Employment Interviews

Although there is some question about the interview as a valid tool for personnel selection, nearly every major position in nearly any field of endeavor requires that the applicant go through an interview. At its worst, an interview can be a waste of time for all parties involved; at its best, an interview can be an integral part of the process of selection and placement. Some of the common criteria for evaluating applicants for most positions are specific abilities, ambition, energy, ability to communicate, knowledge and intelligence, and integrity. A skillfully conducted interview can help the interviewer determine the applicant's strengths in several of these areas; likewise, a skillfully conducted interview can help the interviewee reveal his strengths in many of these same areas.

Assuming then that the interview can be a valid instrument in the selection process, let's consider some of the procedures and methods that are most likely to be beneficial to the interviewer in conducting an interview and to the interviewee in taking part in one.

Responsibilities of the Interviewer

As an interviewer, you are the link between a job applicant and the company. Much of the applicant's impression of the company will be made on the basis of his impression of you. You should know what kinds of information applicants want to know about your company. In addition to the obvious desire for salary information, applicants also seek such information as opportunity for advancement, influence of personal ideas on company policy, company attitudes toward personal life and life-style (political activities, marital status, "volunteer" work), and so forth. Moreover, you have nearly the sole responsibility of determining whether this person will be considered for the position available or whether this person will be kept in the running for possible company employment.

Procedure

For the interview itself, a plan for a highly to moderately structured interview is most likely to draw out the most valid data. In the unstructured interview, the interviewers tend to talk more and tend to make decisions based on less valid data than in structured interviews.[1] Especially if you are screening a large number of applicants, you want to make sure that all have been asked the same questions and that the questions cover a variety of subjects.

Before the interview starts, you should be familiar with all available data about the applicant—application form, résumé, letters of recommendation, test scores if any are available. These written data will help determine some of the questions you will want to ask.

---

[1] P. B. Sheatsley, "Closed Questions Are Sometimes More Valid than Open End," *Public Opinion Quarterly*, Vol. 12 (1948), p. 12.

The Interview

We will consider three parts of the interview itself: the opening, the body, and the closing.

The opening of the interview You should greet the applicant warmly. Call him or her by name, and introduce yourself so that he or she can use your name. A warm handshake is also beneficial to getting things off to a good start. Be open with the applicant. If you are either going to take notes or going to record the interview, let the applicant know why you are doing so.

Should you begin with "warm-up" questions to help establish rapport? Or should you move right into the question schedule? A good interviewer senses the nature of the situation and tries to use a method that is most likely to encourage the applicant to talk and provide adequate answers. Although warm-up questions may help some applicants, most of them are psychologically ready for the interview. As a result, many warm-up questions may be misinterpreted. The applicant may wonder about the motivation for such questions, and they may make him even more nervous. Unless you have good reason for proceeding differently, the best advice seems to be to move into the question schedule right away in as warm and friendly a manner as you can.

The body of the interview The body of the interview consists of the question period. Let's begin with some guidelines for presenting yourself and your questions.

1. *Be careful of your own presentation.*   Talk loudly enough to be heard. Try to be spontaneous. The interviewee is not going to respond well to obviously memorized questions fired in machine-gun fashion. Be sensitive to your own nonverbal communication. The interviewee is going to be looking for signs of disapproval—any inadvertent looks or unusual changes in quality or rhythm may convey a false impression. Remember that you can load a question by giving it a particular tone of voice, so be especially careful.

2. *Do not waste time.*   You have available a wide variety of information about the candidate. Ask questions about information you already know only if you seek some special insights into the information. For instance, if an applicant indicates employment with a particular organization but does not give any detailed account of responsibilities, questions relating to that employment period would be appropriate.

3. *Avoid trick or loaded questions.*   Applicants are always leery of questions that may be designed to make them look bad. Moreover, if a candidate believes that you are trying to trick him, the suspicion may provoke a

competitive rather than a positive atmosphere. Anything that serves to limit the applicant's responsiveness will harm the interview.

4. *Do not ask questions that violate fair employment practice legislation.* Questions directed to a woman about her plans for marriage or, if she is married, about her plans to have children are not only irrelevant but illegal.

5. *Give the applicant an opportunity to ask questions.* Usually, near the end of the interview, you will want to take the time to see whether the applicant has any questions.

Now let's look at some of the specific questions that interviewers usually ask. This list is a combination of questions from a variety of sources and is only representative, not exhaustive. It imposes no limitations on your own creativity but is intended to suggest the kinds of questions you may wish to ask. You might use this as a starter list or as a check list for your own wording of questions. Notice that some questions are open-ended and some are closed, but none is a ''yes'' or ''no'' question.

1. *How did you select the school you attended?*

2. *What are your hobbies?*

3. *How did you determine your major?*

4. *What kind of position are you looking for?*

5. *Why do you think you would like to work for us?*

Applicants are always leery of questions that may be designed to make them look bad.

6. *What do you hope to accomplish?*

7. *What qualifications do you have that make you feel you would be beneficial to us?*

8. *What extracurricular activities did you engage in at school?*

9. *How do you feel about traveling?*

10. *What part of the country would you like to settle down in?*

11. *What kind of people do you enjoy interacting with?*

12. *What do you regard as an equitable salary for a person with your qualifications?*

13. *Does your transcript reflect your ability? If not, why not?*

14. *What new skills would you like to learn?*

15. *Did you help with your college expenses? How?*

16. *At what age did you begin supporting yourself?*

17. *What causes you to lose your temper?*

18. *What are your major strengths? weaknesses?*

19. *What do you do to stay in good physical condition?*

20. *What are your professional goals?*

21. *What kind of reading do you like to do?*

22. *Who has had the greatest influence on your life?*

23. *What have you done that shows your creativity?*

24. *How would you proceed if you were in charge of hiring?*

25. *What are your most important criteria for determining whether you will accept a position?*

The closing of the interview   Toward the end of the interview, you should always tell the applicant what will happen next. Tell him or her about the procedures for making the decision. Who has the authority? When will the decision be made? How will the applicant be notified? These are some of the questions you certainly should answer. Then close the interview in a courteous, neutral manner. You should neither build false hopes nor seem to discourage the applicant.

Responsibilities of the Job Applicant

Interviews are part—and an important part—of the process of seeking employment. Even for part-time and temporary jobs, you will benefit if you approach the interviewing process seriously and systematically. There is no point in applying for positions that are obviously outside your area of expertise. It may seem a good idea to get interviewing experience, but you are wasting your time and the interviewer's time if you apply for a position you have no intention of taking or a position for which you are not qualified.

When you are granted an employment interview, remember that all you have to sell is yourself and your qualifications. You want to show yourself in the best possible light. You should be concerned about your appearance; if you want a particular job, you should dress in a way that is acceptable to the person or organization that may—or may not—hire you. You should be fully prepared for the interview. Two important responsibilities that you must meet before the interview itself are the résumé and the cover letter.

The résumé   Before most employers will even talk with you, they will want to see your résumé. A survey of the recruitment and employ-

When you are granted an employment interview, you want to show yourself in the best possible light.

ment policies and practices of the 500 largest U.S. corporations revealed the following information:[2]

A. *Almost all preferred both a cover letter and a résumé (98 percent)*

B. *Most wanted the cover letter typewritten (67 percent)*

C. *More than 75 percent wanted the following information included in the résumé:*

    1. *Personal information—date of birth, phone, address, marital status, number of dependents (92 percent)*

    2. *Listing of special interests such as accounting, statistics, sales, finance, economics (91 percent)*

    3. *Specific educational qualifications like major, minors, degrees, and the like (87 percent)*

    4. *Willingness to relocate (86 percent)*

    5. *List of scholarships, awards, and honors (86 percent)*

    6. *Previous work experience including jobs, dates of employment, company addresses, reasons for leaving (82 percent)*

    7. *Statement on physical or health status (80 percent)*

    8. *Social data like fraternities, sororities, athletics, clubs, including offices held (76 percent)*

D. *More than 33 percent wanted the following information included in the résumé:*

    1. *Salary requirements (57 percent)*

    2. *Source of applicant's college financing (57 percent)*

    3. *Name of high school, class rank, and date of graduation (48 percent)*

    4. *List of grades in major and minor college subjects (46 percent)*

    5. *Special skills such as typing, fluency in a foreign language, operating computers (41 percent)*

    6. *A list of references (33 percent)*

E. *Although more preferred one- to two-page résumés (35 percent), a significant number preferred only one page (30 percent) résumés*

---

[2]"As You Were Saying—The Cover Letter and Résumé," *Personnel Journal*, Vol. 48 (September 1969), pp. 732–733. This article is a summary of information provided by Harold D. Janes, Professor of Management, University of Alabama.

F. *The cover letter should be short, contain specific areas of interest and availability; it should explain or amplify elements of the résumé; it should be creative; it should be clear, neat, and well-typed.*

Getting ready for the interview   It is a good idea to give yourself a practice session. Try to anticipate some of the questions you will be asked and think carefully about your answers. You need not write out and practice answers; but, before the actual interview, you should have anticipated key questions, and you should have thought about such subjects as salary expectations, possible contribution to the company, and special skills.

The interview   One of the best guidelines for interviewing procedure is a list of some of the common complaints that interviewers have about applicants. Any applicant for employment will find something of value in this list.[3]

The undesirable applicant:

1. *Is caught lying*
2. *Shows lack of interest*
3. *Is belligerent, rude, or impolite*
4. *Lacks sincerity*
5. *Is evasive*
6. *Is concerned only about salary*
7. *Is unable to concentrate*
8. *Is indecisive*
9. *Is late*
10. *Is unable to express himself clearly*
11. *Wants to start in an executive position*
12. *Oversells case*

The list stresses negative points. Let's consider some positive approaches that will help you give the best possible impression.

---

[3]Selected from Charles S. Goetzinger, "An Analysis of Irritating Factors in Initial Employment Interviews of Male College Graduates," unpublished PhD. dissertation, Purdue University, 1954. Reported in Charles J. Stewart and William B. Cash, *Interviewing: Principles and Practices* (Dubuque, Iowa: Wm. C. Brown Company, 1974), pp. 162–163.

1. *Be prompt.*   The interview is the company's only clue to your work behavior. If you are late, the interviewer may conclude that you are likely to be late for work. We suggest that you give yourself at least fifteen minutes' leeway to cover any possible traffic problems.

2. *Look at the interviewer.*   Remember that your nonverbal communication tells a lot about you. Company representatives are likely to consider eye contact a clue to your self-confidence.

3. *Determine if this is a directive or nondirective interview.*   If it is directive, be sure to answer questions completely. Your responses will be compared with those of others who answer the same questions. If the interview appears to be nondirective, open up and talk. The interviewer will be trying to get to know you, and he can do that only if you cooperate.

4. *Give yourself time to think.*   If the interviewer asks you a question that you have not anticipated, give yourself time to think before you answer. It is better to pause and think than to give a hasty answer that may cost you the job. If you do not understand the question, paraphrase it before you attempt to answer.

5. *Don't talk salary.*   Talking salary during an interview can have only negative consequences for you. If you mention a salary that is too high, you can price yourself out of a job that you want; if you mention a figure that is much lower than what the company is willing to pay, the company may lower its offer or reevaluate their impression of a person who has such a low opinion of his worth. One way of handling a salary question is to ask the interviewer, "What do you normally pay someone

If the interview appears to be nondirective, open up and talk.

with my experience and education for this level position?" Such a question allows you to get an idea of what the salary will be without committing yourself to a figure. The time to talk salary is when a company actually makes you a job offer. Then you are in the strongest position to negotiate the salary you consider appropriate.

6. *Don't talk benefits.*   A company is usually interested in people who want to work, not in people who are interested only in reward. Benefits questions are appropriate after the company has made you an offer.

7. *If this is a starting position, do not badger the interviewer with questions concerning upward mobility.*   The interviewer may see these types of questions as personally threatening. You should, however, quickly inquire if this position is a career opportunity. If it is, you can be sure that promotions are available for industrious workers.

8. *Ask questions about the type of work you will be doing.*   The interview is your chance to find out if you would enjoy working for this company. You might ask the interviewer to describe a typical work day for the person who will get this job. If the interview is conducted at the company offices, you might ask to see where you would be working.

9. *Do your homework.*   Do not go for an interview knowing nothing about the company. Knowing about the company shows interest in the company. Know what the company produces or what services it renders; know whether the company is privately or publicly owned. Be aware of its financial health.

Communication Session

Reflection

What do you see as your major interviewing strengths? weaknesses?

Practice

1. Prepare a résumé for a position such as you might apply for after graduation.
2. Working in pairs, each partner will interview the other for the particular job for which the résumé was prepared.

Summary

You are most likely to use interviewing as a means of getting information from an expert for a paper, an article, or a speech. You are most likely to be interviewed when you are looking for a job. In either event, interviewing skills are important to you.

The key skill of interviewing is using questions effectively. Open questions allow for flexible response; closed questions are answered "yes" or "no" or with a few words. Primary questions stimulate response; secondary questions follow up the primary questions. Neutral questions allow the respondent free choice; leading questions require the person to answer in a particular way.

When you are interviewing for information, you will want to select the best person to interview, determine a framework for the interview, conduct the interview according to the framework, and interpret the results.

When you are being interviewed for a job, you will want to learn about the company and prepare an appropriate cover letter and résumé. For the interview itself, you will want to be prompt, be alert and look directly at the interviewer, give yourself time to think before answering difficult questions, and ask intelligent questions about the work.

Suggested Readings

The following two books are especially valuable:

Robert L. Kahn and **Charles F. Cannell.** *The Dynamics of Interviewing.* New York: John Wiley & Sons, 1957.

Charles J. Stewart and **William B. Cash.** *Interviewing: Principles and Practices.* Dubuque, Iowa: Wm. C. Brown Co., 1974.

Chapter 14
Establishing and Maintaining Interpersonal Relationships

PAYOFFS *After you have read this chapter, you should be able to:*

1. *Define a good relationship.*
2. *List and explain the social categories of relationships.*
3. *List and explain the communication levels within relationships.*
4. *List and explain the elements of interpersonal attraction.*
5. *Explain the exchange interactions that occur in testing out and attempting to find mutually satisfying levels of relationships.*
6. *Discuss the criteria for a sound, long-term communication relationship.*
7. *Draw a Johari window.*

We know that people need people, that they need to establish and maintain good relationships with one another, but what *is* a good relationship? Basically, a good relationship is any mutually satisfying interaction—on any level—with another person. Perhaps you are inclined to think of good relationships in terms of male-female interaction, but relationships exist between members of the same sex as well as the opposite sex. They are sometimes determined by the people and sometimes by the context. For instance, Dan may speak proudly of his good relationship with his father, and Alice may speak of a good relationship with her boss—in each of these cases the relationship was contextually determined by being a part of a family or being a member of an organization. On the other hand, Mike speaks of a good relationship with George, and Ann speaks of a good relationship with Jack. In these cases the people were responsible for creating the relationship.

In this chapter we'll explore what relationships are and are not by looking at different kinds of relationships and the various influences that can affect them for better or worse. We'll discuss: (1) the social categories of relationships, (2) the communication levels within relationships, (3) the elements of interpersonal attraction that help to initiate relationships, (4) the exchange interactions that operate in intensifying or cooling off a relationship, and (5) the criteria for a sound, long-term communication relationship.

Social Categories of Relationships

We can have good relationships with many people, but the *nature* of these relationships will differ. These different kinds of relationships may be classified as acquaintance, role, friendship, and deep friendship or intimate.

Acquaintance Relationships

Acquaintances are people we know by name and talk with when the opportunity arises but with whom our ties are loose. We become acquainted with those who live in our apartment house or dorm or in the house next door, who sit next to us in a class, who go to our church or belong to our club. Acquaintance relationships are likely to be a product of a given context. While Ruth and Ann are in biology class, they are friendly, but they make no effort to see each other outside of class, and if they meet it is by chance.

Acquaintances may become friends. Perhaps as Ruth and Ann talk in biology class they find enough in common to extend the relationship beyond the classroom, and in time they may think of each other as friends. On the other hand, when the term ends they may go their separate ways. When they meet on campus, they will recognize each other; and if they do happen to meet somewhere, they will talk.

Role Relationships

Role relationships are also a product of context, even more so than acquaintance relationships. You have a role relationship with your parents, your siblings, your children, your co-workers, your doctor, and so forth. These relationships arise from the interaction of prescribed roles.

Within these role relationships the participants have a great deal of leeway in determining the depth and character of the relationship, but the relationship itself will last so long as they are cast in their roles. With relatives, for example, the role relationships last a lifetime. With co-workers the role relationships last as long as you and the others are employed in the same positions.

You will probably try to make these role relationships good ones. The criteria for a good relationship vary from role to role; a good working relationship with your boss is much different from a good family relationship with your brother or sister.

Friend Relationships

Friends are people we like and who like us; friends seek each other out because they enjoy one another's company. Friendships may be initiated within a specific context. People then *become* friends as a result of a shared interest in a specific activity or a specific line of work. People refer to their tennis friends, office friends, or neighborhood friends because the friendship developed within the context of tennis, work, and so forth.

Within that context people may share ideas and feelings rather freely, but interaction outside the context may be limited. The Marshalls and the Smiths live next to each other. Gayle Marshall and Donna Smith both like to work outside, puttering in the garden. Gayle and Donna become acquainted by virtue of being neighbors. As time goes on and Gayle and Donna find they enjoy each other's company, they become friends. Gayle often drops by during the evening for a few minutes to have a cup of coffee. She becomes acquainted with Donna's husband, Al, in the process, and her husband, Randy, becomes acquainted with both Donna and Al. Donna and Gayle share recipes, give each other advice on handling various family and work problems, and just enjoy each other's presence. And although both couples occasionally go out together, Donna and Gayle's friendship is basically neighborhood bound.

However they may begin, friend relationships are those in which people find satisfaction with each other on many levels. Friends act reciprocally to meet each other's needs. The level of trust between friends is quite high. Friends spend time with each other because they want to. A change of job, a divorce, or a move to another city may not break that friendship. There are some people who see each other only once or twice a year but still consider themselves friends because when they are together, they share ideas and feelings freely and rely on each other's counsel. Yet even friends do not cross some boundaries.

Deep Friendship or Intimate Relationships

Deep friends or intimates are those with whom we share our deepest feelings. A person may have countless acquaintance relationships, a great many role relationships, and many friend relationships, but he is likely to have only one or two truly intimate relationships.

In male-female relationships intimacy is likely to include sex. However, a person can be intimate with a member of the same sex or with a relative without having sex with him or her. Intimacy implies a deep feeling for another person that is marked by the mutual sharing of even the deepest secrets. Intimates are those with whom people usually choose to spend the most important moments of their lives.

Communication Levels in Relationships

The social category of a relationship (acquaintance, friend, and so on) is often determined by or characterized by the communication level that exists between the people involved. The communication level will belong to one of four categories: the phatic level, the gossip level, the idea-exchange level, and the sharing feelings level.

The Phatic Level

On the phatic communication level, you acknowledge or recognize another person and are willing to verbalize this recognition. It is identified by such statements as, "How're you doing?" "What do you say?" and "Great day, isn't it?" With none of these is more than a perfunctory reply expected. If in response to "How're you doing?" the other person were to stop and disclose in detail her current state of health, it is likely that you would be taken aback. Phatic communication is not intended for sharing information; it is used to acknowledge recognition and it leaves the door open for exploration of higher levels of communication at some other time or in some other place. In terms of the communication functions we discussed in Chapter 1, the phatic level serves the important function of meeting certain social expectations.

The Gossip Level

On the gossip level, two or more persons communicate by discussing other persons. Such statements as, "Have you seen Bill lately—I hear he has a really great job" or, "Would you believe that Mary and Tom are going together? They never seemed to hit it off too well in the past" or, "Irene is really working hard at losing weight. I saw her the other day talking with Suzie about the diet she's on" are typical of conversations on the gossip level.

The gossip level is considered a safe level of communication, for you can gossip for a long time with another person without really saying anything about yourself or without learning anything about the other person except the kind of gossip he enjoys. Gossip can be a pleasant way to pass the time of day with people whom you know, but with whom you have no desire or need for a deeper relationship. Sometimes gossip is malicious; more often than not, however, gossip is a way of interacting amicably with others without getting involved personally. You may notice that party conversation is largely gossip. Gossip-level communication is seen in acquaintanceships, role relationships, and some friendships.

The Idea-Exchange Level

On the idea-exchange level, persons share facts, opinions, beliefs, and values. This level of communication is common in role relationships and friendships. At the office, Zeb may talk with Hal about sports, Martha may talk with Ann about sewing, or Pete may talk with Jack about new cars. In more serious circumstances, Bart may talk with Al about the U.S. role in the Far East and Phyllis may talk with Myra about the Equal Rights Amendment. Although the discussions of foreign policy and women's rights may be "deeper" than chatter about sports or cars, both sets of conversations are on the idea-exchange level. On this level, you learn what the other person is thinking; through such conversations you can determine what you have in common, if anything, and you can decide whether or not you would like to have the relationship grow.

Remember the exercise you did on self-disclosure when you had to label disclosures as high-risk, moderate-risk, or low-risk? Most idea-exchange statements are disclosures at the low-risk or moderate-risk level. You can tell what you think about an idea or an action without revealing very much of the "real you." You may discover that many relationships seldom go beyond this level.

The Sharing-Feelings Level

On the sharing-feelings level, persons reveal not only what they are thinking, but also how they feel about the ideas, actions, and behaviors of themselves and others. Although we have discussed the skill of describing feelings as an important part of the sending process on any communication level, the sharing of deep feelings is usually reserved for those whom you regard as close personal friends or intimate friends in an ongoing relationship.

Some achieve this level of communication with only one other person at any one time; many are on this level with members of the immediate family as well as with one or a few others; unfortunately, some seldom if ever achieve this level with anybody. We say "unfortunately" because it is on this level that you come to know and to understand another person. Although it is unrealistic and may be undesirable to have such a relationship with many others, the presence of a sharing-feelings level of communication with at least some persons is regarded as a highly beneficial communication goal.

Elements of Interpersonal Attraction

An old song lamented that "she lived on the morning side of the mountain, and he lived on the twilight side of the hill." The song points out that two people may be just right for each other, but if they never meet it hardly matters whether they are or not. The point is obvious but well taken—people's lives must intersect in some way, or they will never meet. Being in the college, belonging to a club, attending a church, or living in a dorm puts you in a context that enables you to meet people easily. But, whether it be in a course with twenty-five other students or in a dorm with 300, you may be attracted to only a small number of people out of the total. Why? In this section we want to look at the elements of interpersonal attraction other than proximity, that make you move closer to others. Attraction means a drawing together. Attraction is a starting point of interpersonal relationships. Most attraction occurs as a result of one or a combination of the five elements discussed below.

Physical Characteristics

You are probably well aware that the first if not the most important element in interpersonal attraction is physical. Physically attractive people are eye-catching, and giving attention to people solely on the basis of their physical characteristics is an accepted practice in our society. Even though the cliché that beauty is only skin deep is true, many Americans are apparently very much interested in what's on that surface. During almost any hour of television watching you are likely to see one or more ads for commercial products that claim to preserve your attractiveness, make you attractive, or make you *more* attractive. Whether physical characteristics *should* be a factor in developing a relationship is irrelevant; physical characteristics are an inescapable element in interpersonal attraction.

Social Similarity

Another element of interpersonal attraction is social similarity. Although you may first attempt to strike up a conversation with a person on the basis of physical characteristics, you may make a decision about the depth of your attraction—about whether to continue to see that person—on the basis of social similarity. If Holly likes to dance and enjoys parties and movies, she is likely to be attracted to Clark if he likes to dance and enjoys parties and movies. If you are led to believe that a person likes to socialize as you do and you later find that your perception was wrong, that person is likely to become less attractive to you. If Clark confesses to Holly that he doesn't really enjoy dancing and that most movies bore him, she may find her attraction to Clark diminishing.

You are probably well aware that the first if not the most important element in interpersonal attraction is physical.

Task and Professional Similarity

People may be drawn together on the basis of joint work interests. Travis finds satisfaction working with Gwen on research questions of mutual interest: he may begin to wonder whether he can find satisfaction with Gwen in other contexts as well. For some people, work compatibility is a test of the possibility of a long-term relationship. If you want to be attractive to a particular person, you should show interest in that person's work. *Caution*—we are *not* advocating that you fake an interest just to get the person's attention. Although pretense may work in the short run, if you do not actually care about the work the other person will find out soon enough. If the apparent basis for the attraction no longer exists, the relationship is not likely to grow.

Background Similarity

People are likely to be drawn to those who have similarities in background and experience. People who grew up on farms, or went to the same school (or the same kind of school), or spent their summers working at the beach, or who had parents in the service are likely to be attracted to each other. An American visiting, say, Italy may be attracted to a person from his home town simply on the basis of their similar background.

Attitude and Value Similarity

You are likely to be attracted to those who share your attitudes and values. Is your religion vital to the way you conduct your life? Is integrity more important than position? How do you feel about premarital sex? welfare? capital punishment? You are likely to be drawn to those who respond to these questions as you do.

Interrelationship of Elements

How do these five elements interrelate? As we said, people are initially attracted to those whom they perceive as physically attractive. But physical attraction appears to be only a door to developing a relationship. Whether you will work to intensify the relationship is likely to depend on similarities in social interests, work, background, and attitudes and values. Moreover, one or more of these similarities might stimulate a relationship. For instance, Cal and Dorothy work in the same office. Neither is physically attracted to the other until the two are assigned to work on the same project. They find their work interests and work habits are similar. Their work compatibility motivates them to find other common interests. Soon Dorothy may find herself thinking, "Cal never caught my eye before. How did I miss him? He is really very attractive!" Cal finds himself thinking the same thing about Dorothy.

The more people think they have in common, the more they are attracted to each other. Yet what people believe to be true (based on initial perceptions) may not prove to be so; moreover, even when the initial perception about similarities is correct, it may not correctly identify intensity of feeling. When the basis of attraction fades or proves invalid, the relationship is likely to suffer. As we pointed out earlier, when Holly finds out that Clark is not really a dancing and partying man, her attraction to him may fade. Perceptions of intensity follow a similar pattern. For instance, both Sue and Gordon enjoy watching football on television. Their mutual interest in sports—particularly as spectators—has drawn them together. As their relationship intensifies, Sue may discover that her *degree* of enjoyment of televised football is far different from Gordon's. When Gordon insists on watching three football games in a row on a Sunday, Sue may begin to question the basis for her attraction to Gordon. "I enjoy football," she may say, "but Gordon, you're too much." And unless other bases of attraction are strong, football may drive Sue and Gordon apart.

Personality Contrasts

Can a relationship be built on dissimilarities as well as on similarities? Is the saying, "opposites attract" as accurate as, "birds of a feather flock together"? It is true that some people are drawn to others by dissimilarities: Some dominant women seek submissive men, and some introverts are attracted to extroverts. Compelling evidence to support the belief that dissimilarities can be a *major basis for attraction*, however, does not exist. Research on this subject only confirms what we already know: although most people are attracted by appealing physical characteristics and similarities in social and work interests as well as similarities in background and values, some people are attracted by dissimilarities in those same categories.

Exchange Interactions

We have spoken more than once of the importance of exchange theory in explaining why people behave as they do. As you remember, exchange theory claims that we are likely to establish a relationship if the rewards we get from the relationship offset the costs of maintaining it. We are likely to continue in a relationship if the cost/reward ratio we see in alternative relationships is less favorable than in the existing one.

According to exchange theory, relationships move through four stages: sampling, bargaining, commitment, and institutionalization. Each of these stages need not be identifiable as a separate step, nor is it absolutely necessary that a relationship pass through the steps in this order. We believe that an analysis of these stages will deepen your understanding of the nature of relationships.

Sampling is a selection process. As we begin a relationship, we try to find out what we have in common with the other person. If a person shows desirable traits or behaviors, he is pursued. If a person is undesirable for some reason, the relationship is terminated or held at a particular level. In other words, in the acquaintance stage a person makes decisions about whether he or she will find a deeper relationship profitable.

Bargaining is the stage in a relationship at which people determine the kinds of rewards they may expect to get from the relationship and the kinds of costs that will be incurred. Tom finds that if he spends his time and money a certain way he will be rewarded. Tom takes the time to take Phyllis to a museum. If Phyllis doesn't seem to care about what they see, if Phyllis can't share in a discussion of what they see, or if Phyllis doesn't show any appreciation of the time Tom is taking, the cost will exceed the reward. If Tom doesn't get any (or too few) of the needed or expected rewards, he may feel that his total expenditure in time, energy, and money has been wasted. Tom will stop taking Phyllis to museums and, unless he still believes that some potential for reward exists, probably stop seeing Phyllis altogether.

Bargaining also takes place in same-sex relationships. Tom sees a potential friendship developing with George because both like to play racquetball. But if George can't get enough free time to play with Tom, or if George can play only at hours when Tom can't, or if George is too poor or too good a player to make an enjoyable game, or if their game is about equal but Tom just isn't getting the pleasure he expects, the racquetball friendship will not develop, will stagnate, or will deteriorate.

Commitment is the stage in a relationship at which a person gives up other relationships in favor of a particular one. Jack and Margaret go out a few times and enjoy themselves. Each is benefiting from the relationship. The relationship has progressed so well and the rewards have been so high that they begin to spend even more time together. Although other relationships may be maintained during this time (Margaret continues to go jogging with Andrea), relationships of the same kind will be limited (Jack was also dating Nancy, but no longer).

Institutionalization is the stage in the relationship at which two people formally ratify their commitment. In a male-female relationship this stage is most often marked by marriage. In another kind of relationship, it could be marked by signing a contract, by forming a partnership, or by any other act that is appropriate for that particular relationship.

Communication Session

Reflection

Consider a person with whom you have a close interpersonal relationship. Does the above discussion help to explain the success of this interpersonal relationship? If so, how? If not, why not?

Discussion

With a close friend, discuss the similarities and differences in your perceptions of your behavior. What accounts for any differences that might exist?

Criteria for a Sound Communication Relationship

At this point in your life, you may have a solid friendship or close personal relationship with at least one person and perhaps with several others. Once a mutually satisfying relationship has been achieved, it becomes all too easy to be complacent. Some people assume that, because of mutual love and respect, a particular relationship will go on indefinitely; they may discover, however, that various stresses and strains can weaken and perhaps destroy even the strongest relationships. What is needed to help us withstand the inevitable assaults on our relationships with others? In sorting out suggestions from philosophers, psychologists, and communication experts, we believe that you stand an excellent chance of maintaining a sound, long-term communication relationship if three qualities are present: openness in communication, sensitivity in placement of realistic demands, and restraint of the need to control.

Openness in Communication

In Chapter 5, we defined openness as a willingness to self-disclose and a willingness to receive feedback. A communication relationship is strengthened by the existence of a mutually satisfying blend of self-disclosure and feedback. How can you tell whether you and another are sharing enough to keep the relationship growing? The best method is to discuss it. As the basis for a worthwhile discussion, we suggest the drawing and analsis of Johari windows.

The Johari window (named after its two originators, Joe Luft and

Harry Ingham)[1] is a tool that you can use to examine the relationship between disclosure and feedback. The window is divided into four sections or panes as shown in Figure 14-1.

Open	Hidden or Blind
Secret	Unknown

Figure 14-1

The first quadrant is called the "open" pane of the window. The open pane is used to represent everything about a person that he or she knows and freely shares with others. It also shows others' observations of him or his behavior that he is aware of. For instance, most people are willing to discuss biographical data, the kind of car they drive, where they go to school, their favorite restaurant, and countless other items of information. Moreover, most people are aware of certain of their mannerisms that others observe. A person may be well aware that he reddens when he is embarrassed or that he walks with a slouch when he is tired. If you were preparing a Johari window that represented your relationship with another person, you would include in the open pane all the items of information that you would be free to share with that other person.

The second quadrant of the window is the "secret" pane of the window. The secret pane is used to represent all those things a person knows about himself that he does not normally share with others. For instance, many people are less likely to share items of information that they regard as personal. This information may run the gamut from items like where Charley keeps his clean socks or why he does not care for squash to deep secrets that seem very threatening to him. If you were preparing a Johari window that represented your relationship with another person, you would include in the secret pane all the items of information that you are unwilling to share with that other person. Secret information moves into the open part of the window only when you change your attitude about revealing that specific information. If, for example, Kathy was engaged at

[1]Reprinted from *Group Processes: An Introduction to Group Dynamics* by Joseph Luft. By permission Mayfield Publishing Company (formerly National Press Books). Copyright © 1963, 1970 by Joseph Luft.

one time but usually does not tell people that fact, it would be in the secret part of her window. If for some reason she decided to disclose this information to you, it would move into the open part of the Johari window that she drew to represent her relationship with you.

The third quadrant of the window is called the hidden or blind area. The hidden pane is used to represent information others know about a person that he is unaware of. Most people have blind spots—behaviors that are observable to others but for some reason unknown to the person himself. If Charley snores when he sleeps, if he always wrinkles up his nose when he does not like something, or if he gets a gleam in his eye when he sees a girl he would like to get to know, these may be nonverbal behaviors that he is blind to. Information in the hidden area of the window moves to the open area through feedback from others. We are constantly getting feedback, but some of us are more receptive to that feedback than others. If you were preparing a Johari window that represented your relationship with another person, the size of the hidden or blind pane would depend on how receptive you are to the verbal or nonverbal feedback of that person. For instance, if Ken draws Charley for a roommate at the dorm, he might announce to Charley that he snores or he might "feed back" information to Charley in a more subtle manner. If Charley does not choose to "hear" what Ken tells him, the blind spot continues. On the other hand, if Charley is receptive to such feedback, the blind or hidden pane gets smaller and the open pane enlarges.

The fourth and last quadrant of the window is called the "unknown." It represents information about a given person that is not known to anyone—not even the person himself. If no one is aware of this information, how do we know it exists? We know it exists because the unknown manifests itself on occasion. This manifestation might be called the "ah ha!" experience. For instance, let's suppose that you have never thought of yourself as a leader (therefore, your leadership capability is unknown to you) and let's say that your friend has never thought of you as a leader either. Now, let's further suppose that some emergency arises and you are forced to assume a leadership position. If your friend has an "ah ha!" experience and realizes how well you led the group, the information about your leadership abilities moves from the unknown part of the window to the hidden part of the window, where it is known to him but not to you. If your friend then shares this new-found perception of you with you by means of feedback, this information moves into the open part of your window, where it is known to both you and your friend. The second way the unknown becomes known is by means of your own unaided realization—after assuming this leadership position *you* might realize that you are a good leader. In this case, the information about your leadership ability moves into the secret part of the window, where it is known to you but not to your friend. Should you disclose this realization to your friend, it then moves into the open part of your window.

As you can see, with each bit of self-disclosure or feedback the sizes and shapes of the various panes of the window change. For each relationship you have with another person you can construct a window that represents the nature of that relationship in terms of the behaviors we have been discussing. Let's look at four different representations and consider what they mean.

Figure 14-2 shows a relationship in which the open area is very small.

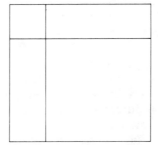

Figure 14-2

The person is not sharing much information about himself and is blind to what the other person knows or thinks about him. This window is typical of a relationship during the first stages of getting to know a person; it is also typical of a person who keeps to himself and does not want, desire, or need to interact on more than a superficial level with others.

Figure 14-3 shows a relationship in which a person is willing to share his thoughts and feelings but gets or is receptive to very little feedback from the other person. Such a person may perceive himself to be very open in his communication. Yet his communication is limited by his unwillingness or lack of interest in learning about what others observe.

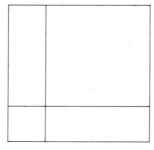

Figure 14-3

Figure 14-4 shows a relationship in which a person seeks out and is very receptive to feedback but is quite reluctant to share much of himself.

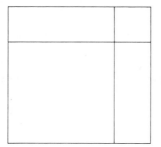

Figure 14-4

He wants to hear what others have observed, but he is not willing or is afraid to disclose his observations or feelings.

Figure 14-5 shows a relationship in which a person both seeks out and is very receptive to feedback and is willing to share information and feelings he has. This is the kind of window we would expect to see depicting a close relationship of friends or intimates. Even though Figure 14-5 is the best model of communication for friends and intimates, the windows of Figures 14-2, 14-3, and 14-4 depict most of our communication relationships. Although no one need share every idea or feeling with others and no one need be receptive to every person's reaction to him, having a relatively large open pane is conducive to good interpersonal communication.

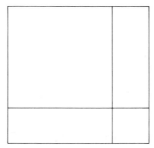

Figure 14-5

Communication Session

Reflection

For persons with whom you communicate on a more or less regular basis, does the open part of your window tend to be large or small? Explain.

Practice

Working with an intimate or a close friend, each of you draw a window that represents your perception of your relationship with the other. Then each of you draw a window that represents what you perceive to be the other's relationship with you. Share the windows. How do they compare? If there are differences in the representations, talk with your friend about them.

Sensitive Placement of Realistic Demands

It is unlikely that two people can be close to each other for very long without one or both seeing in the other behaviors that he or she would like to see changed. In a good interpersonal relationship, participants may place demands on each other, but the demands must be realistic and sensitively communicated.

Realistic demands are those that each person is capable of fulfilling without harm to the individual. A woman may demand that her husband give up sports—a man may demand that his wife give up seeing her women friends. Neither of these demands is realistic. Although each of these demands may be capable of being fulfilled, neither is likely to be fulfilled without hurting the other individual. It may well be realistic, on the other hand, for the woman to demand that her husband limit the total hours he gives to sports or for the man to demand that his wife limit the total hours she spends with women friends.

How such demands are placed is every bit as important as the nature of the demands themselves. Descriptiveness (rather than judgment), provisionalism (rather than dogmatism), and equality (rather than superiority) are all communication skills that should be used in the phrasing of these demands. We have already seen that defensiveness is easily aroused when discussion centers on a subject one or both persons feel very deeply about.

Restraint of the Need to Control

In each person the control need varies from strong to weak. Yet even persons with relatively low control needs may attempt to exercise control when they perceive that the behavior of the other person is changing the nature of the communication relationship. All too often, unfortunately, when two people enter into a relationship, they firmly believe that both (especially the other) will forever be as they were at the beginning of that relationship. Have you never heard comments like, "She wasn't interested in going back to school when I first met her" or, "He's a different person—he joined Kiwanis and now he wants to spend all his free time 'doing good'"? Sometimes changes in one person in a relationship are so great that the relationship cannot be maintained. Some deterioration in marriages may be attributed to such developments. When a person perceives herself threatened by changes in another, she may experience a strong desire to place controls on the other person in order to halt or alter the perceived change.

We must recognize, however, that change is a part of growth. Just because two persons are joined in a relationship does not preclude the need or desirability of change. What are the alternatives to trying to control the other person? If the relationship is to continue, the threatened person must either change with the other or adapt to the particular change. If the wife goes back to school to study for a degree, either the husband must involve himself in the subject matter she is studying or he must change his approach to his wife. Either the wife must share her husband's interest in Kiwanis or she must adapt to his change in time priorities.

Summary

An effect of—if not the primary reason for—communication is developing relationships. Although at times we seem to fall into and drift out of relationships without rhyme or reason, there are identifiable elements underlying the success or failure of a relationship. A good relationship is any mutually satisfying level of interaction with another person.

People are inclined to view their relationships in the social categories of acquaintances, roles, friends, and deep friends or intimates.

Communication in relationships will occur on the phatic level, the gossip level, the information-exchange level, and the sharing-feelings level. Although phatic communication and gossip are most associated with acquaintances, they both occur in all social categories. Sharing-feelings communication, the highest level, is likely to occur only with close friends and intimates.

Relationships are begun on the basis of interpersonal attraction. We are probably first attracted to each other on the basis of physical characteristics. Attraction is also a product of similarity of social interests, task or professional interests, background, and attitudes and values. Although most people are attracted by similarities, some are attracted by contrasts.

People test out relationships through sampling, bargaining, commitment, and institutionalization. Most relationships stay in the sampling and bargaining stages, or perhaps we should say that as a result of the sampling and bargaining process we determine with whom we will seek more intensive friendship and intimacy.

When a loving relationship is formed, there are certain qualities that must be present to maintain the relationship at that level. Three of the most important of these are openness in communication, sensitivity in placing realistic demands, and restraint of the need to control.

Suggested Readings

Sidney M. Jourard. *Healthy Personality.* New York: Macmillan Publishing Co., 1974. Although the entire book is worth reading, you should find Chapter 10, "Personal Relations and Healthy Personality," especially valuable.

Joseph Luft. *Group Process: An Introduction to Group Dynamics.* Palo Alto, California: Mayfield Publishing Co., 1970. Contains a complete explanation of the Johari window.

Paul Watzlawick, Janet H. Beavin, and **Don D. Jackson.** *Pragmatics of Human Communication.* New York: W. W. Norton & Co., 1967.

Lawrence S. Wrightsman. *Social Psychology,* 2d ed. Monterey, California: Brooks/Cole Publishing Co., 1977.

Appendix A
Glossary of Basic Communication Skills

Skill	Definition	Use	Procedure	Example
Accuracy (pp. 121–122)	Selecting words to represent thoughts and feelings that are recognized by others in our culture as symbolizing those thoughts and feelings.	To increase the probability of receiver decoding message accurately.	**1.** Before you speak, ask yourself whether word is most accurate representation. **2.** Make your statement. **3.** If used wrong word, correct it.	"Bill, would you go get my watch off the [thinks 'hutch' mentally corrects] buffet?"
Arbitration, Seeking (p. 218)	Finding an impartial person who, after hearing both sides of a conflict, will weigh and evaluate the alternatives and make a decision for you.	To resolve conflict when other methods have failed.	**1.** Agree on an arbitrator. **2.** Make sure arbitrator is competent to make decision. **3.** Make a verbal contract to abide by arbitrator's decision.	"I can see that we're deadlocked. How about asking Dr. Wright's opinion and going along with what she says?"
Assertiveness (pp. 136–139)	Learning to state ideas and feelings openly in interpersonally effective ways.	To show clearly what you think or feel.	**1.** Identify what you are thinking or feeling. **2.** State it in the most interpersonally sound way.	(Believing you have been overcharged) "I have never been charged for a refill on iced tea before—has there been a change in policy?"
Crediting Others (pp. 128–129)	Verbally identifying the person whose ideas you are using.	To give credit to others in order to confirm them and to avoid possible hard feelings.	When you are using ideas you got from others, include their names—give credit to them—when you state the ideas.	No credit: "We've got to make some changes in our course offering. I think we should offer a course in attitude change." Crediting: "We've got to make some changes in our course offerings. Laura suggested we offer a course in attitude change, and I agree."

Skill	Definition	Use	Procedure	Example
Crediting Self —Making "I" Statements (pp. 129–130)	Identifying *yourself* as the source of a particular idea or feeling.	To transmit information accurately, to help receiver fully understand, to avoid creating defensiveness, to acknowledge personal responsibility, and to avoid allness.	When an idea, an opinion, a feeling is *yours*, say so.	Instead of saying "Maury's is the best restaurant in town," say "*I* believe Maury's is the best restaurant in town."
Dating (pp. 117–118)	Including a specific time reference that indicates *when* a fact was true.	To avoid the pitfalls of language that allow you to speak of a dynamic world in static terms.	1. Before you make a statement consider when observation was true. 2. If not based on present information, include when it was true.	When Jake says, "How good a hitter is Steve?" Mark replies by dating his evaluation: "*When I worked with him two years ago,* he couldn't hit the curve."
Describing (pp. 105–106) (See Describing Behavior *and* Describing Feelings.)	Putting sensory data into words.			
Describing Behavior (pp. 162–164)	Accurately recounting specific observable actions of another without labeling the behavior as good or bad, right or wrong.	To create a supportive climate, to give helpful feedback, and to help support descriptions of feelings.	1. Become aware of what you see or hear. 2. Report only what you observed. 3. Refrain from judging the merit of the observation.	Instead of saying "She is such a snob," say "She has walked by us three times now without speaking."
Describing Feelings (pp. 130–134)	A sender statement that puts emotional states into words.	For self-disclosure; to teach people how to treat you.	1. Get in touch with the feelings you are having. Identify them—hate? anger? joy? 2. Credit your feelings —make an "I" statement. 3. Make sure the statement contains an emotion. 4. Describe the specific cause of the feeling, if known.	"I'm depressed and discouraged because I didn't get the job." "I'm feeling very warm and loving toward you right now."

Discussion (p. 212) (See also, Problem-solving method.)	Verbal weighing and considering of the pros and cons of the issues in conflict.	To resolve conflict.	1. Be cooperative, not competitive. 2. Be objective in presentation. 3. Be open in stating feelings and beliefs. 4. Be open to possible solutions. 5. Paraphrase others' statements.	"Now if I understand what you've been saying, you think we should get married in September because by then we will both have graduated. I guess that makes sense, but I'm afraid if we wait that long it will hurt our relationship . . ."
Empathizing (pp. 89–93)	Being able to detect and identify the immediate affective state of another. Responding in an appropriate manner.	To create or to promote a supportive climate.	1. Listen actively to what the person is saying. 2. Try to recall or to imagine what you would feel like under those same circumstances. 3. Say something that indicates your sensitivity to those feelings.	When Jerry says, "I really feel embarrassed about wearing braces in college," Mary empathizes and replies, "Yeah, I can understand that—I remember the things I had to put up with when I wore braces."
Equality (pp. 107–108)	Seeing others as worthwhile as oneself.	To create or promote a supportive climate.	1. Consider what you are about to say. 2. Consider whether it contains words or phrases that indicate or imply that you are in some way superior to the receiver. 3. If so, recast the sentence to alter the tone.	Instead of saying "As you gain maturity, you'll learn how to cope with these situations," say "That was a difficult one. But handling difficult ones helps you gain the experience—and we all need experience to help us with special cases."

Skill	Definition	Use	Procedure	Example
Feedback, Giving (pp. 171–174)	Responses to a person that provide that person with new information about himself. Takes the form of description of behavior, praise, and criticism.	To give people new information about themselves. To help them see themselves as others see them.	1. Make sure context allows for criticism. 2. Precede negative with positive if possible. 3. Include description of behavior. 4. Focus on only one behavior. 5. Be specific. 6. Direct to behavior that can be changed. 7. Include means of improvement. 8. Proceed with caution.	Carol says, "Bob, I've noticed something about your behavior with Jenny. Would you like to hear it?" After Bob assures her that he would, she continues, "Well, the last few times we've all been together, whenever Jenny starts to relate an experience, you interrupt her and finish telling the story."
Feedback, Receiving (pp. 102–104)	Creating a climate in which others feel comfortable giving you feedback.	To get information that will help you better understand yourself and your effect on others.	1. Ask for feedback only when you are really willing to hear it—outline what you are willing to hear feedback on. 2. Avoid verbal-nonverbal contradictions. 3. Paraphrase what you hear. 4. Show others that you are appreciative of what they have told you.	Mary asks, "Tim, when I'm in a group do I talk too loudly?" Tim replies, "Now that you mention it, Mary, you really do—and it's kind of embarrassing to me." "Thank you for being honest with me, Tim."
Fluency (pp. 124–127))	Speaking in smooth, uncluttered sentences. Avoiding such nonfluencies as vocal interferences, "you know," and empty expletives.	To avoid antagonizing the receiver; to decrease noise; to improve message reception.	1. Become aware of the nonfluencies you use. 2. In practice sessions, see how long you can talk without using a nonfluency. 3. In conversation, mentally note usages.	"Will you get me, uh, you know, a glass of water? Let me try that again—Will you get me a glass of water, please?"

Skill	Definition	Purpose	Guidelines	Example
Indexing (pp. 118–120)	Mentally or verbally accounting for individual differences.	To avoid allness in speaking.	**1.** Before you make a statement, consider whether it pertains to specific object, person, or place. **2.** If not based on knowledge of the specific, include some statement that acknowledges that.	**George:** "He's a politician, and I don't trust him." **Bill:** "Whether politicians are dishonest in general or not, we don't know Petrowski, and he may be honest."
Interpreting (pp. 154–156)	Attempting to point out an alternative or hidden meaning to an event.	To help a person see the possible meanings of words, actions, and events.	**1.** Consider your motives for interpreting. **2.** Phrase an alternative to the sender's interpretation—one that is intended to help the sender see that other interpretations are available. **3.** When appropriate, preface the interpretation with a supportive statement.	**Pam:** Sue must really be angry with me—Yesterday she walked right by me at the market and didn't even say, 'Hi.'" **Paula:** "Maybe she's not angry at all—maybe she just didn't see you."
Listening (pp. 145–148) (*See also* Paraphrasing, Supporting, Questioning, Interpreting.)	Making sense out of what you hear.	To receive oral communication.	**1.** Get ready to listen. **2.** Shift from speaker to listener completely. **3.** Listen actively. **4.** Withhold evaluation.	[Not applicable.]

Skill	Definition	Use	Procedure	Example
Negotiating (pp. 217–218)	Resolving conflict through trade-offs.	To resolve conflict when people will not change their positions.	1. Determine whether activities in conflict cannot both be accomplished. 2. Are negotiable elements of fairly equal importance? 3. Suggest a compromise position or suggest that if one person's idea is followed now the other's will be followed next.	"You've got to get to the store, and I've got to get this paper done. I'll drive you to the store tonight and help you with the shopping if you'll help me by typing my paper tomorrow morning."
Openness (See Self-Disclosure *and* Feedback, Receiving.)				
Paraphrasing (pp. 157–161)	Restating a message in your own words.	To increase listening efficiency; to avoid message confusion; to discover sender's motivation.	1. Listen carefully to the message. 2. Determine what the message means to *you*. 3. Restate the message using your own words to show the meaning you got from the message.	**Julia:** "I saw the best movie— you have to see it." **Tony:** (content paraphrase) "I take it that you really like the plot." (feelings paraphrase) "Sounds like the movie really made you happy."
Perception Checking (pp. 165–167)	A verbal statement that tests your understanding of how another person feels.	To clarify the meaning of nonverbal behavior.	1. Watch the behavior of another. 2. Describe the behavior to yourself or aloud. 3. Ask yourself: what does that behavior mean to me?	**Gary:** "I think we should rent costumes for the party." **Allan:** (Knits his brow and frowns as Gary talks.) **Gary:** "I get the feeling that you are not pleased with the idea of renting costumes."

Skill	Definition	Purpose	Example / Procedure
			4. Put your interpretation of the nonverbal behavior into words. 5. Check to see whether your perception is accurate.
Persuasion (pp. 187–197)	The conscious, usually verbal act of influencing attitude or behavior.	Bring about change.	Use the available means of persuasion: reasoning, motivating through emotional appeal, and credibility.
Problem-solving Method (pp. 267–270)	An organized procedure for solving problems.	To settle conflicts cooperatively; to help individuals and groups solve problems.	1. Identify the problem. 2. Analyze the nature of the problem. 3. Suggest possible solutions. 4. Select the solution that best meets the needs. 5. Implement the solution. See detailed example on pp. 269–270.
Provision-alism (pp. 106–107)	Phrasing ideas tentatively rather than dogmatically	Allows you to express your opinion, but recognizes that others may have valid ideas; helps create or maintain a positive communication climate.	1. Consider what you are about to say. 2. Determine whether it contains a wording that shows an attitude of finality, positiveness, or allness. 3. If it does, add a qualifying statement that recognizes (a) that the statement is your opinion or (b) that the statement may not be entirely true or only true under these circumstances. Instead of saying "That was a horrible movie," say "Others may have liked it, but I didn't care for it at all."

Skill	Definition	Use	Procedure	Example
Questioning (pp. 152–154)	Getting additional information.	To help get a more complete picture before making other comments; to help a shy person open up; to clarify meaning.	1. Determine motives for questioning. 2. Determine what kind of information you need to know. 3. Phrase question(s) to achieve the goal. 4. Make sure paralanguage is appropriate.	**Mary:** "Well, it would be better if she weren't so sedentary." **Sue:** "I don't understand—what do you mean by *sedentary?*"
Self-Disclosure (pp. 97–100) (*See also* Describing Feelings.)	Sharing biographical data, personal ideas, and feelings that are unknown to the other person.	Necessary to the initiation and development of a relationship.	1. Disclosure should be an acceptable risk. 2. Should move to deeper levels. 3. Should be part of an ongoing relationship. 4. Should be reciprocal. 5. Should consider receiver's ability to handle the disclosure.	May tells her current boy friend, "I've been engaged three times before."
Specific, Concrete Words (pp. 122–124)	Using words that indicate a single item within a category or a single representation of an abstract value.	To help receiver picture a thought analogous to sender's.	1. Before you speak ask yourself if the word or phrase is specific and concrete. 2. Make your statement. 3. If used more general or abstract than necessary, correct it with specific or concrete word.	Instead of saying "Get that junk off the table," say "Get the toys off the table." Instead of saying "He drives a cool car," say "He drives a red Jaguar convertible."
Supporting (pp. 150–152)	Saying something that soothes, reduces tension, or pacifies.	To help the sender to feel better about himself or what he has said or done.	1. Actively listen to the message. 2. Try to empathize with the person's feelings. 3. Phrase a reply that is in harmony with these feelings. 4. Indicate your willingness to be of help if possible.	"I'm so disappointed I didn't make the team." "I can understand the disappointment; you worked so hard."

Appendix B
Glossary of Communication Problems

Problem	Defined	Cost	Suggestions for Solving
Aggression (pp. 211–212)	Attempting to force another to accept your ideas through physical or psychological threats or actions.	Conflicts are created or escalated.	1. Resist the urge to threaten. 2. Describe your feelings.
Competitive Attitude (pp. 205–208)	Viewing conflict as a win-lose situation.	Creates or escalates conflict. Heightens competitive feelings in others.	1. Approach situation cooperatively. 2. Demonstrate your desire to resolve perceived conflict in a mutually beneficial way.
Defensiveness (pp. 105–106)	A negative feeling and/or behavior that results when a person feels threatened.	Interferes with open communication.	1. Be descriptive rather than evaluative. 2. Be problem-solving rather than control oriented. 3. Be spontaneous rather than strategic. 4. Be empathic rather than neutral. 5. Be equal rather than superior. 6. Be tentative rather than dogmatic.
Evaluative Responses (pp. 170–171)	Statements that judge a person's ideas, feelings, and behaviors.	Creates defensiveness.	Be descriptive rather than evaluative.
Gaps (pp. 244–263)	Communication distances between persons or groups of people.	Message distortion, stereotyping, prejudice.	1. Recognize that communication becomes more difficult as differences between communicators are increased. 2. Build bridges between *individuals*. 3. Index statements carefully.
Hidden Agenda (pp. 109–110)	A reason or motive for behavior that is undisclosed to the other participant(s).	May destroy trust between individuals; causes defensiveness; is manipulative.	1. Sender should self-disclose motives. 2. Receiver should describe behavior and perception check.

Problem	Defined	Cost	Suggestions for Solving
Inappropriate Responses (pp. 168–171)	Responses that do not meet the expectation of the other person, or responses that disconfirm the other person.	Cause defensiveness.	Substitute paraphrasing, questioning, interpreting, or supporting.
Incongruous Responses (p. 170)	Messages whose verbal cues conflict with the nonverbal cues.	Cause defensiveness.	1. Sender should be honest and describe his true feelings. 2. Receiver should perception check.
Information Overload (pp. 140–141)	Receiving more information than you can process at that time; or sending more than the other person can process.	Loss of at least part of the message. Possible frustration.	1. Receiver should use selective perception and if possible paraphrase. 2. Sender should limit details, group ideas, and emphasize key points.
Interrupting Response (p. 169)	Breaking in before the sender has finished.	Creates climate of superiority.	Allow person to finish sentence or complete thought.
Irrelevant Response (pp. 168–169)	One that bears no relation to what has been said.	Tends to disconfirm, to make person question his own value.	Listen to what other person has to say; at least acknowledge that you heard.
Noise, Internal (p. 9)	When thoughts and feelings of the participant interfere with meaning.	Overrides or interferes with message reception.	Turn up power of concentration.
Noise, External (p. 8)	External factors clogging the channels of communication.	Overrides or interferes with message reception.	1. Receiver can eliminate the noise or turn up powers of concentration. 2. Sender can compensate for the noise.
Noise, Semantic (pp. 8–9)	Decoding with a different meaning from what sender intends.	Distortion of meaning.	1. As sender, determine meanings, encode with care, analyze receivers to determine whether they are likely to understand language you have selected. 2. As receiver, listen actively and paraphrase if possible.
Surrender to Conflict (pp. 210–211)	Giving in to another for sole purpose of avoiding conflict.	Can become martyr.	1. Describe your feelings. 2. Credit your feelings.

Term	Description	Suggestions
Suspicion (p. 97)	An unhealthy fear of the unknown, the unusual, or people in authority.	Tremendous psychological pressure; prohibits open interaction.	1. Build a climate of trust. 2. Practice placing responsibility in others. 3. Take note of benefits of trusting behavior.
Tangential Response (p. 169)	Statements that change the subject without appropriate response.	Imply that sender's statement is not important enough to deal with.	Consider why a person makes a statement; then, before you change the subject, deal with the implications of the statement.
Transfer Stations (pp. 139–140)	Chain-link communication that passes through several receivers before getting to destination.	Message distortion. Usually the greater the number of transfer stations, the greater the distortion.	1. Create face-to-face settings whenever possible. 2. If message must be sent chain-link fashion, each receiver should paraphrase carefully.
Withdrawal (pp. 209–210)	Removing one's self physically or psychologically from setting.	Conflicts are not resolved, only put off.	Resist urge to withdraw; describe feelings.

Index

To the student:

We hope that *Inter-Act* has helped you develop the kind of interpersonal communication skills you think are important. We designed the book hoping to meet your needs—we can know how successful we've been only through your comments. With that in mind, would you take a moment to fill out this postage-free questionnaire and mail it back to us. We'll look forward to hearing from you and to using your suggestions in future editions of *Inter-Act*. Thank you!

School _____ Instructor's Name _____

Course Title and Number _____

1. What did you like *most* about *Inter-Act*? _____

_____

2. What did you like *least* about *Inter-Act*? _____

_____

3. Which skills did you consciously try to develop? _____

_____

4. Which skills do you feel you succeeded in developing? _____

_____

5. Were there any skills you did not find useful? _____

_____

6. Are there any interpersonal communication skills you think are important that were not covered in the book? If so, what skills would you like to see added to *Inter-Act*?

_____

7. Did you find the appendixes helpful? _____

8. Were there any chapters or sections in the book you were not assigned to read? Which ones? _____

9. Did you use the Communication Sessions often? Which types of questions did you find most helpful? _____

_____

10. How did you feel about the cartoons and graphics in the text? _____

_____

11. In a separate letter please make any additional comments you think would be useful. We'll be delighted to hear from you. Thank you for your help.

Optional

Your Name _____ Date _____

May Wadsworth quote you in future promotion of *Inter-Act*?   Yes ☐   No ☐

Sincerely,

Rudolph F. Verderber
Kathleen S. Verderber

FOLD HERE

FIRST CLASS
PERMIT NO. 34
BELMONT, CA

BUSINESS REPLY MAIL
No Postage Necessary if Mailed in United States

Dr. and Mrs. Rudolph F. Verderber
c/o Wadsworth Publishing Company
10 Davis Drive
Belmont, CA   94002

CUT PAGE OUT